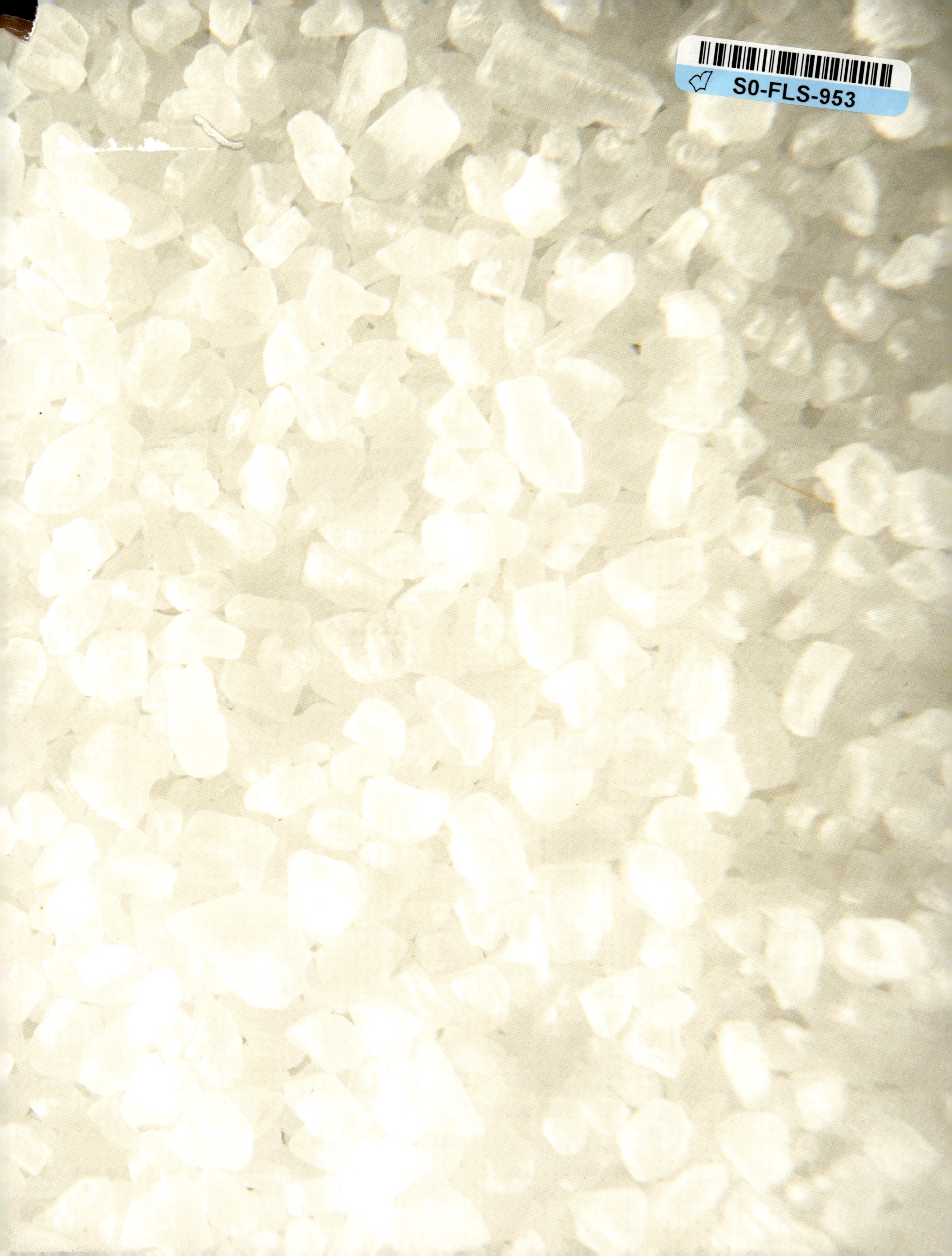

HAM

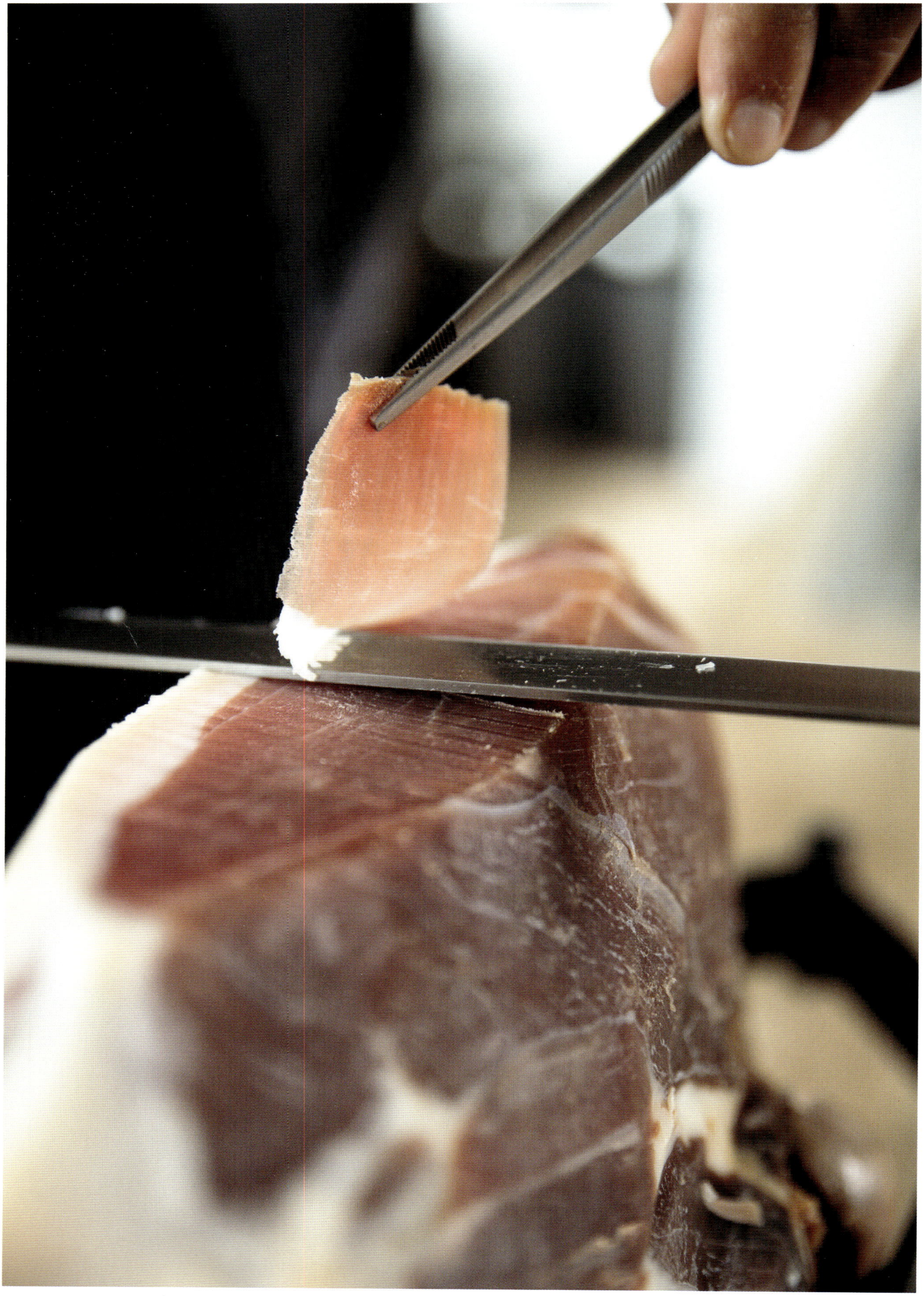

H

Prime Hams of Europe
Stories and Recipes

A

STEFAAN DAENINCK

M

LANNOO

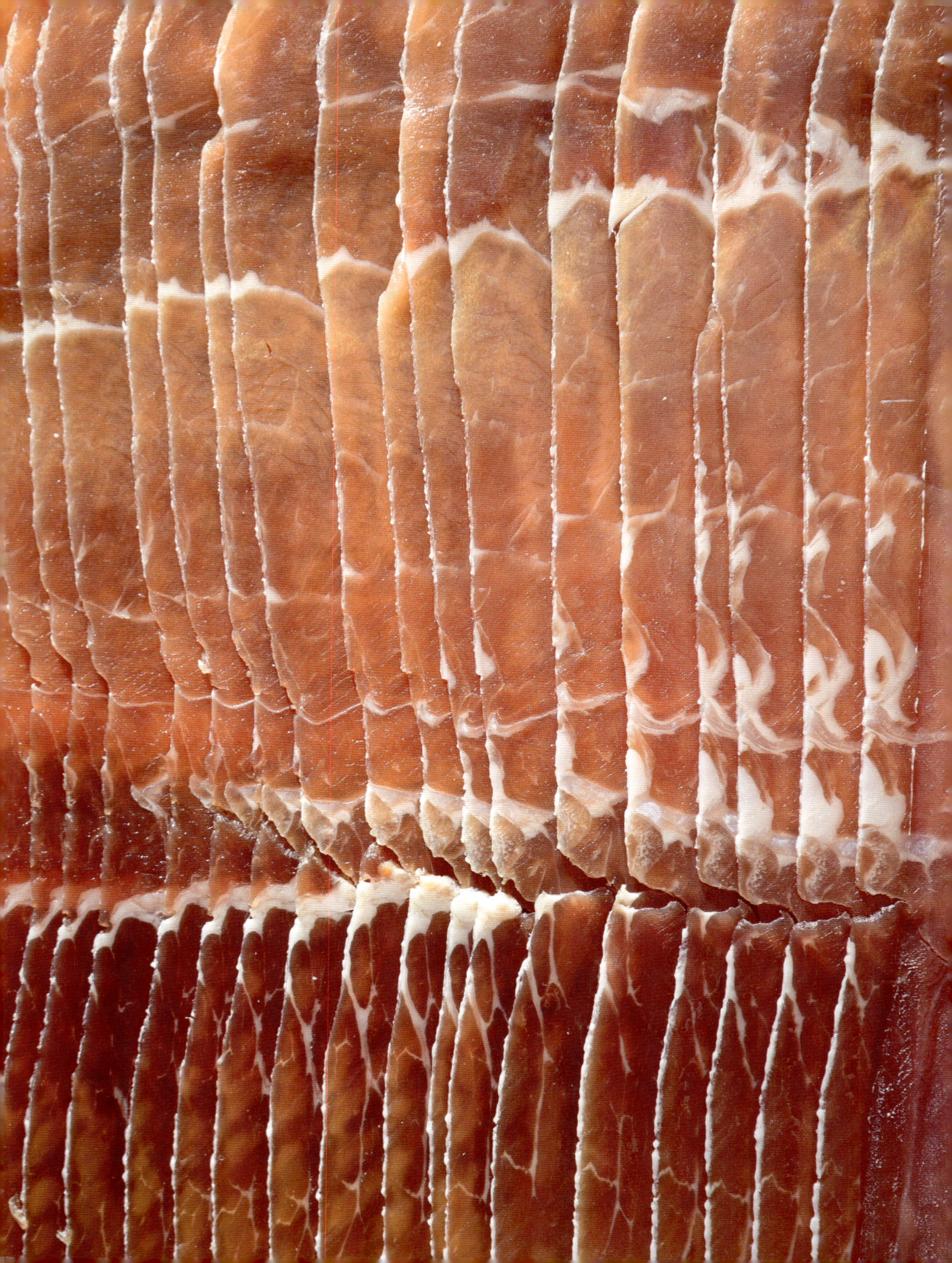

A RICH TRADITION WITH MUCH RESPECT FOR THE BASIC PRODUCT

Start with a quality piece of 'terroir' pork that has a story. Add salt of course and give it the necessary time to develop the taste (nuances). This is a rich tradition with much respect for the basic product, a tradition that goes back more than a thousand years …

The book *Ham* by Stefaan, dedicated to this tradition, is something I can be enthusiastic about. It is an ode to the product, the craftsmanship and the animal, the pig. Let a ham slowly ripen, dry and then hope that after many months of patience this results in a tasty and delicately scented ham. Magnificent!

There is much that binds ham producers together. In the end, they all make the same delicacy. Yet every producer has his own story and history, and each ham retains its own identity. There is more than enough material here to fill a book about ham.

Add the various viewpoints and recipes of three top chefs, plus the 50 creative and tasty recipes of Stefaan, and you have a true reference book for ham lovers, a book that appeals to foodies, hobby chefs and professional chefs!

At Ganda Ham we have been salting and drying Belgian hams in the traditional way for about 30 years. All this time, we have been working without preservatives to produce a genuine and pure Belgian product. Recently we have also been doing the same with exclusive types of beef, because we noticed that there is a demand for these new products with a story.

This book introduces you to our colleagues throughout Europe. I am persuaded that this reference work will help you realize what a beautiful and delicious product dried ham is. It is also an invitation to enjoy ham even more intensely in the future.

Enjoy reading and enjoy ham!

Dirk Cornelis
Managing director of Ganda Ham

CONTENTS

HAM

My reasons for writing this book	8
What is (raw) ham?	10
The history of pigs	12
Pig breeds	14
The history of raw ham	26
Quality labels	31
From pig to ham	32
Manufacturing process	37
Factors that determine taste	48
The importance of salt	56
European hams	59
The art of slicing ham	82
Different types of packaging	86

THE CHOICE OF TOP CHEFS 88

GEERT VAN HECKE
Ham, a culinary mainstay, ideal ingredient and tasty condiment — 91
- Ganda Ham with oysters — 93
- Fine cream of green asparagus with Ganda Ham and morel mushrooms — 95
- Wild salmon topped with Ganda Ham, poivrade, artichoke and wild garlic sauce — 96
- Cheese terrine with Ganda Ham and raisins — 99

MASSIMO BOTTURA
Come with me to Italy — 101
- Tartar of Chianina, Parma ham foam — 102
- Ice cod, katsuobushi broth, Parma ham — 102
- Ravioli bathed in tomato sauce — 103
- Asparagus, Parma ham, Parmesan cheese — 104
- The taste of the river — 105
- The garden of Italy, the best of fruits and vegetables — 105

PIET HUYSENTRUYT
'With a dish, not only the taste and the appearance are important, but also the aroma.' — 107
- An open sandwich from Flanders — 108
- My Blood sausage — 111

CULINARY HAM

- Breakfast — 114
- Breakfast new style — 115
- Apple cucumber shot with Black Forest ham — 116
- Bell pepper gazpacho with Serrano ham — 118
- Fennel Bayonne ham salad, the sun on your plate — 121
- My favourite bruschetta — 122
- Green asparagus, cheese sauce and Mangalica ham — 124
- Spring rolls — 127
- Bouillon of mushrooms with courgette and San Daniele ham — 128
- Ham with cauliflower — 130
- Plate of Iberico ham with guacamole and sage — 132
- Tomato carpaccio with burrata and Serrano ham — 135
- Pea soup with ham froth — 136
- Parma rolls, Pesto Genovese and Grana Padano cheese — 138
- Tarte Tatin with tomato and Bayonne ham — 141
- Gazpacho full of flavour — 142
- Grilled scallops with dried ham — 144
- Spanish sardines with Serrano ham — 147
- Stewed scallops, beetroot, San Daniele ham — 148
- Scampi, ham and chicory — 150
- Potato pie with Parma ham and poached egg — 153
- Oysters, Bayonne ham and basil emulsion — 155
- Jambon d'Ardenne, red chicory, squash and radicchio — 156
- Carpaccio made with omega bass, Iberico ham and cavaillon melon — 158
- Semi-cooked salmon and Bayonne ham, avocado, melon and port wine — 161
- New potatoes, farm ham and fried eggs, farm style — 162
- The Volcano — 165
- Bruschetta party — 166
- Potato, olive oil and Iberico de Bellota — 167
- Aubergine puffed in the oven with Grana Padano cheese and Parma ham — 168
- Snack of grilled green asparagus and Black Forest ham — 171
- Watermelon with Ganda Ham — 172
- Zeeland mussels, Ganda Ham, tomato and saffron — 175
- Southern ratatouille … from the cartoon — 176
- Risotto with Parma ham, tomato and mozzarella di bufala — 179
- Caramelised chicory, Jambon d'Ardenne, three kinds of cheese from Chimay — 180
- Scrambled eggs, Ganda Ham, and ketchup — 183
- Little rolls of Bayonne ham and Basque piperade — 184
- Puff pastry with Bayonne ham and spinach — 186
- Rolled pork tenderloin roast, Chimay cheese and Jambon d'Ardenne — 189
- Lentils with ham rolls — 191
- My favourite herring — 192
- Ravioli with mushrooms and Parma ham — 195
- Ganda Ham roll-ups — 198
- Wrap rolls with Ganda Ham and Le Larry goat cheese — 198
- Rolls of ham — 199
- Oriental Ganda cannelloni — 199
- Crispy Ganda Ham roll-ups — 200
- Savoury strudel — 200
- Bruschetta Ganda Ham with green olives — 201
- Ganda Ham with tasty tapenade — 201
- Sweet-salty-sour, my jam pastry — 203
- Salad and toast with mushrooms and Iberico ham — 204
- Salad Niçoise — 206

MY REASONS FOR WRITING THIS BOOK

My constant search for the most exquisite dishes and the tastiest foods ...

My wonder when I see my daughter Ella enjoying a piece of dried ham ...

My roots: being from West Flanders, I cannot ignore the importance of pigs ...

I have long heard it said: 'In West Flanders there are more pigs than people.' Investigation confirmed that this is true. For every resident of West Flanders there are several hundred pigs ...

The first vivid memory from my early childhood was waking up before dawn as a four-year-old kid when my father and our butcher-neighbour left for the pig farm to slaughter 'our' pig. Indeed, our pig. Every year, a friend who was a pig farmer fattened up a pig especially for us. I anxiously looked forward to the slaughtering. They could not leave without me, because I was selected to do a special job. At a young age I was given a big responsibility as the 'blood man'. As the man who took care of the blood, I was responsible for the main ingredient of the black pudding. Specifically, this meant that I was expected to keep stirring the warm blood so that it would not congeal. It was a big assignment. I rolled up my sleeves, and my whole arm disappeared in the lukewarm blood. I thought this was great. No one could carry out this task more conscientiously than I did. A few hours later I was the proud owner of about two metres of black pudding, and whoever wanted some could buy it from me ...

In the meantime I watched with wide-eyed amazement the butcher slaughtered the pig and cut it into many pieces: large pieces, small pieces. The pig seemed like a puzzle with a hundred pieces. The animal was cut up completely. The different pieces were carefully stored in plastic bags and they were each given a well-deserved resting place. There they waited patiently until they could be used in the most delicious culinary preparations.

Two important pieces stayed behind at the butcher's shop: the hams, the pig's hind legs. These two huge pieces were washed and were given a special place. Then, after a few weeks, they emerged but then disappeared again for six months in our cellar.

And then it was time for a feast. Family, friends and acquaintances were summoned and the delicious raw ham was sliced off with a passion. It was finger-licking good … The memory of that pure taste has stayed with me throughout my whole life. Perhaps that stimulated my culinary interests in what has become and remains my hobby and my profession to this day: good food!

Stefaan Daeninck

WHAT IS (RAW) HAM?

The 'ham' discussed in this book refers specifically to the back leg of a pig where the best quality ham is found.

The raw ham discussed can be described as the salted meat from the back thighs of a pig. Raw hams originated from the need to preserve the ham of a pig longer after slaughter.

Dried ham has existed throughout the centuries in many countries and regions, and with a wide range of flavours. These vary because of the local ingredients and herbs used for brining and / or salting and drying, the method of preparation, the ripening period and the specific circumstances in which this occurs. And of course everything starts with the pig itself. The specific breed and the food that the pig has eaten during the course of his life are of paramount importance with regard to the taste and quality of the final dried raw ham.

There is also shoulder ham, that is often cooked. There are different types of cooked ham, the main distinction being between 'gammon' and 'leg ham'. Leg ham comes from the part that can be found at the bottom of the leg. Cooked ham can also be subdivided into 'artisan' and 'industrial' ham. Artisan cooked ham usually contains less water and fewer additives.

Today, raw shoulder hams are becoming increasingly popular, especially in Spain and Italy. This is mainly because these hams are perfect for cutting by hand, coupled with the popularity of the *cortador* or ham slicer. Some types of shoulder ham are lighter, somewhat fattier in texture and very fine in taste due to the particularly tasty, veined meat. More and more shoulder hams are being dried in the south of Europe and gradually they are becoming popular with our consumers as well.

THE HISTORY OF PIGS

The chicken or the egg? The pig or man? Which came first?
This is a question that we will probably never be able to solve.
Are there two living beings with more in common?
Where evidence of man has been found, the pig is also there, and vice versa.

About four million years ago, the first ape-like creature appeared that walked on two rather than four legs. Australopithecus (literally 'southern ape') appeared in Africa and was much smaller and had more hair than people of today.

In about the same period, but in another part of the world, the wild boar came into being. This animal appeared in southeast Asia and spread to other areas. About two million years ago, the boar managed to colonize the mainland of Eurasia.

A good million years ago, the European and Asian swines separated from each other, among other things, because of the successive ice ages that resulted in a massacre among the many genetic variants. Particularly in parts of southern Europe, various pig populations managed to survive.

In prehistoric times, the wild boar (the primal pig) was the most important source of food for humans. When some 6,000 years ago, human beings (first in Asia-minor and afterward in Africa and Europe) changed from a roaming to a sedentary existence, the pig was perhaps their first domesticated animal. And that would have been true, of course, not only because of the companionship of this social animal but especially because of its tasty and nutritious meat.

The wild pig was easy to domesticate. Taming this animal was an obvious choice for prehistoric man because by having the pig as his friend he could prevent it from eating everything in sight!

Another factor that contributed to the taming of the wild pig was the fact that the pig supplied large quantities of edible meat.

Dans le cochon, tout est bon.

[In a pig, everything is good]

Around 5000 BC, the territory of present-day Belgium consisted mainly of wooded areas. Wild boars and wild pigs ran rampant and could feed on an abundance of wild roots, fruits, grasses, ferns and all kinds of nuts, such as walnuts, beech nuts, acorns and chestnuts. These nuts, along with the lush grasslands, were an ideal source of food for large herds of pigs that populated our regions.

At that time, the hunters could easily capture enough animals without endangering the population. They were fond of the taste of pork and treated the animals with respect. Already, the Celts understood that the unrivalled taste of pork was due to the food pigs could find in the forest. As the hunters developed into farmers who stayed in one place, the pig became a welcome guest, a friend of the family. The pigs were allowed to roam free, albeit in demarcated areas, so the animals had sufficient room to move about and develop delicious muscle fat. This was common practice in our region around 3500 BC, and it is still done today in the rugged Huelga in southwestern Spain where the famous Iberico pigs can roam free in gigantic areas and feed on acorns and wild roots. Acorns are an important flavour component for pork and consequently also for ham. Acorns are also responsible for fat that melts in your mouth and they supply various flavours and flavour components.

About 6,000 years ago, in parts of Asia, especially in Anatolia, large herds of pigs were bred. These bred animals were introduced to Europe by farmers. There, farmers also began to keep and domesticate local swine.

In the early AD period, the pig became increasingly important in Europe. Due to the population growth, the demand for meat continued to increase, and the pig turned out to be a useful animal for breeding. For millennia the pig, which was still roaming around, paired with wild boar so that the gene pool was constantly being replenished. Thus, the genetic variation in domesticated pigs is even greater than in wild boars.

The pig was a versatile farm animal. Not only was it a supplier of meat, but the animal was also used to plough the fields, and it provided fertilizer for soil that was often poor. Thus, the pig was not an expensive boarder. In addition to providing food for the table, it processed the farm's nutrition-rich waste materials into valuable manure.

For religious reasons, the pig was not bred in the Jewish or the Islamic world.

PIG BREEDS

Many pig breeds have developed during the course of history. Originating from their wild ancestors, as time went by, various breeds were crossed, which has resulted in a number of remarkable varieties.

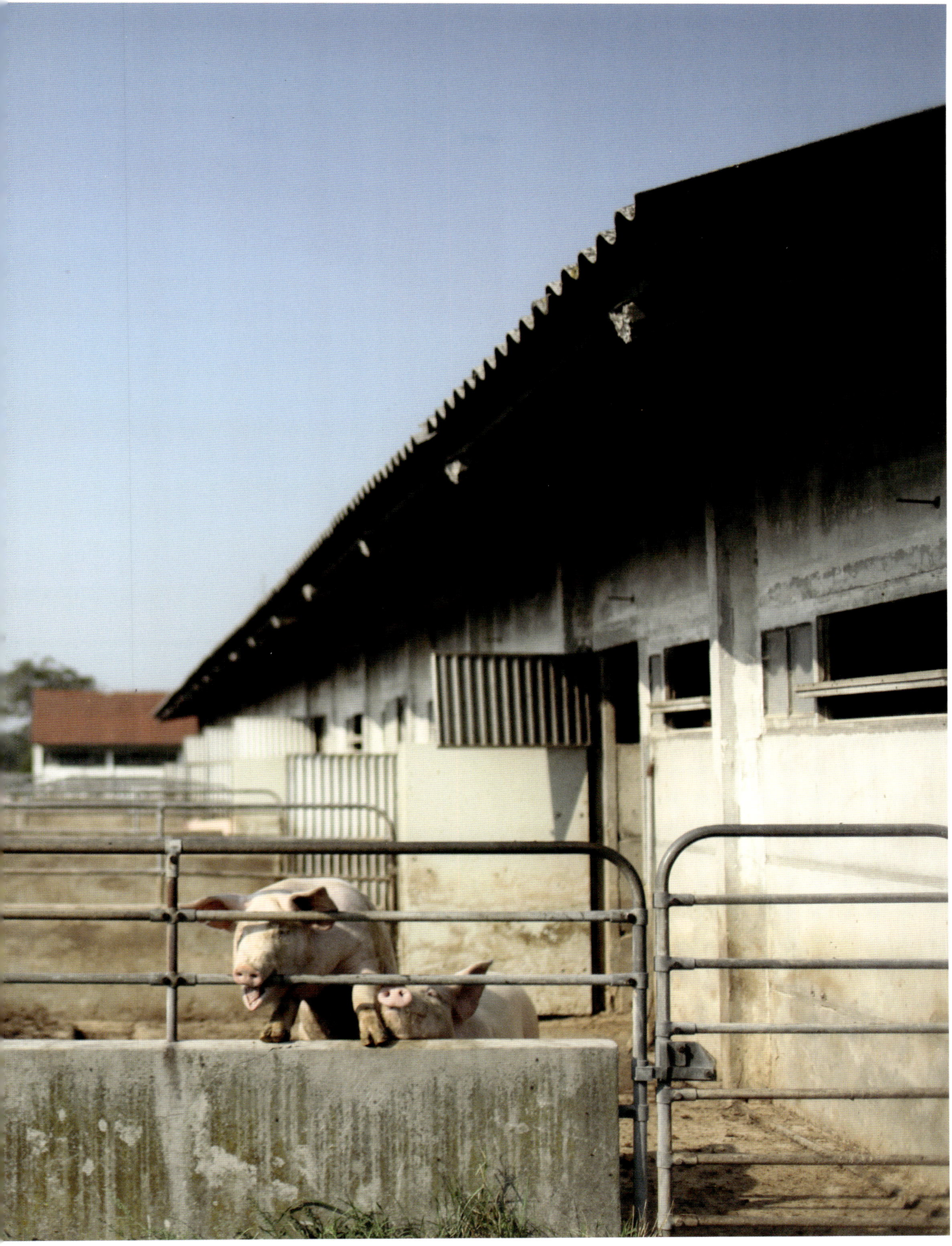

PIÉTRAIN
THE MOST MUSCULAR PIG BREED IN THE WORLD

Piétrain is a well-known Belgian pig breed that existed only in and around Piétrain near Jodoigne between 1920 and 1950. The breed originated from an intensive crossing of the Belgian Landrace with English Berkshires.

This English breed was introduced into Belgium in the period after the First World War because, at that time, the demand for pigs far exceeded the local supply. These English pigs quickly became popular in Belgium due to their specific rich meat flavour. By crossing them with Belgian pigs, a new variant emerged that immediately scored well.

The Piétrain pig, with a high slaughter productivity and low fat content, soon broke through, first in the province of Brabant and then in the rest of Belgium. After the Second World War, the demand for leaner meat became increasingly greater. As prosperity increased, less heavy physical labour had to be performed, so the lean meat of the Piétrain pig became very popular.

Because of its sturdy build, this pig is very suitable as a meat pig. The Piétrain pig is also a carrier of the large-ham gene, which means that all pigs of this breed have an extra-large set of hams. In the past, the breed was promoted as 'the pig with four hams'.

The breed is considered the most muscular pig breed in the world. Characteristic of the breed are the black spots on the body and the small upright ears. These animals also have strong teeth with large canines. The canines are filed down when the pig is in captivity on a meat farm.

Around 1960, the first Piétrain pigs were exported to the Netherlands.

Because Piétrain pigs are very stress-sensitive animals, in 1980 breeders decided to cross them with Large Whites (see below). Because of this crossing, a sub-breed was created, the Piétrain Rehal.

The Piétrain pig is less suitable for being kept in a stall and does best when it can roam freely on a fenced-in piece of ground and root in the ground with its snout. The animal remains popular in the meat industry, but is also popular with hobby farmers and on children's farms.

The Confrérie de l'Ordre du Cochon Piétrain was established in January 1992. The members of this order want to preserve the old recipe of Noix de Piétrain ham, prepared with seven herbs and sea salt.

DUROC
THE MOST AGGRESSIVE PIG OF ALL

The Duroc breed is called 'the most aggressive pig in the world'! Many theories circulate about the origin of this imposing animal. According to some, the breed originated in Africa and ended up in America via the slave route. Another source states that none other than Columbus brought the breed from Africa to Nova Scotia.

What seems certain is that the current Duroc pigs are descended from a cross between the Red Duroc pig from New York and the Jersey Red pig, and that the breed originated around 1800.

In the 19th century the Duroc pig caused an international furore. At the World Fair of 1893, a Duroc show was organized that garnered great acclaim. This was the beginning of a success story and the popularity of the breed increased everywhere.

The Duroc pig has a dark-reddish-brown coat and an elongated body. According to the breed standard of a pure Duroc pig, white spots are prohibited but some black spots are allowed. The red in the coat may have different shades. There are also Duroc pigs of an almost light golden to yellow shade with a reddish sheen.

In addition to its aggressiveness, this variety is also known for its high fertility. The sows have many piglets at once, which quickly grow to full maturity.

The hams of the Duroc pig are – like the shoulders – wide, the hair is long and dark, and the hooves are black. Characteristic are also the drooping ears that distinguish this pig from its peers.

Because of its very aggressive nature, the Duroc pig is not suitable as a farm animal or for a children's farm.

LARGE WHITE
(YORKSHIRE) THE BEST-KNOWN PIG BREED

The Large White is a pig breed that originally came from Yorkshire and sometimes also gets the name of this northern English county (such as 'York' or 'Great Yorkshire'). The breed was officially recognized in 1868 and the first studbook was opened in 1884. In the 19th century, the Large White was often imported from England. From the beginning, the breed was known for its good meat characteristics, high fertility and good maternal traits.

The Yorkshire pig is a large pig breed with white skin and firm upright hair. According to the breed standard, the Large White must have a broad snout with light jaws. The ears are medium, wide and fairly long, upright, fine and slightly turned outwards. Soft hairs should be present on the edges of the ears. Large Whites have a strong bone structure. They are very stress-resistant, which makes them very suitable for the farm and the children's farm.

Because of its high fertility, the animal is very popular in the meat industry, where it is often used for modern, intensive pig farming. The quality of the meat is highly regarded. Often, the animal is also used for crossing with other breeds to make them more resistant to stress.

BERKSHIRE
A PRESTIGE BREED

The Berkshire is a typical meat breed from the English county of Berkshire. These animals are black, with a white snout and white feet, and they have a very good meat quality. It is an old breed that has been refined by breeding and crossing. It has been featured in Queen Victoria's stables. She was the proud owner of The Ace of Spades, the most famous Berkshire boar of all.

The meat of this animal is very tender and dark, and its taste is highly regarded. Typical are the sweet taste and the marble-like structure. In terms of appearance, according to some, this meat can be compared to wagyu beef. The fat content of this animal is up to three times higher than average, which contributes to the rich character of the meat. The special properties of this prime meat are due to a high pH value, a finer and shorter fibre structure and good fluid retention that makes the meat lose little moisture even after cooling for several days. The meat of this pig shrinks little during baking.

The breed was threatened with extinction until it was revived in our region. It was rediscovered by a Dutch breeder and was crossed by Stefaan Lambrecht of the Flemish pork production firm Danis. He has put The Duke of Berkshire on the culinary map in Europe.

This new breed comes from the crossing of a rare boar of the Berkshire breed and a sow with the authentic genes of two old English landraces. The motto: the taste of the future, with the memory of the past.

Farmers who breed Berkshire pigs must feed them much more than a Piétrain. And they also must be willing to deal with their stubborn character. The pigs are bred in a closed circuit and are fed a vegetarian multigrain diet.

In scientific studies, the Berkshire breed has become famous for its physiological and taste-technical qualities.

EUROPEAN LANDRACES

We find landraces everywhere in Europe. These varieties have been frequently crossed and, in addition to common characteristics, they have also developed distinctive local characteristics.

THE BELGIAN LANDRACE

The Belgian Landrace (also called the Belgian native pig) is a very muscular breed that is mainly used for meat production.

The Belgian Landrace originated from crossings between different breeds of the landrace type, including the German and Dutch native pigs and some English landraces.

The sows of this robust breed are very fertile and have good maternal traits. The meat of these animals is somewhat lean. The pigs are short and wide built with large, drooping ears.

Members of this breed are always white. The sows weigh up to 250 kg and the boars weigh up to about 300 kg.

THE DUTCH LANDRACE

The Dutch Landrace has an elongated body with large muscles and flat hams. The animal has very strong bones and hanging ears. The skin colour is white, and the tail must have a curl to meet the breed standard.

In the Netherlands, this has become a rare pet breed that is threatened with extinction. The reason for this is simple: since the Second World War, the Dutch Landrace has been increasingly crossed with other breeds to produce new varieties that could guarantee a higher meat yield at a lower cost.

THE DANISH LANDRACE

The Danish Landrace is also a native pig with high fertility and a good maternal instinct of the sow, which has an average of fourteen piglets per litter.

This breed originated from crossings of the Jutland Landrace and various English pig breeds, with the Large White being the most noticeable.

This type of pig is rather elongated and is strong with a solid bone structure. The meat is lean in structure. It is appreciated all over the world, and is therefore a common export product.

The Danish native pig has a white breast and skin, a long body and an elongated head. According to the breed standard, the pigs may in some cases have light-grey, almost invisible spots. The animal has long hanging ears. Danish native pigs grow rapidly, almost a kilogram per day.

THE FINNISH LANDRACE

The Finnish Landrace is a native pig breed with a very strong bone structure and firm muscles. These animals are generally in good condition and the sows are also very fertile, with an average of twelve to fourteen piglets per litter.

These animals grow quickly and are known for their good meat quality.

THE NORWEGIAN LANDRACE

The Norwegian Landrace is often used to improve pig breeds in general and in the many variants of the European Landrace. This is because the Norwegian Landrace is fuller, more elongated and has more flesh on the shoulders than most of its kind. These animals also have strong bones, high fertility and caring sows.

THE SWEDISH LANDRACE

The Swedish Landrace is closely related to the Norwegian and Danish native pigs. These pigs are also popular breeding animals for improving other breeds.

THE GERMAN LANDRACE

The German Landrace is also known for its good fertility and rapid growth with good maternal characteristics in the caring sow.

These animals have white, light-pink skin, long ears and they are large in size. The specimens of this impressive German variety have firm muscles and produce high-quality meat. They can reach a shoulder height of 80 to 90 cm and the boars are clearly larger than the sows. The weight of this breed varies between 250 and 320 kg.

THE ENGLISH LANDRACE

English Landrace pigs are known worldwide for their quality. They are very popular because of their high fertility, the caring nature of the sow and their strong growth rate.

The fat percentage of this pig's meat is average and the taste is unanimously experienced as very good.

The bones of this pig are very strong, which also makes the animal suitable for travelling farther for the purpose of breeding.

The English Landrace is the textbook example of a breed that is very suitable for crossing with other breeds. Many varieties have also been bred with it.

THE ITALIAN LANDRACE

The Italian Landrace has, just like most other European landraces, very high fertility with sows that take good care of the piglets. The growth rate of these pigs is optimal and the meat quality is greatly appreciated.

THE RELATIONSHIP BETWEEN TAPAS AND HAM

Anyone who says tapas in Spanish immediately thinks of ham as well. Many stories circulate in Spain about the origins of this combination. We do not want to deprive you of one. According to one of these stories, King Alfonso XIII stopped on his return from a visit to Cádiz at a bar by the sea and asked for a glass of sherry. A violently rising wind threatened to blow sand into the glass, so the panicked owner of the bar covered the sherry with a slice of dried ham. The king thought it was supposed to be so and ate the ham before drinking the sherry. The monarch enjoyed it so much that he proudly introduced the custom to his court.

THE IBERIAN PIG

The Iberian pig is a semi-wild pig breed that has run around on the Iberian Peninsula for centuries. The animal stands quite high on its legs and is very mobile.

Most pigs of this breed are dark-grey, but brown tints also occur. Pata negra ham owes its name to the black hooves of the animal.

Traditionally, these pigs are fed with acorns. The animals fatten themselves naturally with acorns, which ensures a high content of unsaturated fats in their meat. This fat is stored in the muscle tissue and gives the meat a particularly fine, marbled structure. Some Iberian pigs are the basis for the world-famous Pata Negra. Now the name Pata Negra may be used only for the black label, the highest grade, the 100% Ibérico Bellota Pata Negra.

There are four regions in southwest Spain where Iberian pigs (Bellota) are found: Huelva, Extremadura, Córdoba and Salamanca. These Iberians are divided into four different categories (see pages 75-76).

MANGALICA

The Mangalica pig is a typical Hungarian pig. This animal stands firmly on its legs and is physically well-armed against the combination of cold and severe heat on the Hungarian Pannonian steppes (from -30° C in winter to +30° C in summer). The animal is resistant to many diseases and is very resistant to stress.

During the winter, the coat of the Mangalica pig (except for the muzzle) is covered with thick, long, woolly hair up to its ears.

In terms of breed, Mangalica pigs are related to Spanish Iberian pigs. The animal is of a friendly nature and lives on a natural diet of corn, grains and grass.

When ready for slaughter, the animal is almost twice as heavy as our varieties. The meat is richly veined with fat and has its own distinctive taste.

PORC NOIR DE BIGORRE

This black pig, described as noble, was abundant in the landscape of the French Bigorre region at the time of the Romans. The animal flourished as a noble pig breed with the famous Cistercian monastery of Escaladieu in the background.

The animal almost went into oblivion in the course of the 20th century, however, after a count of Mediterranean pig breeds in 1980, researchers sounded the alarm. Only a handful of these pigs still lived in their natural habitat.

The Padouen collective intervened and sixty united breeders managed to give the Noir de Bigorre a new future. Under the motto 'grow together' a scenario was drawn up in which strict requirements for the pig 'Noir de Bigorre new style' were drawn up. For example, this animal must be purebred and crosses with other breeds are strictly prohibited. The animals may be reared with up to 25 per hectare, and the feed is exclusively made up of grass from the meadows on the basis of clover and grains such as barley, rye and wheat, supplemented with chestnuts and other natural food that the animals find on the spot.

All steps of the pig's life cycle, from birth to slaughter, cutting, salting and commercialization take place under the strict supervision of the collective.

FOSSILIZED HAM FROM TARRAGONA

Historians have learned that the Romans knew and had perfected methods of drying ham. In remnants of the old city of Tarragona, a fossilized ham was found, showing that the Romans had mastered the technique of salting pork.

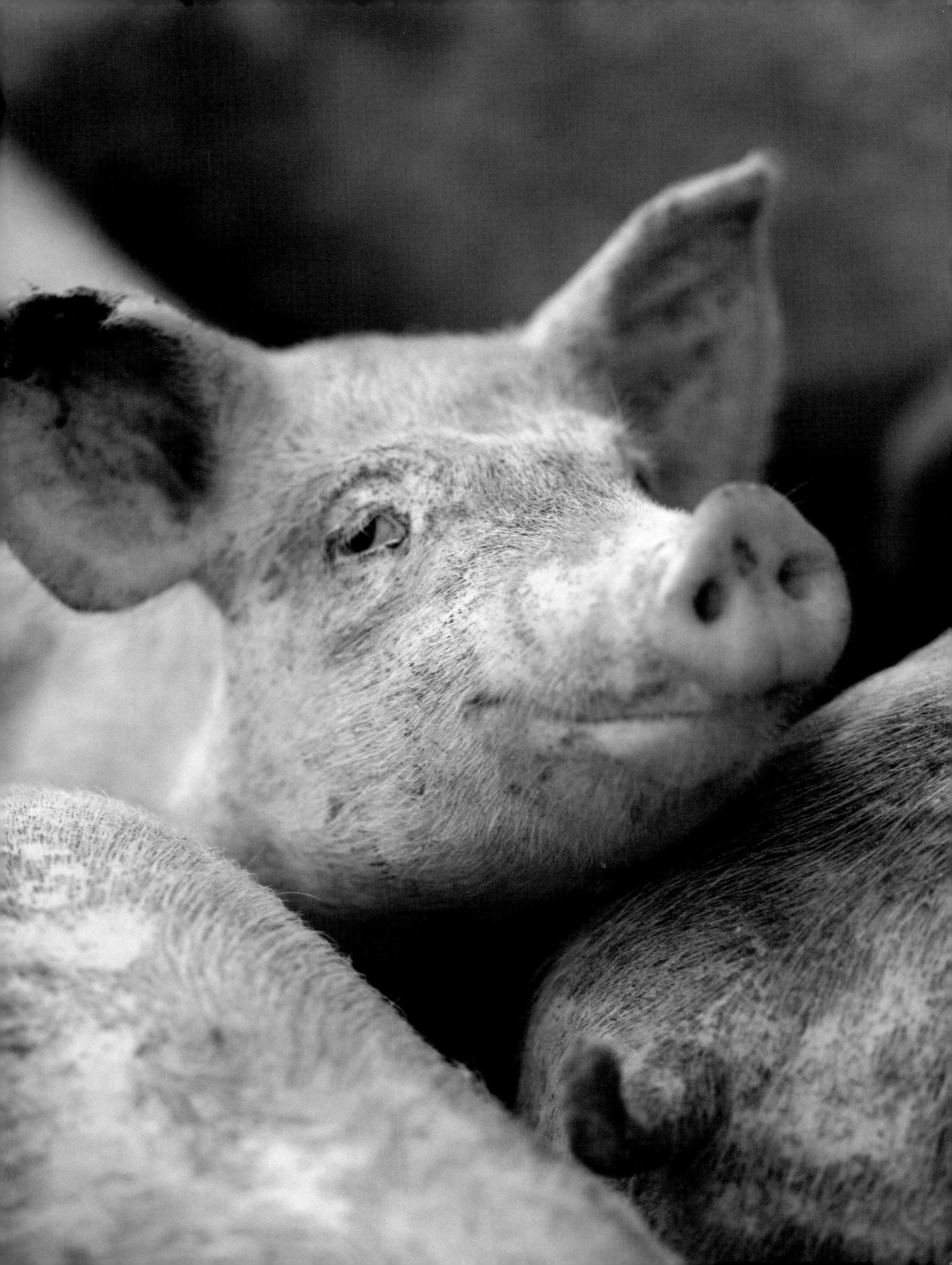

THE TRIGG COUNTY HAM FESTIVAL

The largest ham festival in the world takes place every year in October in Trigg County, Kentucky. Tens of thousands of people from all over the world come together to enjoy quality ham. Every year there are numerous competitions, including the selection of the best hams, a pig competition and a competition where one tries to catch a pig smeared with oil.

THE HISTORY OF RAW HAM

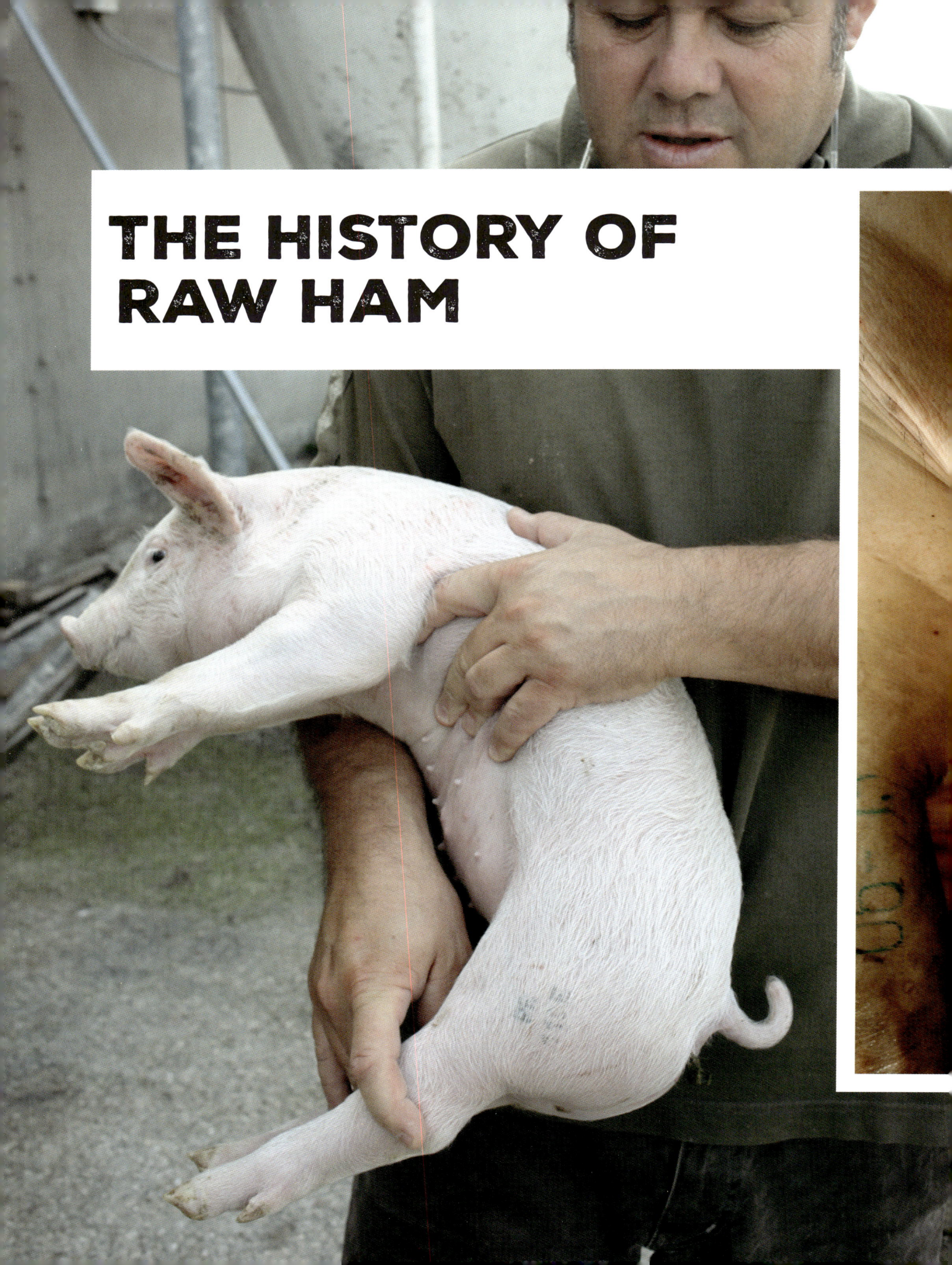

Pigs were the ideal food source for the Celts, and hams were considered an exceptional delicacy. This did not escape the notice of the Roman occupiers who fought numerous great battles with the Celtic tribes. Many Roman historians mentioned that our region was overpopulated with wild pigs. In his *De Bello Gallico*, Julius Caesar called the 'Belgae' the bravest of the Celts and referred to our pigs as 'wild, strong and barbaric'.

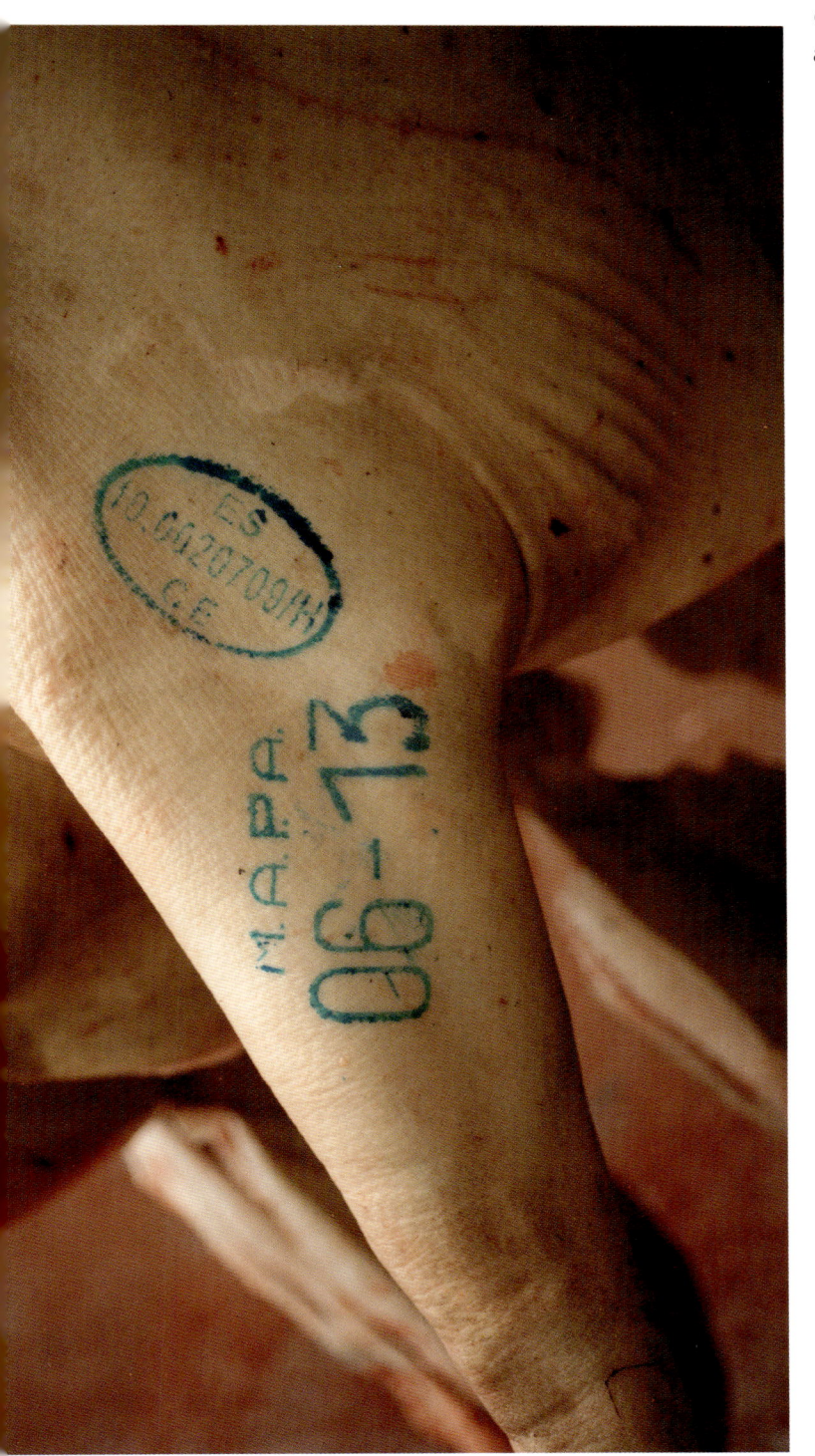

The Romans also learned to enjoy our hams and they were exported to Rome in large quantities where they were dried. Soon there was a lively export and Belgian ham was viewed as a luxury product to indulge the patricians and the legionaries.

Around 200 BC, Cato the Elder wrote that there were four thousand pork sides and hams from 'Belgica' hanging to dry in underground storage places in Italy. The Roman geographer mentioned in a passage about salted pork in 'Belgae': 'Their pigs may roam freely in the wild. They are remarkable because of their size, fighting spirit and mobility.'

Conversely, the ancient Belgians learned the use of salts and brine from the Romans. They saw how the hardened legionaries had dried meat with them that could be kept for a long time. They adopted this usage and modified it. For example, herbs were added to the brine water in the wooded areas, resulting in an additional taste experience.

During the conquest of large parts of Europe, the Romans introduced the technique of salting and drying everywhere. To this day, the technique of brining and drying parts of the pig, and especially the ham, is still being applied.

According to tradition, the origin of raw ham lies in our regions and more specifically in the Ardennes. It was in these wooded areas that the first local pigs were domesticated.

The Ardennes have a microclimate that enhances the great taste of the meat. There are also numerous natural caves and spaces where the wind has free play, which facilitate the drying and the processing of ham. The thick butts and the bacon of the pigs were first brined and salted, with the addition of local herbs. After a few days, the hams were dried, first in caves and in caves where fires were lit to promote drying and then in chimneys in the first rudimentary houses. This smoking technique came about naturally, and it was soon discovered that the meat could be kept longer in this way. This type of ham is still known today as Jambon d'Ardenne.

MENAPIAN HAM

During the first four centuries AD, modern-day Flanders was part of the large Roman Empire. The region between the coast and the Scheldt river was the territory of the Menapians, a farming community where the pig was highly regarded. They integrated few Roman influences in their way of life, but the Menapian pig was so well-liked by the Romans that the well-to-do patricians were willing to pay a fortune for it. Especially the Menapian ham was appreciated. It was redder than other types of ham.

This ham was the oldest export product on the tables of Rome. The tradition of producing hams may go back even farther in time. In the 1st century AD, the Roman author Martialis praised the quality of Menapian hams. Emperor Diocletian, who, after an inflation in 302, set maximum prices for some products in Rome, explicitly mentions Menapian ham. The price was set at 20 denarii per Italian pound (327.5 grams). By comparison, the price for a kilo of wheat was 12 denarii. These sources suggest that the import of high-quality Menapian hams was a large-scale activity.

Other ancient authors mention that in the forests of the northern part of the province of Gaul, to which the Menapian area belonged, large groups of large, semi-wild pigs were kept. Recent archaeological research shows that the relatively poor sandy soils were covered with large areas of forest, including an extensive zone to the north of Ghent. Forests at that time were certainly not unprofitable economically, because they were very suitable for pig farming. It was the natural biotope where the animals could feed on acorns, nuts, tubers, roots, mushrooms and leaves.

The pigs were semi-domesticated wild boars. These animals were very important to the Menapian farmers. Not only was the killing of this fast, dangerous beast a sign of strength and masculinity, it was also honoured and associated with the cult of the hearth. These fireplaces, centrally located in the wooden farms of the families, were flanked by two ceramic elements that supported a

Maybe it will soon be possible to taste authentic local hams ...

lattice and were decorated with a pediment with stylized wild boars.

It is not known exactly how the hams were produced. Both smoking and salting, or a combinationof the two, are possible. There was certainly plenty of wood, and the Menapians, who lived near the coast, specialized in the production of salt. The many traces of salt transport found in excavations of Menapian farms show that salt was available in large quantities in the interior.

The tradition of pig farming in the northern Flemish forests continued to exist until the Middle Ages. Some written documents show how in the 9th century the abbey of Sint-Baafs in Ghent hunted hundreds of pigs in the woods to the north of Ghent. This shows that ham production is one of the oldest traditional skills in Flanders and that ham is one of the oldest export products.

The Menapian pig had disappeared from our regions, but now it is back! A collaborative project of an experienced pig breeder, Ruben Brabant, in co-operation with various departments of Ghent University, and with the support of Dirk Cornelis among others, has resulted in the re-establishment of the animal. After years of research and careful re-breeding using old breeds and even wild boars, the Menapians are walking around in Flemish fields once more. It is already possible to taste the meat and we are looking forward to the opportunity of feasting on these authentic local hams.

For more information: *www.menapii.be*

PGI
(PROTECTED GEOGRAPHICAL INDICATION)

The European Commission awards the Protected Geographical Indication (PGI) label to products that are produced, processed or prepared in a specific geographical area. There must be a link between the individuality or the familiarity of the product and its geographical origin. It concerns products prepared according to local methods within a defined geographical area. Examples of hams:

- **Belgium:** Jambon d'Ardenne
- **Germany:** Schwarzwälder Schinken
- **France:** Jambon de Bayonne, Jambon sec des Ardennes
- **Italy:** Prosciutto di Norcia
- **Austria:** Tiroler Speck
- **Portugal:** Presunto de Barroso
- **Spain:** Trevelez, Serón

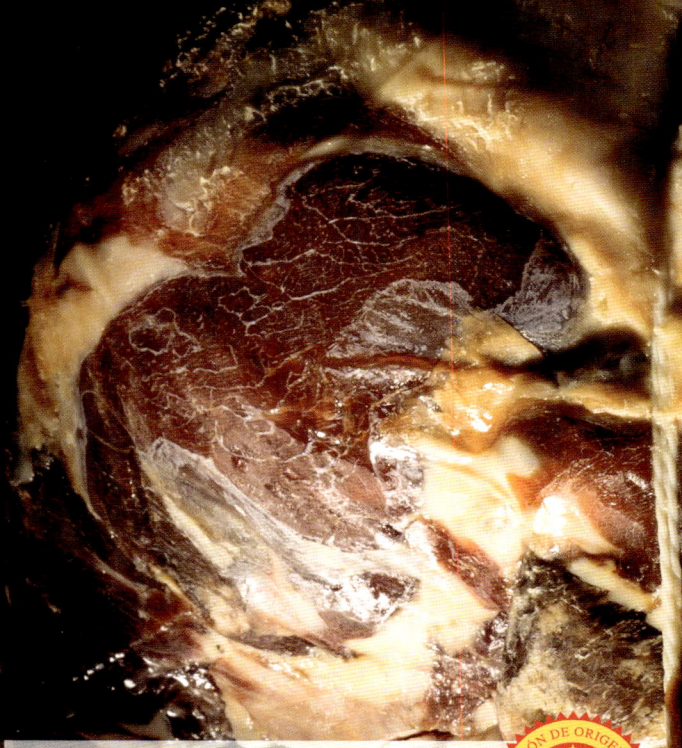

PDO
(PROTECTED DESIGNATION OF ORIGIN)

The European Commission grants the Protected Designation of Origin (PDO) to products whose production, processing and preparation take place within a certain geographical area. This must be done according to a recognized and controlled method.

Examples of hams:

- **Spain:** Dehesa de Extremadura, Guijuelo, Jabugo, Los Pedroches, Jamón de Teruel
- **Italy:** Prosciutto di Carpegna, Prosciutto di Modena, Prosciutto di San Daniele, Prosciutto Veneto Berico-Euganeo, Prosciutto di Parma, Prosciutto Toscano, Culatello di Zibello, Valle d'Aosta Jambon de Bosses, Speck dell'Alto Adige, Cinta Senese
- **Portugal:** Presunto de Barrancos
- **France:** Noir de Bigorre

QUALITY LABELS

Three major quality labels in Europe guarantee the protection of many quality products. A large number of hams are protected by these labels.

TSG
(TRADITIONAL SPECIALITY GUARANTEED)

The term Traditional Speciality Guaranteed (TSG) does not refer to the origin of the product but to the traditional product composition or production method. 'Traditional' means that the product has been available on the EU market unchanged and demonstrably for at least 30 years. Examples of hams:

- **Spain:** Serrano

REGIONAL PRODUCT

The term *Regional Product* used in Belgium has five definitions:
- Made with local ingredients and/or ingredients that are considered to be local.
- Generally accepted as a traditional local product.
- Produced artisanally according to traditional local methods.
- A regional product must correspond with the region of production, both in the processing of the end product and in the regional designation.
- Long-term or historical reputation as a regional specialty.

Belgium: Ganda Ham, Bruges Ham, Grega, St-Eloy, Maasland Farm Ham, West-Flanders Farm Ham, Kempen Dried Farm Ham

FROM PIG TO HAM

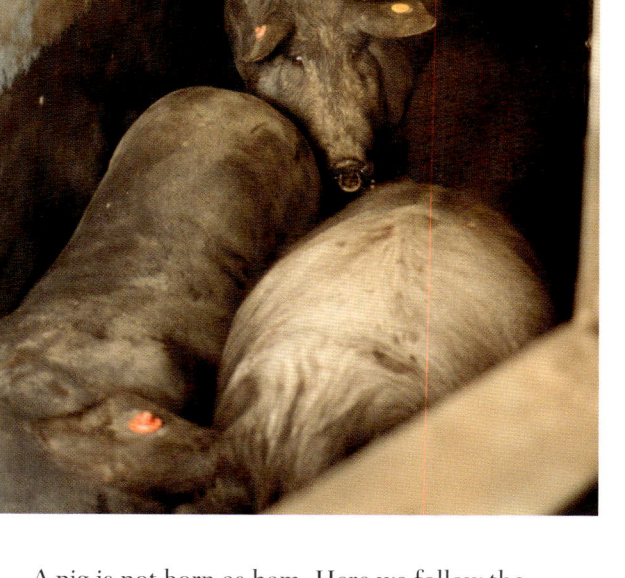

A pig is not born as ham. Here we follow the slaughter in the slaughterhouse of Jabugo. This is done at night to disturb the animals as little as possible.

After being raised, which differs for each type of pig, the pig must be slaughtered. Today this is done as animal-friendly as possible in a way that is approved by EU legislation and that subjects the pig to the shortest possible agony.

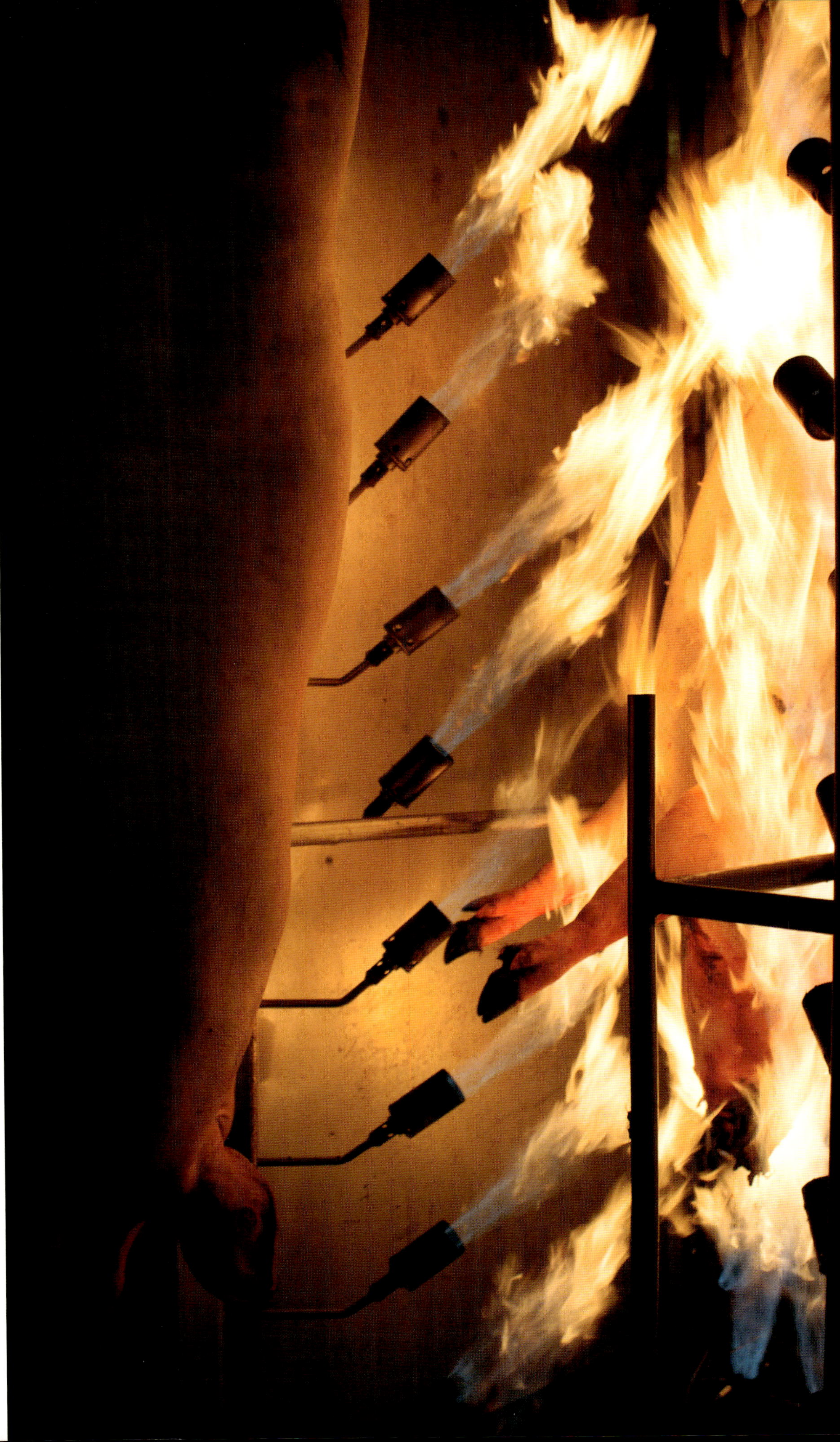

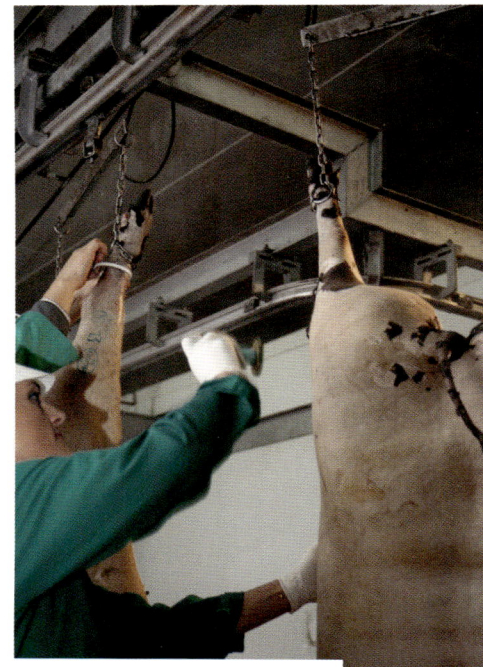

The pig is processed as soon as possible after slaughter. Reference samples are taken and quality inspections are performed.

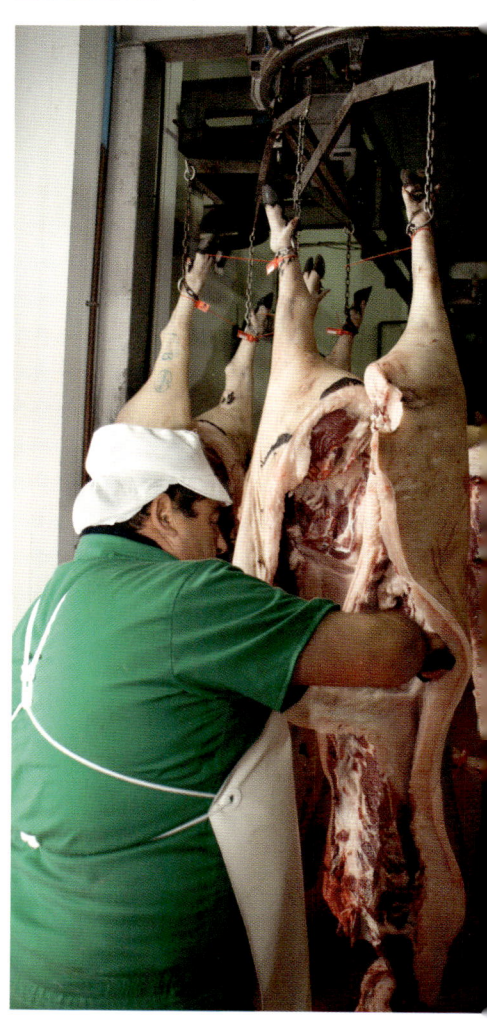

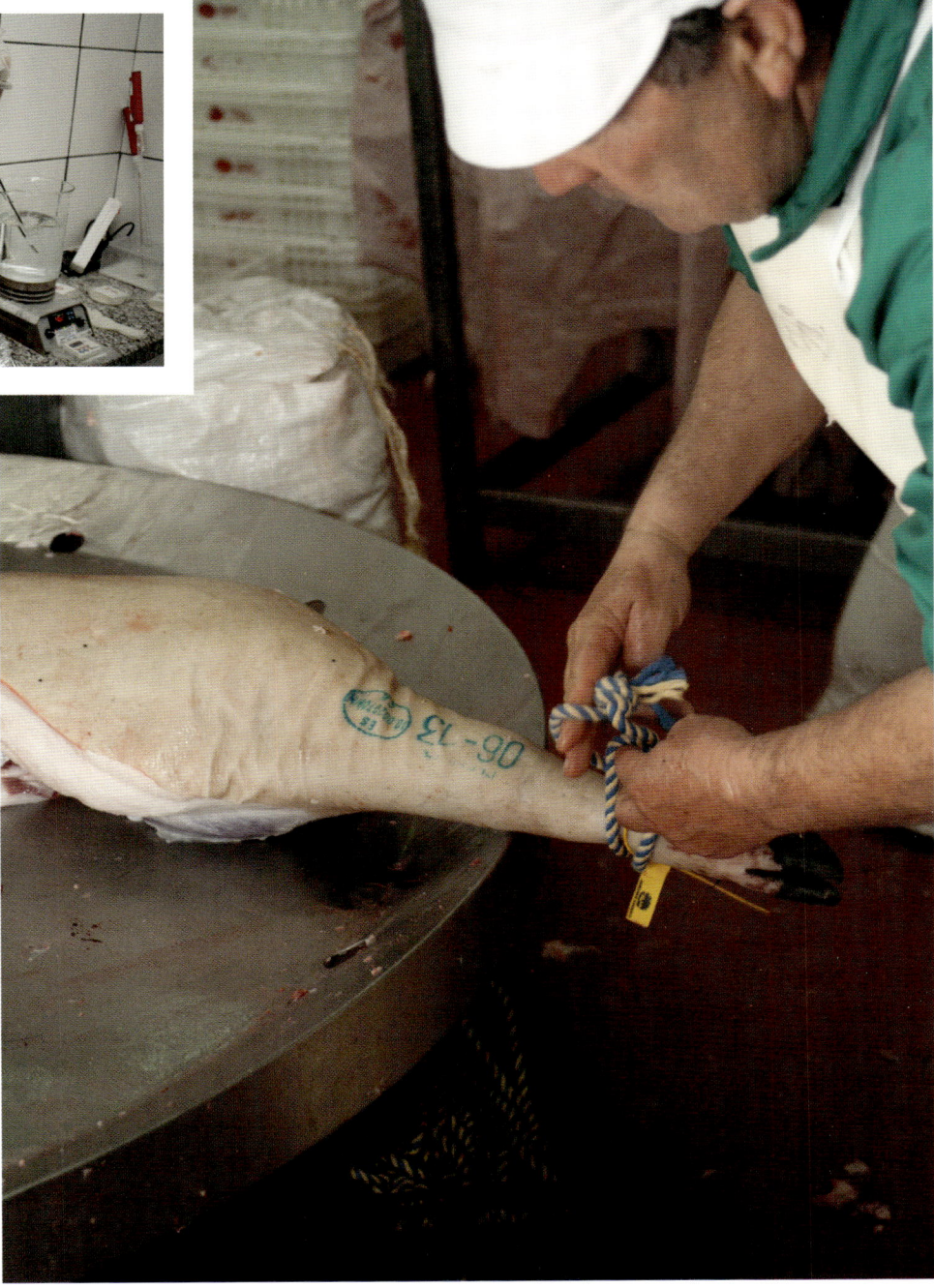

The hams are inspected and then stamped so they can be traced. Stamps with quality mark, slaughter date, farm of origin and type are applied.

Each type of ham is cut up differently, the cutting off of the skin and fat takes place in a different way, and the foot and the lower leg may or may not be retained. Here you can see how Iberian pigs are cut up in Huelva.

MANUFACTURING PROCESS

We can illustrate the manufacturing process of dried ham nicely with Ganda Ham. There are many aspects that go back to the traditional methods of pig farmers in our region.

After the slaughtering process, selected hams are checked for their quality. Every ham is given a label when weighed to ensure traceability. The fresh hams are first acclimated to the cooling room for 1 to 2 days to give them the same core temperature.

THE FIRST SALTING

Residual blood is forced out of the veins of the hams and the rinds (the skin of the ham) and the meat are rubbed with sea salt. A salting machine sprinkles an extra layer of dry sea salt on the hams, which are then manually salted again.

The hams then go to the salt chambers for a week at a temperature of 1 to 4 or 5° C. During this period, the salt extracts moisture from the meat, dissolves it and penetrates the meat, with the extracted water partially evaporating.

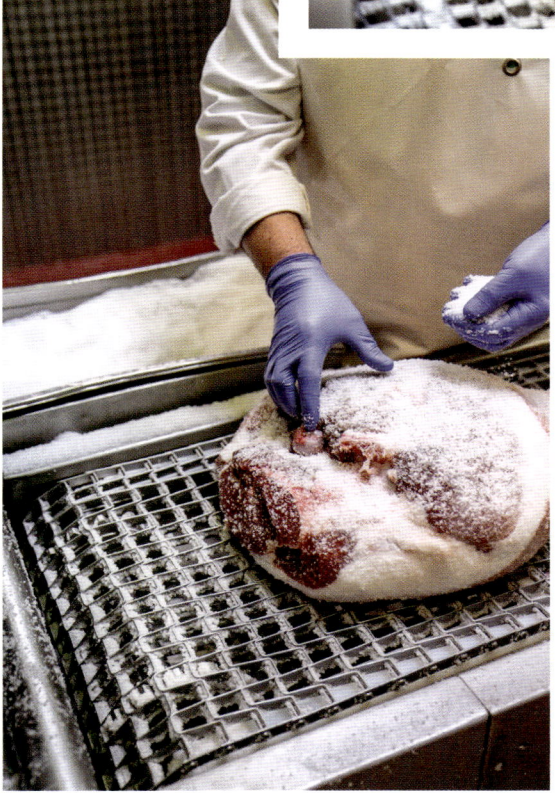

SECOND SALTING

After a week, the salt that remains on the hams is blown away. To make it easier to absorb the salt, the meat is made supple again by massaging it. In the past, the pig farmers and butchers did this by rolling the hams, but now there are machines that take care of this task.

After massaging, the hams will rest again for 2 weeks.

DESALTING, WASHING AND MATURING

In the past, the hams were brushed clean. With Ganda Ham, the dry, salted hams are blown clean and then hung up. This differs from the industrial brinning process where the hams are stacked.

The hams now mature for 2 months in cooled ripening rooms. This gives the salt a chance to penetrate deep into the ham. During this ripening process, the water on the surface of the ham evaporates, forming fine salt crystals on the outside. They are washed away at the end of this phase during an extra 'shower'.

DRYING

The farmers used to dry their hams in the barn, where the refined aroma could develop further. With Ganda Ham, drying takes place in slightly ventilated special drying chambers at a temperature of about 17° C. Drying out slowly is a process that takes place through the combination of cooling elements, ventilation and a constant temperature. This is a meticulous task because the optimal bacteriological balance in the drying rooms is only reached after several years. This balance allows the natural yeasts to do their work and to start a slow, enzymatic process that could be described as 'bacteriological magic' …

LARDING

After about ten weeks of drying, a dry crust begins to form on the side of the ham. For this reason, the leg is rubbed along the side with a mixture of smout (lard), flour, pepper and salt.

The ham is dried for at least another 10 months. During this drying process, the quality of the ham is constantly monitored. The curing master pricks the meat with an awl made of horse bone. By pulling the pointed bone out of the meat and holding it under his nose, this expert can immediately determine the maturity of the ham by the rich aroma.

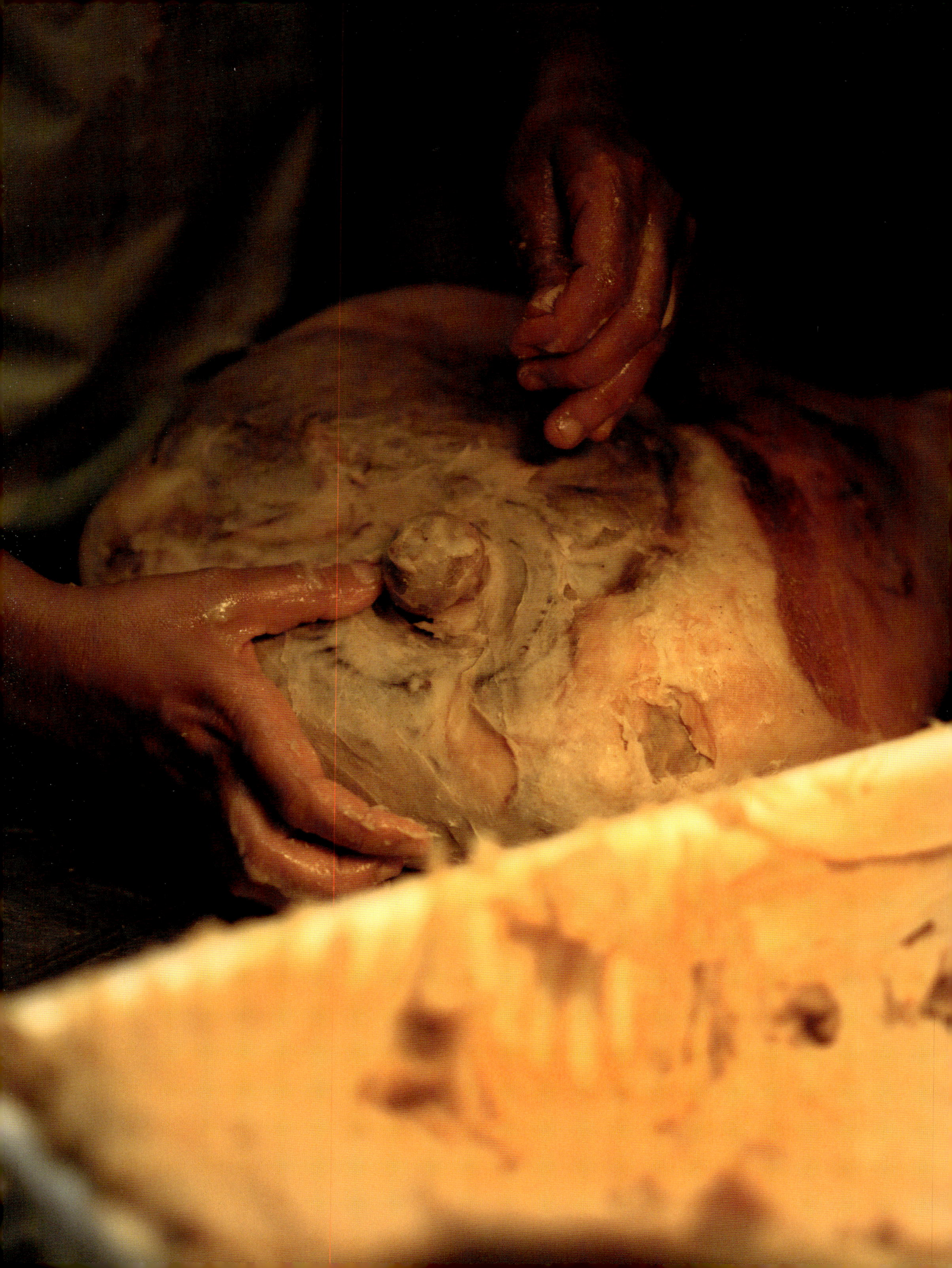

The larding is often a company / family secret. The basis for the larding consists of lard (pig fat) and flour. Usually rice flour or buckwheat flour are used so the ham will be a gluten-free product. Some ham houses also use salt, local pepper (black or white), paprika powder, chilli or other spices or herbs. This photograph is from Parma in Italy.

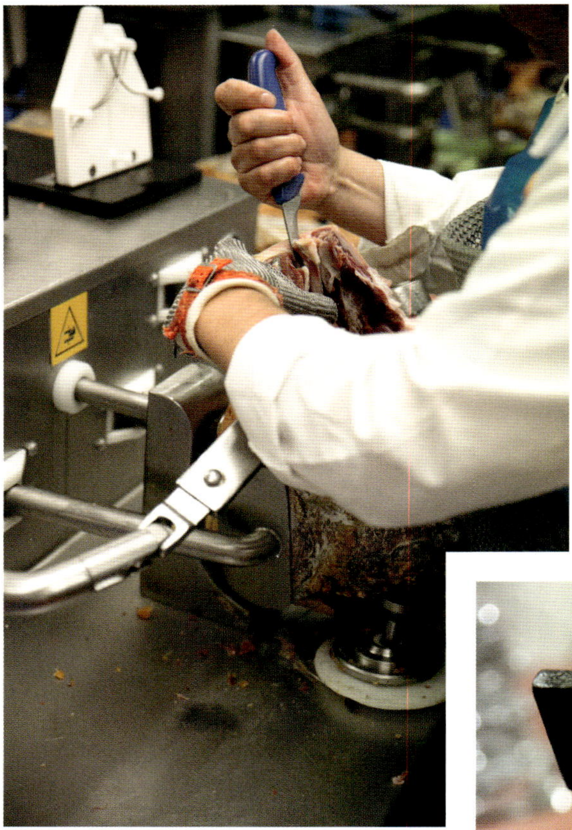

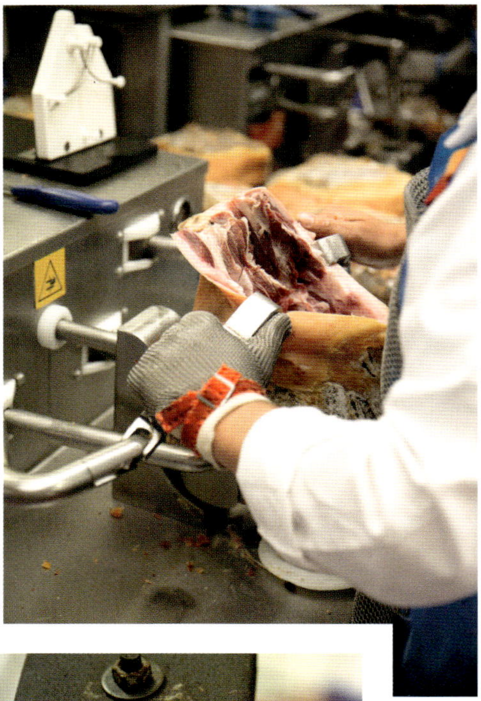

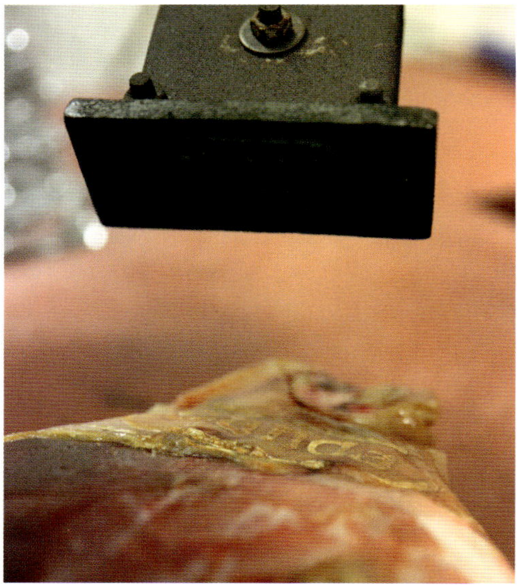

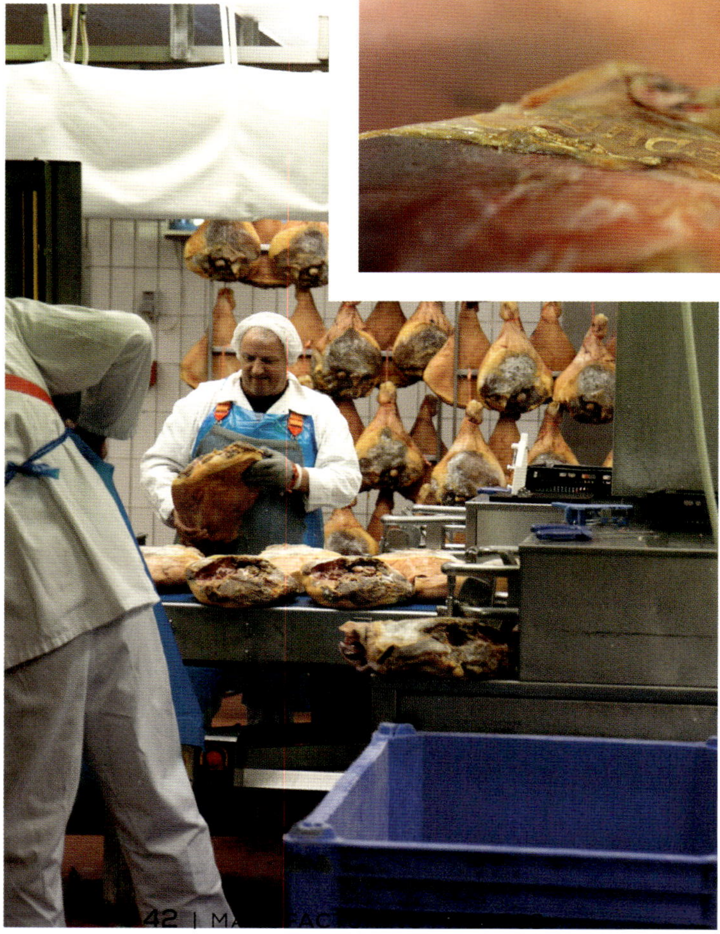

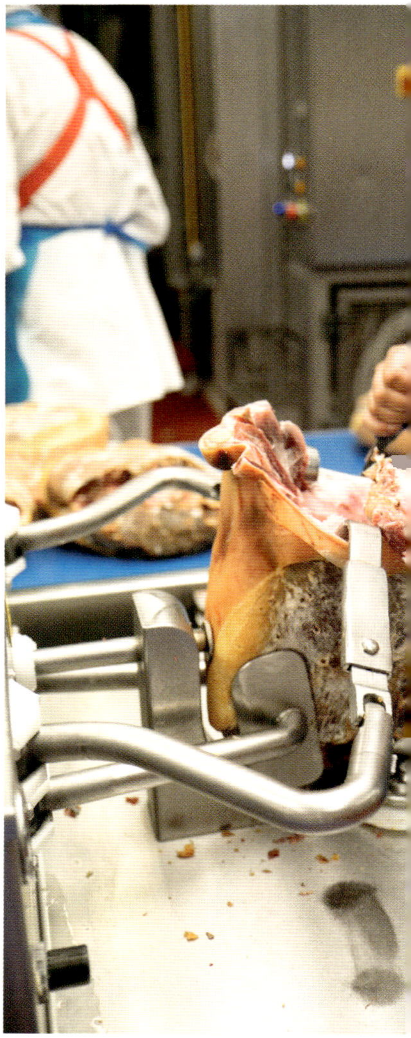

WASHING AND (POSSIBLY) DEBONING

After this period, the hams are washed again to remove the lard layer. Larger hams continue to ripen until they are 10 to 14 months old. Then the hams are finally ready to be sold – with or without bone.

The deboning of the ham takes place in the 'deboning room'. After the bone is removed, the ham is cleaned to remove the off-flavour of oxidised fat formed during the drying process. It is sewn together, pressed into a mould, provided with the Ganda brand name and then finally vacuum packed. Each ham receives a strict quality control. Hams that do not meet the strict requirements are irrevocably removed.

In the shipping room, the packaged hams are provided with the necessary labels, placed in a net and sent, on their way to the connoisseurs.

ONLY THREE INGREDIENTS ...

Only three ingredients are used for the production of naturally dried Ganda Ham: pork, sea salt and ... time. No nitrites, flavourings or colourings are added to the ham. The traditional process of salt drying and the natural ripening create a specific mature and rich aroma that makes Ganda Ham unique.

Ganda Ham is easily digested and contains less than 10% fat, which also consists of 54% unsaturated fatty acids with a cholesterol content of 85 mg per 100 g. The Ganda Ham firm supports a healthy, creative cuisine by co-operating with chefs in the development of innovative recipes and by sponsoring culinary competitions and promotional activities.

100% BELGIAN

Ganda Ham prides itself on working only with hams from Belgian breeders who guarantee that their animals grow up in the traditional way. It involves a selection of pig farms that meet strict criteria. For example, they must be able to submit a well-defined breeding method with controlled feeding conditions.

Only heavier hams (10 to 12 kg) are eligible. This is a deliberate choice because these hams produce stronger, more mature meat, and also contain a little more fat, which is an important seasoning for meat.

Round hams are refused because they do not lend themselves optimally to the technique of salt drying.

Ganda encourages growers to raise their pigs in animal-friendly conditions and with natural food. This benefits the quality of the end product. A natural product is also much more attractive to the consumer, who is increasingly interested in quality.

SEA SALT: AN ADDED VALUE FOR THE HAM

It is no coincidence that Ganda uses only sea salt for salting the hams.

The main function of salting is still 'to preserve the meat well' for a long time. As with the traditional pig breeders of the past, the salt in the ham serves mainly as a preservative and only in the second instance for the taste.

In the process of fine-tuning the optimal manufacturing process for Ganda Ham, manager Dirk Cornelis and his team did not cut any corners. They experimented patiently and for a long time with various types of salt and salting techniques. For the specific process of salt drying, the use of sea salt turned out to have special advantages. Sea salt, in contrast to rock salt, contains very small amounts of impurities in the form of minerals and trace elements. These 'irregular' elements are precisely what provide the beautiful, stable colour and the soft taste that make Ganda Ham unique.

INTEGRAL QUALITY ASSURANCE

The pursuit of quality is central to the mission of Corma, the company behind Ganda Ham. A traditional approach is combined with modern technology. Ganda is continually involved in scientific research on themes such as health, salt reduction in meat products, the composition of fatty acids, the processing of waste products, etc.

As early as 1992, the company started to develop integrated quality assurance in a structured way, and in 1993 Ganda became the very first Belgian company in the meat products sector to obtain the ISO 9002 certificate, the guarantee of an officially recognized quality system. Afterwards, the BRC Global Standard for Food Safety and the IFS Food Standard were also achieved. These two standards are intended for suppliers of private label products to retailers with the main objective of assuring food safety and hygiene in the food processing industry.

Ganda has developed a system of self-checking so that all aspects of the production, processing and distribution of the hams comply with the legal regulations on food safety, traceability and quality. This is based on the Autocontrol Guide, a document approved by the Federal Agency for the Safety of the Food Chain (FASFC) with clear guidelines.

In addition to products that meet their own stringent quality requirements, the company also markets around 100 to 200 hams per week that come from bio-certified pigs. The term 'organic' is legally protected and there is a compulsory check on the products that the company puts on the market as 'bio'.

WHY ARE HAMS HUNG FROM THE CEILING?

An obvious reason for hanging hams from the ceiling is to let them dry. In many bars, restaurants and wineries they now hang mainly as a decorative element. In Spain, however, this had another reason at the time of the great persecution of the Jews in the Middle Ages. Owners of eateries wanted to make clear that they were not of Jewish origin by ostentatiously hanging a ham, and this usually exempted them from further suspicions or police investigations.

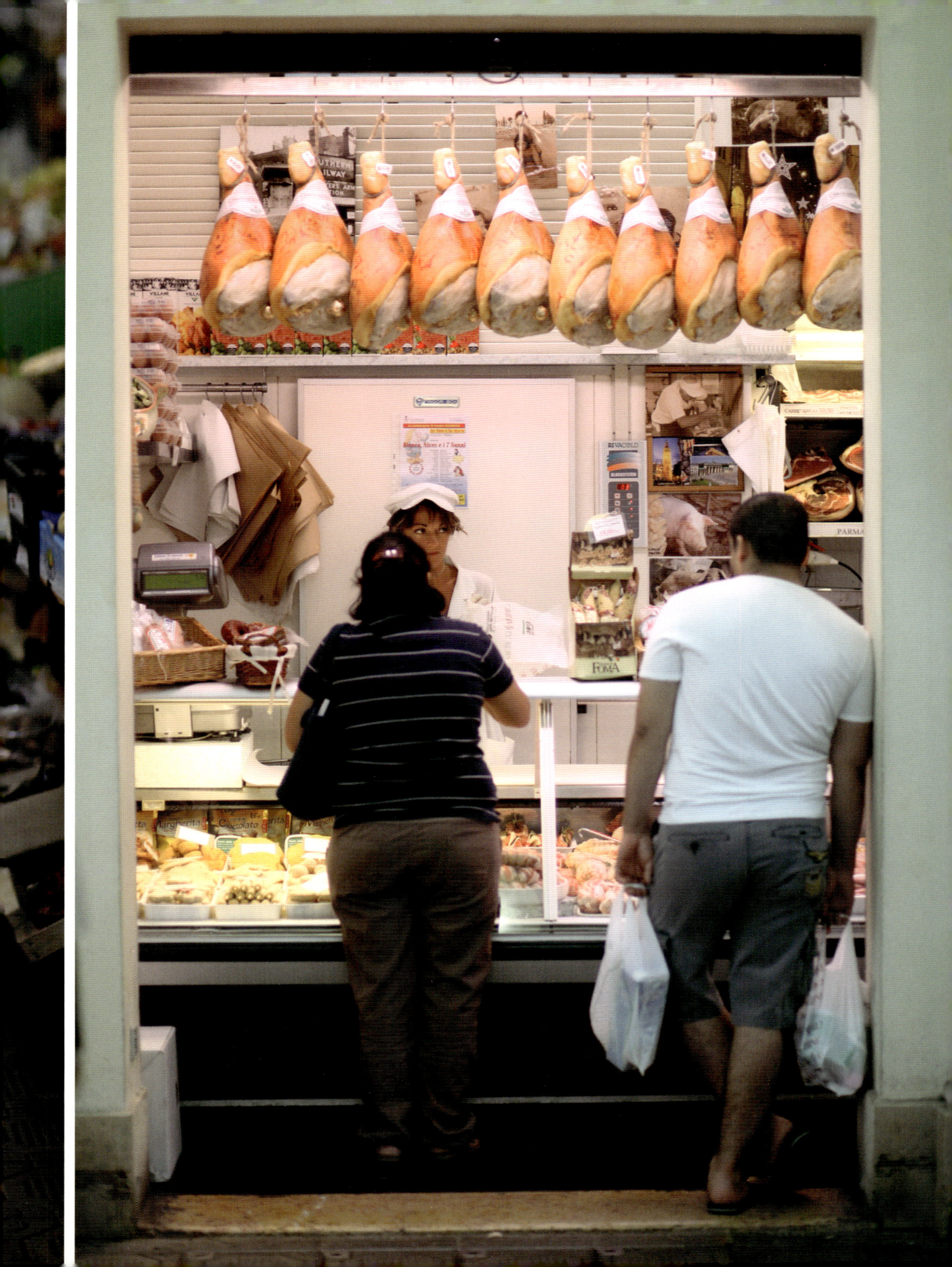
RIVACOLD
PARMA

FACTORS THAT DETERMINE TASTE

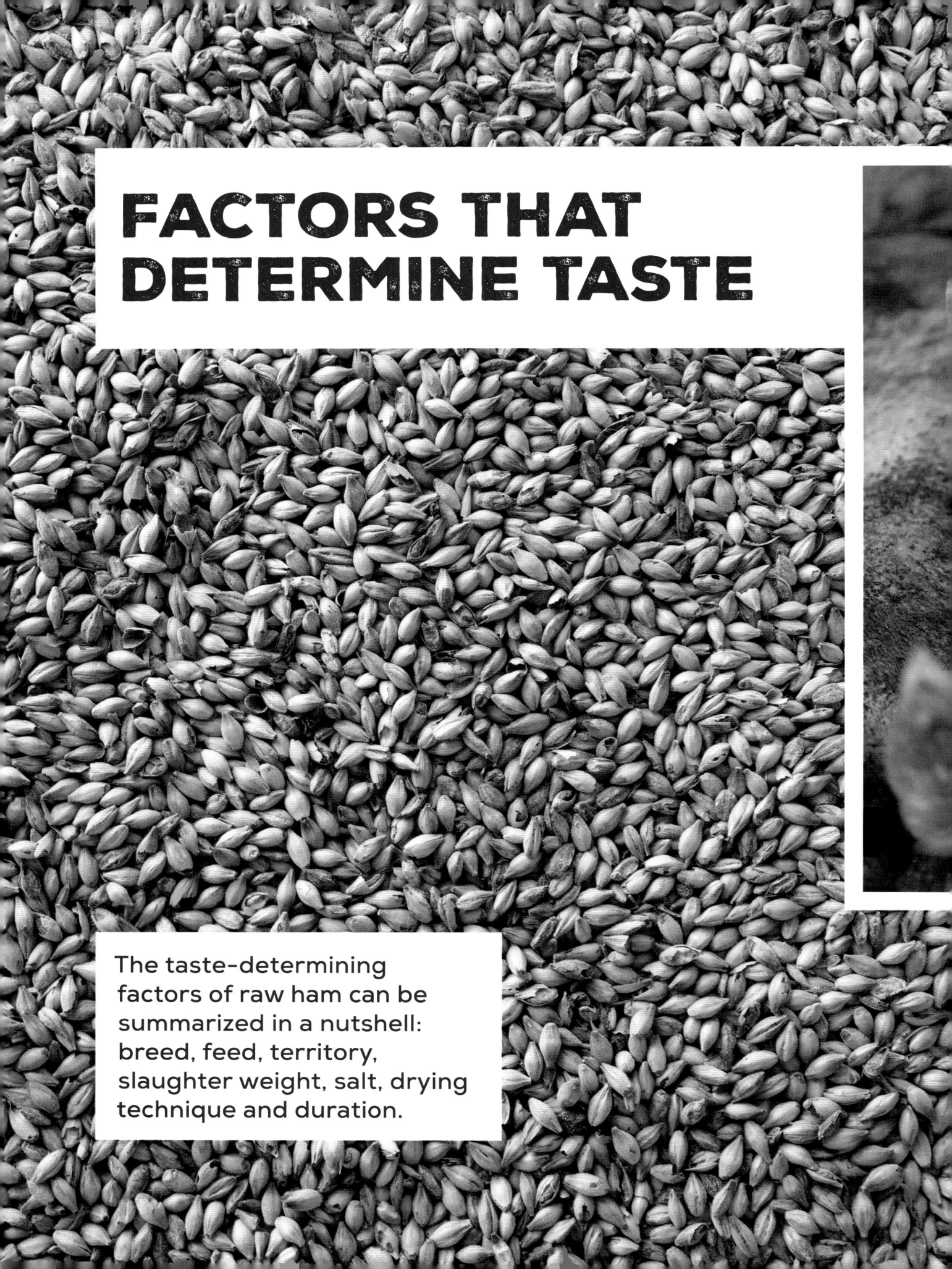

The taste-determining factors of raw ham can be summarized in a nutshell: breed, feed, territory, slaughter weight, salt, drying technique and duration.

Of course everything starts with the pig. As mentioned above, this animal is perhaps one of the oldest companions of human beings, and in the course of history many varieties have developed around the world.

When humans began to breed pigs, only animals that best met the local conditions and taste preferences of the local population were retained. Exchange of animals over long distances was rare, creating local breeds with their own specific characteristics. Only the strongest animals survived diseases and climatic conditions, which automatically 'purified' the different breeds.

Through the process of trial and error, man tried to cross different breeds through the ages, but the scientific basis for this is only recent.

In Belgium, at the end of the 19th century, extensive thought had been given to the improvement of pigs. For example, a commission was established in 1898 by the Ministry of Agriculture with the task of creating a more economical pig with more and better meat qualities. This committee came to the conclusion that, among other things, an average specimen of the white Yorkshire breed should be used to give our native pig an injection of quality. In the period up to 1930 this led to a mix of pigs in Belgium with the main categories being the 'bacon pig', a very fat pig with a slaughter weight of 150 kg, and the 'meat pig', a lean pig with a slaughter weight of 90 to 100 kg.

Between 1900 and 1930 the first programs of carefully organized selection originated in Belgium, which were then adopted by other countries as well. The user made more and more demands on the pig, especially in the area of leaner meat. The breeders tried to meet these wishes and therefore increasingly imported carefully selected foreign breeds to cross with their own best pigs.

In addition to the animal itself, the diet of the animal also plays a major role in the final taste of the meat in general and of ham in particular. The pigs of yore and free-range pigs fed on what they found and could find on the spot. Pigs are notorious omnivores. Indeed, purely biologically speaking, the pig is an omnivore with teeth that are suitable for eating both plants and meat. With a set of premolars and large canines, the pig can handle not only grasses and forest fruits, but also larvae, carrion and even smaller mammals. The premolars are suitable for both grinding and cutting this varied diet, and the large canines are useful for rooting in the soil for food.

For pigs grown on a commercial scale, there are extensive feeding programs that vary according to the age of the animal. Piglets have different needs than sows or pigs being fattened. There is a specific standard diet for each of these groups.

In the classic feeding trough of a commercially grown pig you will find basic raw materials such as corn, soy, grains and all kinds of remains from the food industry, such as pulp from sugar beets. Residues such as potato peelings or sunflower seeds can also be added.

Basic pig feed must contain just enough easily digestible carbohydrates to prevent the animals from getting too fat. Inadequate nutrition not only gives the pig a deficiency of necessary nutrients, but also creates an unsatisfied feeling of hunger, resulting in deviant behaviour.

Production pigs that receive concentrated food usually have to expend little effort. This does not match their natural need to look for food. Complementing their rations with fibre-rich roughage such as grass and hay is therefore advisable.

AUSTRALIAN HAM

If you eat ham with a bone in Australia, it is a local specimen or an illegally imported ham. For reasons of hygiene, Australian law prohibits the importation of hams with a bone.

Just as with the cultivation of grapes for an excellent wine, the territory where the pig grows up also plays a role. Pigs that roam freely in the woods eat plants such as acorns and grasses. These create a unique taste in the meat, which is more reminiscent of game than of pork as we know it.

By running around freely in nature, the muscles of these pigs are also much more developed. This makes the fat infiltrate nicely into the body of the animals, which benefits the taste.

The slaughtering weight of pigs is clearly evolving and has an influence on the taste of the meat. For example, the average slaughter weight in 1990 was 83 kg per pig but has now increased to 93 kg. The reasons for producing more meat-weight per pig are varied. However, pig farmers also want to bring costs and yields into line with ecological sustainability. Heavier pigs offer economic benefits, and the Flemish 'Agentschap voor Innovatie door Wetenschap en Technologie' (Agency for Innovation by Science and Technology – IWT) is financing a study in this context (carried out by the Belgian ILVO Animal Unit and ILVO Agricultural and Society Unit). For example, a simple calculation model was developed that would allow pig farms to determine an ideal slaughter weight on the basis of a number of company-specific data.

In the production of raw ham, salt is the only physical addition to the meat. Naturally, the salt itself is essential, but so is the specific salting process that can vary from ham to ham.

According to a French legend, this conservation process goes back to two Gallic farmers who saw one of their pigs disappear in a pond filled with salt water. When months later, after a prolonged warm period, the pond became dry, the animal turned out to be remarkably well-preserved and the meat also tasted good. This story can be taken with … a grain of salt, but the fact is that the Gauls did perfect the technique of salting.

52 | FACTORS THAT DETERMINE TASTE

In our time, with scientific precision, these techniques have been developed further on a hygienic level.

Another determining flavour factor that follows the salting is the drying of the ham. The specific drying time varies from region to region depending on climatic conditions and the taste that the producer wishes to achieve. The presence of certain bacteria and fungi in combination with the specific characteristics in the air and the air movements all contribute to the development of the taste of a dried ham.

Worldwide, hams are matured for different lengths of time. Exactly how many months a ham ripens has an unmistakable influence on the taste. Longer ripening does not necessarily mean that the ham is 'better', but 'different'. It is similar to the aging of a malt whiskey in the barrel: the taste changes depending on the maturation period but that does not mean that everyone will appreciate it.

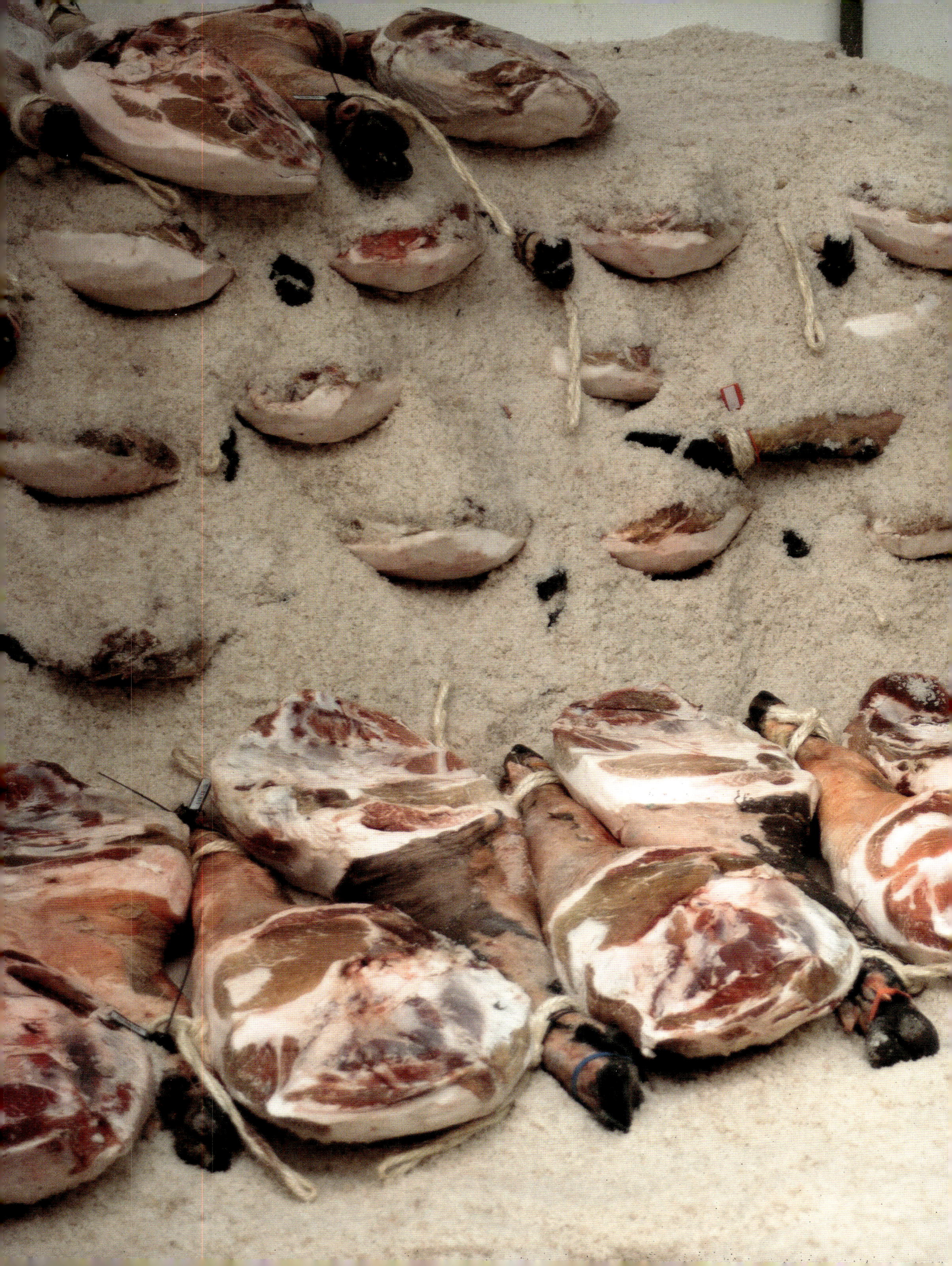

In Huelva in Spain, the hams, here palettas or shoulder hams, are stacked together during the salting process. The salt master determines how and for how long; this may vary by a few days. The minerals in the salt are already a first taste-determining factor.

THE IMPORTANCE OF SALT

The importance of salt in the process of storing, drying and curing meat or ham cannot be emphasized enough. Salt is, in addition to the meat itself and together with the element of time, the most essential part of a good ham.

Worldwide, salt is extracted along the coastlines. This is done, for example, on the Atlantic Ocean and along the Mediterranean Sea. One of the most important salt areas in the world is the Camargue. After concentration and drying in the reservoirs, a million cubic metres of salt are extracted annually from a total surface area of salt extraction sites of around 12,000 hectares. This makes the Camargue the largest salt extraction area in Europe.

In the area that stretches along the foot of Aigues-Mortes lies the oldest salt pan of the Mediterranean. Salt has been extracted here for centuries. This raw material generates the economic strength of the city and the region.

Four hundred years ago, some fifteen foresighted salt producers entered into a partnership under the leadership of a merchant from

Montpellier. From this initially rudimentary collaboration, the company Les Salins du Midi came into being in 1856.

Long before the emergence of the current ideological trend, the traders of this company produced salt in an environmentally conscious manner. This is evident because the salt production takes place in a natural environment that is important for the quality of the salt. The company also draws its energy from the surrounding elements of nature such as wind and water.

The salt is extracted in evaporation basins. These salt pans are flooded with fresh seawater at high tide. Before the water evaporates and the salt starts to crystallize, a thin layer of salt is formed on the surface of the water. This happens only with the right weather conditions, water temperature and salt balance. This crust floats only briefly on the surface of the seawater. It must be manually dipped off at the right time, after which it is dried in the sun. This creates fleur de sel. The salt layer is indeed reminiscent of a thin layer of ice with ice flowers.

Salt production is not only economically important for the region but also has its usefulness in maintaining biodiversity.

Lakes too can be sites for salt extraction. In Senegal, 25 km from the capital Dakar (where the Paris-Dakar rally formerly finished) we find Lac Retba (Pink Lake). This lake has a high salt content and is separated from the Atlantic by dunes. The name refers to the pink colour of the water. This colour can be explained by the presence of red plankton and microorganisms such as bacteria. The high concentration of salt ensures that the sunlight is diffracted in a different way. This also contributes to the pink appearance of the water.

The high salt concentration makes life in the water virtually impossible and just like in the Dead Sea you can float on this water. The lake is about three metres deep, one and a half metres of which consists of salt. The water flows through underground 'channels' from the ocean under the dunes and is purified in this natural way.

Salt from Cádiz in Spain and from the Adour river in France

In the region, salt extraction is one of the main sources of income. The work is mainly done by labourers from other African countries such as Mali, Niger and Benin.

Other areas known for their salt extraction include Kilold's mines near Carrickfergus (Northern Ireland), Cheshire and Worcestershire (England), Rheinberg (Germany), Wieliczka and Bochnia (Poland), Hallstatt and Salzkammergut (Austria), Tuzla (Bosnia), Cacica, Salina Turda and Praid (Romania), Provadia (Bulgaria), Racalmuto and Petralia Soprana (southern Italy), Khemisset (Morocco), Khewra and Warcha (Pakistan), the Detroit Salt Company with an underground salt-mine complex of 10 km² and the Sifto salt mine in Goderich (Canada), currently the largest working salt mine in the world.

Clockwise: Celtic sea salt, fleur de sel, Portuguese sea salt and English sea salt

- AMMERLÄNDER SCHINKEN
- GANDA HAM
- GREGA
- BRUGSE HAM
- WESTFÄLISCHER SCHINKEN
- MAINZER SCHINKEN
- JAMBON D'ARDENNE
- ENAME ABDIJHAM
- ST. ELOY
- SCHWARZWÄLDER SCHINKEN
- JAMBON D'AUVERGNE
- UZERCHE SALAISONS
- JAMBON DE BAYONNE
- JAMBON NOIR DE BIGORRE
- JAMÓN BIANCO SERRANO
- JAMÓN BLANCO TERUEL
- IBERICO JAMÓN IBÉRICO GUIJUELO
- JAMÓN IBÉRICO DEHESA DE EXTREMADURA
- JAMÓN IBÉRICO LOS PEDROCHES
- JAMÓN BLANCO DE SERÓN
- PRESUNTO DE BARRANCOS
- JAMÓN IBÉRICO JABUCHO
- JAMÓN BLANCO TRÉVELEZ

EUROPEAN HAMS

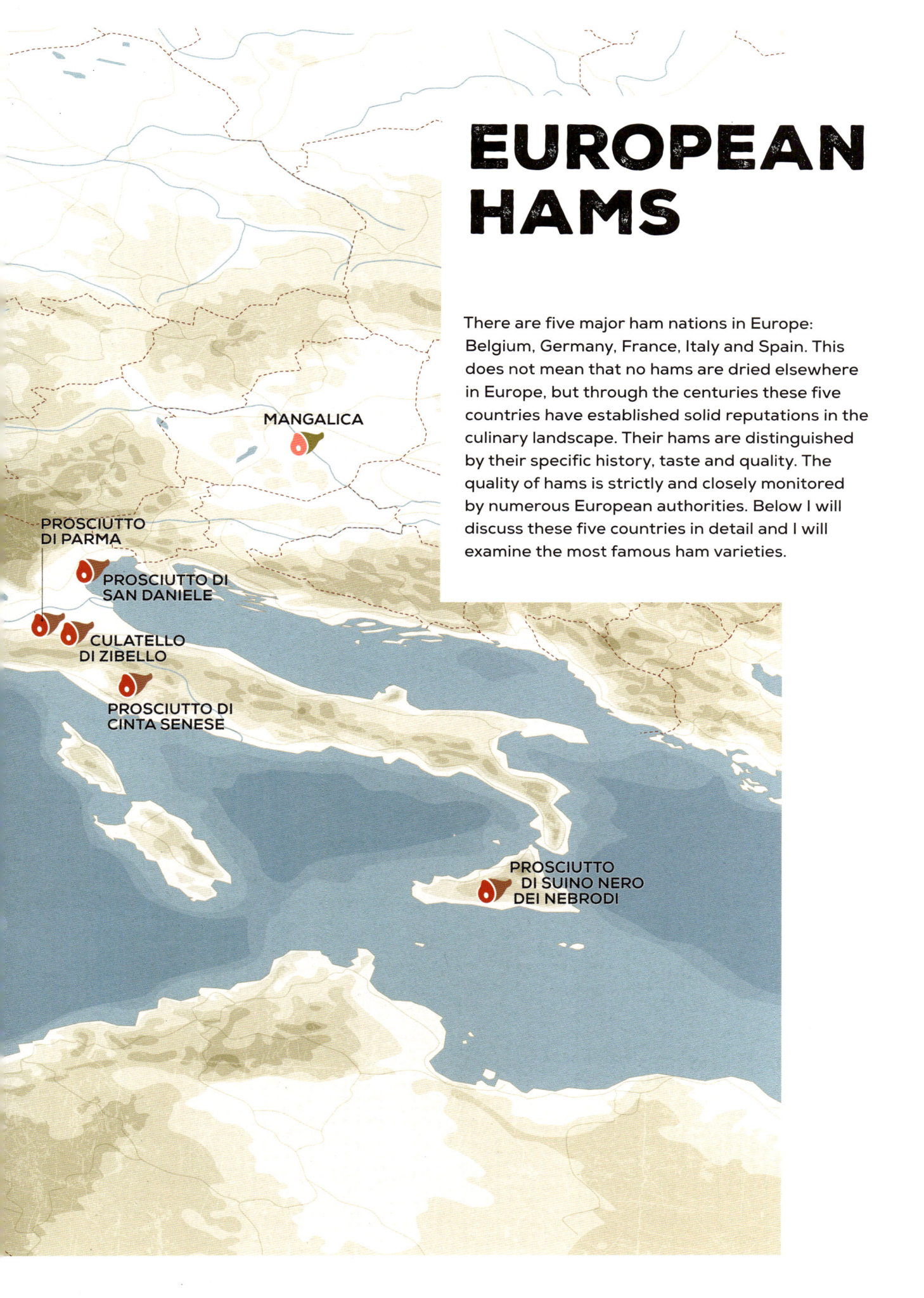

There are five major ham nations in Europe: Belgium, Germany, France, Italy and Spain. This does not mean that no hams are dried elsewhere in Europe, but through the centuries these five countries have established solid reputations in the culinary landscape. Their hams are distinguished by their specific history, taste and quality. The quality of hams is strictly and closely monitored by numerous European authorities. Below I will discuss these five countries in detail and I will examine the most famous ham varieties.

- MANGALICA
- PROSCIUTTO DI PARMA
- PROSCIUTTO DI SAN DANIELE
- CULATELLO DI ZIBELLO
- PROSCIUTTO DI CINTA SENESE
- PROSCIUTTO DI SUINO NERO DEI NEBRODI

BELGIUM

Belgium has a solid reputation to maintain as a ham nation. The export of Belgian pigs, fresh pork, hams and sides goes to all parts of the world. And the quality of Belgian meat is renowned. Every self-respecting butcher in Belgium makes his own charcuterie. And, if possible, he also dries his own ham. This is something to be proud of ...

As described above, the pig was highly regarded in our region at the time of the Romans. These were tame breeds that had been crossed with wild breeds that had more fat and meat. For centuries these pigs roamed our forests where they lived on a diet of acorns, chestnuts and other nuts. Gradually, stricter regulations came into force and free breeding was restricted in order to obtain pure, meat-rich varieties with great taste.

It was no accident that the technique of making hams was refined further in wooded areas where a suitable microclimate for the drying and ripening of the hams prevailed. In our region that was primarily in the Ardennes.

Everywhere, local recipes were created for making dried ham, usually with a number of common characteristics. For example, the hams were first marinated from several days up to a week in a preparation with herbs and salt and then they were brined. Afterwards the hams underwent a process of smoking and drying for months, either cold or not cold, in a sheltered place or in the chimney high above the hearth. Finally, a maturation of several months followed in places with natural air circulation such as caves.

JAMBON D'ARDENNE

A prime example of this is Jambon d'Ardenne, a ham with an ancient history that is the pride of Wallonia. According to historians the Ardennes region is the cradle of dried hams …

For centuries this ham has been an indispensable ingredient of every feast. There was no menu from the 19th or 20th century for the nobility and the bourgeoisie on which Jambon d'Ardenne did not play a prominent role.

A Royal Decree of 1974 established the authenticity, the production method and the geographical position of this ham. In this way the name was protected against wild growth and abuse. According to this Royal Decree, the ham, after being dry-salted or wet-brined, must be smoked with wood or wood chips without the use of coniferous or recycled wood.

Jambon d'Ardenne can only be produced in the province of Luxembourg and some cantons of the provinces of Liège and Namur, namely Beauraing, Gedinne, Rochefort, Dinant, Ferrières, Stavelot, Malmedy, Saint-Vith, Louveigné, Spa and Eupen. This means that the pigs from which the ham originates must also be raised there. Since 1996, Jambon d'Ardenne is the only Belgian ham to have a European provenance, the PGI (Protected Geographical Indication). For connoisseurs, Jambon d'Ardenne is a true delicacy due to its specific taste characteristics and distinct character.

For this ham, only the heart with the lower butt and nut (with or without bone) is used. The minimum weight of the hams is 4 kg.

The salting time, dry or wet, varies between 12 and 21 days and occurs with the addition of aromatics such as garlic, thyme, bay and rosemary …

The drying process lasts for a period of at least 3 months.

The ham can be smoked with different local woods (with the exception of resin-bearing trees / conifers), with the addition of juniper or thyme.

A total of 21 companies have been recognized as producers of Jambon d'Ardenne.

GANDA HAM

This famous ham from the Ghent region can be called the Heinz or the Coca-Cola of hams. Or how a brand name became a quality product with a name …

In the 1950s, Roger Cornelis and his wife Maria Mattheeuws opened a modest butcher's shop in Wetteren in East Flanders. The shop soon became too small and after a few years the business was moved to a larger building in Mariakerke. In 1954, Roger Cornelis decided to sell his butcher's shop in Destelbergen to start the meat company Corma (a contraction of Cornelis and Mattheeuws). This company specialized in the production of cooked meats and salted hams.

Corma created their first 'farm ham' in 1978. After their son Dirk joined the company and after many experiments with salting and brining processes, Ganda Ham was born in 1985.

'Ganda' is the old Celtic name for Ghent and literally means 'merging' (of the Leie and Schelde rivers). With regard to ham, this is translated into the merging of Flemish perseverance and know-how with the natural character of the hams.

Ganda Ham has become a hallmark in itself. Every ham that finds its way to the consumer after a strictly controlled selection procedure is given the branding of the Ganda logo as a sign of quality and artisan tradition. Corma produces over 100,000 hams annually.

Full hams are used for Ganda Ham. The bone is sometimes removed before sale. The minimum weight of the hams is 10.5 to 13 kg.

The hams undergo a double salting. They are first salted for 1 week, then the salt is blown away and they are salted again, then the hams rest for 2 weeks.

The drying process of the small hams is at least 9 months, for the larger hams it is between 12 and 14 months.

The bone is removed only after hams are ordered.

Ganda Ham can be obtained in different types of packaging.

The producer follows the specifications of the Meesterlyck quality mark. This label applies the strictest standards in terms of production, such as low salt content, a ban on the addition of nitrites, phosphates and substances foreign to the product (flavour enhancers and dyes).

BRUGES HAM

In addition to Ganda Ham, Corma also participates in the production of Bruges Ham, a ham that was saved from oblivion. In 2008, Corma took over the Hoste Meat Products company in Maldegem. At Hoste Meat Products, dried and smoked artisanal hams are prepared with the main ingredients being Belgian pork and … time. The hams are recognized as a regional product by VLAM. Hoste Meat Products has also obtained the IFS Food Standard label and performs self-checking.

The hams are salted in a traditional way with an old spice and undergo a gentle ripening process. The brine is stored and used as long as it is good, giving the hams a more intense taste.

Afterwards, the hams are dried, and some are smoked. About half of the hams undergo a smoking process with oak and beech wood.

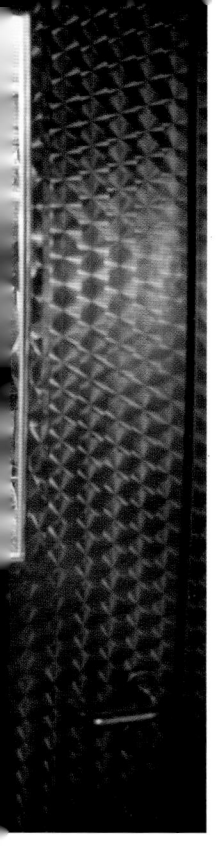

COBURG

These hams are cut into rectangles and are salted with the addition of herbs such as juniper and laurel (according to the firm's secret recipe). Afterwards, the hams rest stacked for about 20 days. After being brushed, they dry for 10 weeks and they are smoked cold with a mixture of beech and oak. After this, the hams are pressed into shape and obtain their typical rectangular appearance.

The ripening time is about 12 to 16 weeks.

GREGA MEAT PRODUCTS

Based in Buggenhout, the Van den Berghe-Vermeir family started in the 1950s with the production of dried ham in their family shop. The first hams were dried in a 'potato loft'. Today Grega has grown into a modern company that works according to traditional salting and drying processes. They produce about 100,000 hams per year. The ripening time of these hams varies from 9 to 24 months, depending on the quality of the ham.

ST. ELOY HAM

In 1960, Camiel Van Hoe, in the third generation of a family of traditional butchers in the Oudenaarde area, started with the traditional drying of hams from selected pigs from the region.

Today St. Eloy ham is a recognized local product and the fourth generation of the Van Hoe family has been added. The hams of St. Eloy are dried for at least 5 to 11 months, depending on the weight. Tradition and craftsmanship make the St. Eloy hams unique in structure and taste.

ENAME ABDIJHAM

In addition to the production of the St. Eloy ham, the Van Hoe family also handles the production of Ename Abbey ham. The hams find their origin in the Saint Salvator Abbey of Ename in the Flemish Ardennes. The hams are salted with sea salt in a traditional way. They ripen at least 9 to 12 months depending on the weight, and are dried with the bone in the ham. The curing master regularly pricks a piece of bone from a horse leg into the meat to check the quality. A conscious choice, because horse bone is very porous and can retain the odours.

After a final inspection, the ham is deboned, formed into the distinctive Ename ham shape and sewn up.

FARM HAM WITH BONE

The hams undergo strict control on the basis of acidity, colour and fat content. They then undergo a traditional salting process. This means that they are dry-salted and brined. The brine is not injected, but is naturally absorbed by the hams in a brine bath.

MATURE FARM HAM

To obtain this product, the hams are hung in drying rooms where the same temperature and humidity prevail. The natural ripening provides the traditional flavour, and after 6 to 7 months the ham is ready for consumption.

OTHER BELGIAN HAMS

In addition to Corma, there are a number of producers of raw hams in Belgium that each have their own character.

HAM AND ART

Ham also inspires artists. Enfant terrible Jan Fabre caused the customary controversy when he covered eight large pillars at the entrance of Ghent University in the Voldersstraat with slices of ham as part of the Over-the-Edge / On-the-Corner art project. He used no less than 360 kg of Ganda Ham for this. The choice of this quality product was not accidental. According to the artist, 'the dark-red colour and the capricious white patches of fat look like the marble pillars'.

Artist Dwight Kalb from Chicago also used ham to make a statue of Madonna. He needed 90 kg of ham for this.

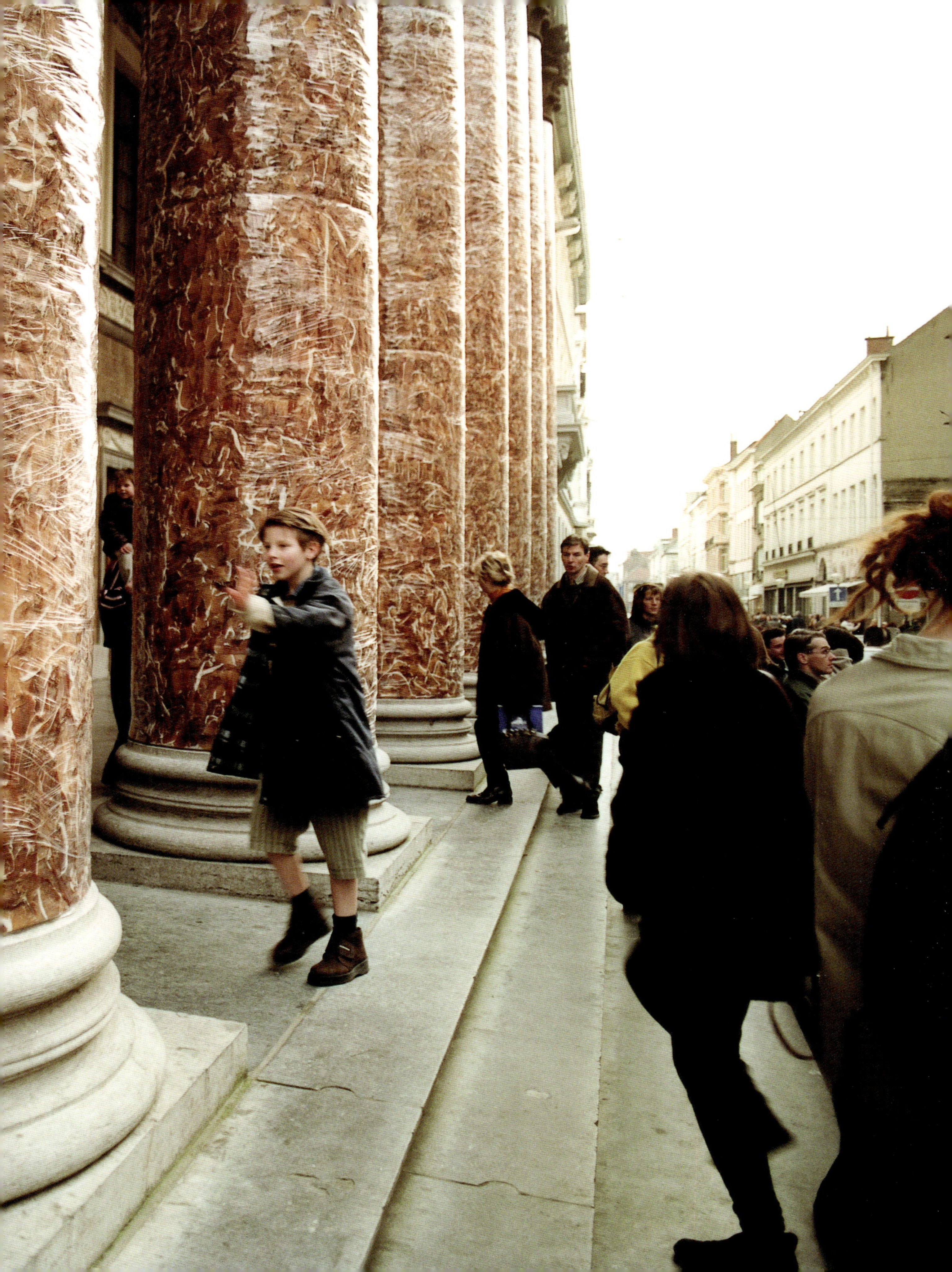

GERMANY

German hams are usually marketed without a bone.
The bone is removed before the salting process, which results in a flat butt.
German hams are usually dark in appearance and very aromatic in taste.

SCHWARZWÄLDER SCHINKEN

This ham is really unique. It originated centuries ago in the German Black Forest where pigs were allowed to get big and fat. These pigs fed well on the cones of the pine trees, but also on fresh herbs, which guaranteed a rich taste.

The bacon layer of the pigs is specific to this type of ham that is also recognizable by the black exterior and powerful red flesh inside.

Typical for this ham is the flat butt with a muscle piece. It is always deboned. The minimum weight is 7 to 8 kg after deboning.

The hams, which are always deboned before drying, undergo a 1-week process of dry salting along with aromatics: pepper, garlic and juniper berries (according to a secret recipe of the house). Then the hams go into an extra wet brine for 1 week according to the same recipe. The drying process takes 2 to 3 weeks in smoking rooms (cold smoking at 25° C on pine with extra herbs according to the family secret), then another 3 to 7 weeks in rooms or natural spaces at 15° C.

The selected producers use a logo on the ham of a pine tree with red balls. The ham has the EU designation PGI (Protected Geographical Indication).

AMMERLÄNDER SCHINKEN

This ham gets its specific flavour and aroma from the wind that blows in the country between the Ems and Weser rivers. Through the centuries, large pigs were converted into the Ammerländer pig breed that has a lot of fat.

This ham consists of a flat butt with a muscle piece, it is deboned and has a minimum weight of 12.5 kg.

The salting time is 6 weeks with dry salt or brine, with aromatics such as chili, brown sugar and juniper (according to a secret recipe of the house). This is followed by a drying process of 2 to 3 weeks in the open air under thatched roofs, which is then followed by 10 weeks of cold smoking on beech wood at a temperature of 25° C. Then there are still 6 weeks of aging at 15° C.

This ham is black on the outside and a beautiful red on the inside with a very specific taste and aroma.

The ham has the EU designation of PGI (Protected Geographical Indication).

WESTFÄLISCHER SCHINKEN

Another tasty prime ham from Germany with a unique character is the Westfälischer Schinken. In terms of time, this is perhaps the longest smoked ham in the world.

This ham has a flat butt with a muscle piece, is deboned and has a minimum weight of 10 kg.

The hams undergo 5 weeks of salt drying with aromatics according to the secret recipe of the house. They are stacked in the salt. This is followed by a drying process of 5 months in smoking rooms (cold smoking at 25° C on beech wood with extra herbs according to the family secret). Then they are cured for 3 more months in rooms or natural spaces at 15° C.

This ham is brownish-black on the outside and dark-red on the inside. The ham has a very specific strong taste and a pronounced aroma.

MAINZ-HAM

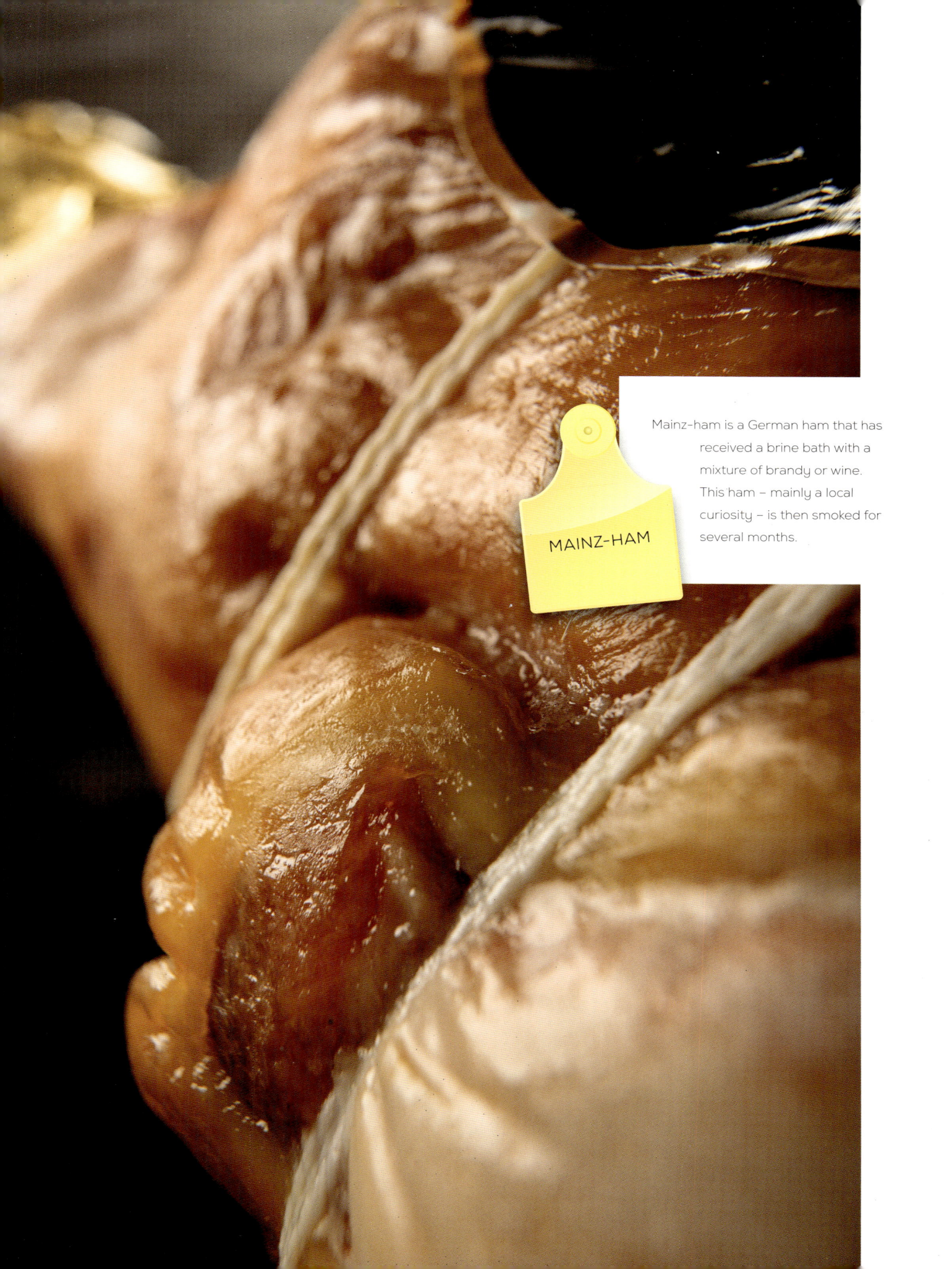

Mainz-ham is a German ham that has received a brine bath with a mixture of brandy or wine. This ham – mainly a local curiosity – is then smoked for several months.

OBELIX'S LOVE FOR WILD BOAR

The Gauls were also fond of ham. It is no coincidence that the favourite hobby of Asterix's companion Obelix is to eat wild boar. Preferably fresh and in its entirety, but a dried ham is always included. For the classic feast at the end of each story, pork must be included on the menu.

FRANCE

Typical for French hams is the use of aromatics such as garlic, clove, cinnamon, marjoram and the specific herbs of the region. Each department in the middle and south of France has its own traditional raw ham. This is mainly marketed and consumed locally, and every self-respecting restaurant has its own ham on the menu.
In addition to all these local hams, four French hams have also penetrated the international market.

JAMBON DE BAYONNE

The region of Bayonne in southern France is one of the most famous origins of French hams. From this port city the various hams from the area have always been shipped. Eventually the products of a collection of small ham producers were united into one known type of ham.

The Ham Feasts in the Easter period are world-famous. Every year a champion is crowned and a grand procession takes place in honour of the Bayonne ham.

This type of ham consists of a complete hind ham without the foot.

They are hams from white pigs such as the Duroc and the Large White Landrace. The pigs come from Aquitaine. Midi-Pyrénées and Poitou-Charentes and from the neighbouring departments of Hautes-Pyrénées, Landes and Gers. These pigs are fed mainly with corn.

The minimum weight of the hams is 10 kg.

The salting time consists of 3 weeks of hand-salting according to the secret recipe of the house with aromatics such as clove, cinnamon, basil, chillies and salt from the region around Bayonne. The hams are stacked in Sel de l'Adour, which is salt from the Salines de l'Adour.

The drying process consists of 8 weeks of aging and then drying for at least 9 to 12 months. This drying takes place in rooms along the river Adour where a wind blows from the Atlantic Ocean that has a favourable influence on the taste of the ham.

The producers include no fewer than 1,700 pig breeders and 41 meat-product producers.

JAMBON D'AUVERGNE

The Jambon d'Auvergne is 'the small ham that is hard to come by'. The ham is so delicious that people from the region would rather eat it themselves … The ham is protected by the Label Rouge which is a French quality seal for traceability and authenticity.

This is a rear ham, round cut, without pubic bone and foot, from Duroc or Piétrain pigs. The minimum weight is 9 kg.

The authentication checks occur at the time of slaughter and after the ripening process.

The hams undergo a process of 10 to 12 days of manual salting with sea salt and garlic. Immediately afterwards they are dried for 7 months or exactly 210 days. This happens in the caves of Auvergne where the famous cheeses also age, but then in open areas. There is no ripening or smoking process.

This ham loses practically a third of its weight during drying, yielding hams of up to 6 kg.

The producers do not supply more than 400,000 hams per year.

JAMBON NOIR DE BIGORRE

This ham is quite similar to Bayonne ham with the difference that only the Noir de Bigorre breed is used. This is a typical black pig breed that has developed at the foot of the French Pyrenees. This variety received the Protected Designation of Origin (PDO) on 15 September 2017.

The production zone consists of the departments Hautes-Pyrénées, the Comminges and Haute-Garonne and the surrounding l'Astarac in the Gers. This region corresponds to the cradle of this historical breed. The mild climate ensures a good interaction between sun and rain with little wind and gentle temperatures, the ideal habitat for the pigs, which are able to live in the open air.

This ham consists of the complete rear ham without foot. The minimum weight of the hams is 8.5 kg.

The salting time is determined by the weight of the raw fresh ham. The salting with salt from Salines de l'Adour takes place at low temperature for 10 to 16 weeks, during which the ham loses a lot of moisture.

Drying proceeds at a mild, constant temperature of 10 to 12° C for a period of 10 months. During this process the hams are rubbed with lard. The drying process of the hams has been established at a minimum of 20 months.

The consortium has only one ham preparer / refiner who has been selected by the various producers who let their hams dry together.

The finishing of the hams takes place over a period of 10 months in smoking rooms with windows so that the wind from the mountains can freely pass through the ripening rooms.

UZERCHE SALAISONS ('LA PERLE DU LIMOUSIN')

Since the beginning, dried hams at Uzerche Salaisons have been produced with the utmost respect for tradition and craftsmanship. The company was founded in 1964 by the Trarieux family, but was sold in 1988. In the meantime, the company has come under the auspices of Corma, the producer of Ganda Ham.

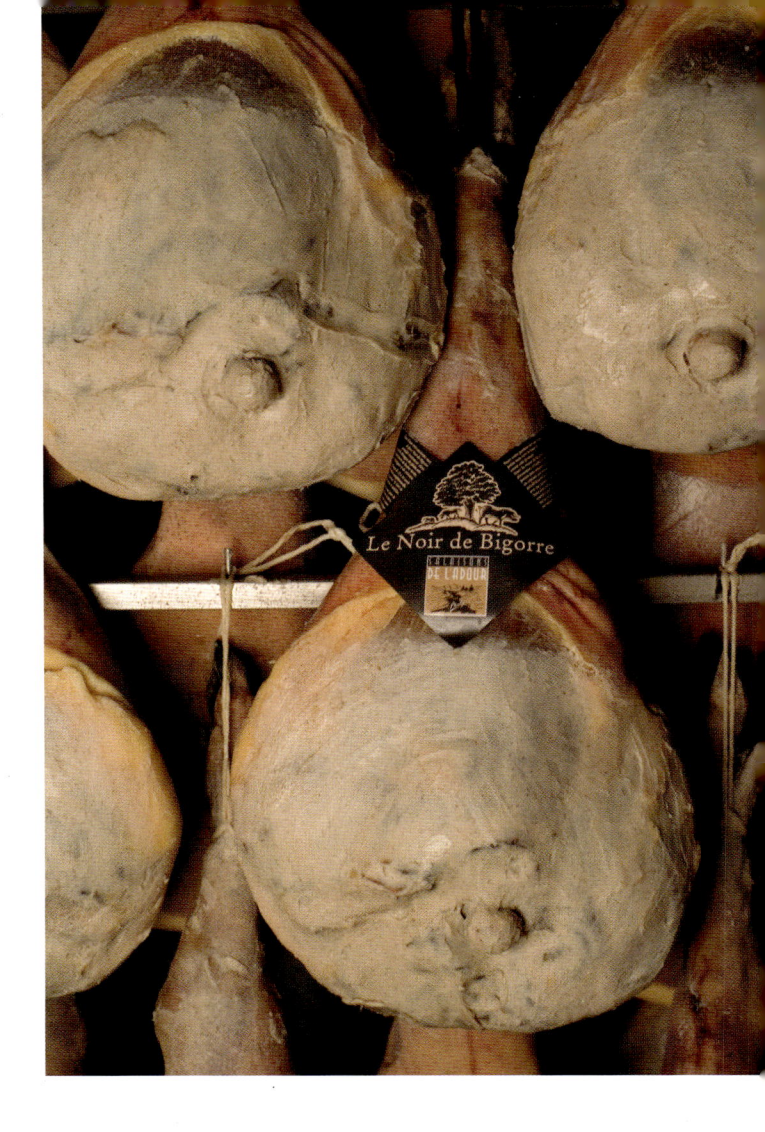

The workshops and drying rooms are located in the picturesque village of Uzerche in the Corrèze, a quiet place with a serene beauty that touches every passer-by. Because of the beautiful location in a rocky bend of the meandering Vézère, this place got the nickname 'la Perle du Limousin'.

All hams are salted by skilled staff and then dried in the mild climate of the Limousin. Drying takes 7 to 9 months and afterwards the bones are removed from the hams.

The ham gets its delicate taste and refined aroma from the long ripening period and a spice mix according to an old secret family recipe.

ITALY

Italy is an important ham country historically.
The Romans obviously had something to do with that.

PROSCIUTTO DI PARMA

The term Parma ham refers to traditionally dried, raw ham from the province of Parma. It is a protected name where the ham must meet a number of conditions. No preservatives or additives may be used, and consequently Parma ham consists only of meat and sea salt.

The ham must be made from pigs born and raised in Italy, more specifically from the provinces of Emilia-Romagna, Veneto, Piedmont, Lombardy, Umbria, Abruzzo, Tuscany, Marken and Lazio. The pigs must be at least 9 months old and weigh 160 kg. Part of the food of the animals must consist of the whey left over from the production of Parmesan cheese.

The ham must have been dried in the mountain winds for at least 12 months and may only be made in the province of Parma (due to the specific climate).

Parma ham can be recognized by the five-pointed crown on the ham or the packaging. The consortium Consorzio del Prosciutto di Parma ensures that all conditions are met.

There may also be ham from Parma that cannot officially be called Parma ham. This ham, which often uses imported meat, is usually of lower quality.

PROSCIUTTO DI SAN DANIELE

The village of San Daniele in Friuli is located on a hill by the Tagliamento River, close to the pre-Alpine slopes. Here the cool air of the north meets the warm, iodine-rich sea breeze of the Adriatic Sea.

The pigs used for San Daniele ham come from eleven selected regions where they are born, bred and slaughtered, namely Friuli-Venezia Giulia, Veneto, Emilia-Romagna, Piedmont, Tuscany, Umbria, Marken, Lazio, Abruzzo and Molise.

The pigs must have a minimum weight of 160 kg, be at least 9 months old and supply hams of at least 11 kg. The pigs must originate from one of the traditional breeds (Large White or Landrace). They may be a cross with the Duroc breed, but these pigs must meet the requirements of the national genealogical book of the Italian big pig. The breeders must tattoo the piglets at birth on both hind legs, so that the farm and the month of birth can be found quickly.

With the ham (out of respect, among other reasons) the hoof is retained. The butcher must check in advance whether the grower has complied with the production regulations and places a stamp on the hind feet.

The salting time is 14 to 16 days and afterwards the hams are pressed or tied up. Tying up is typically Italian and is done to obtain a much better quality. They are salted through for 36 to 42 days. The minimum drying time is 12 months and is usually 24 months. The super quality ripens up to 36 months.

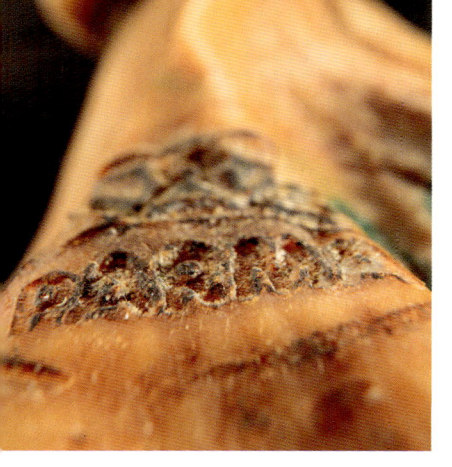

CULATELLO DI ZIBELLO

In Italian, culatello means 'nice ass' …

This ham comes from pigs that were born, bred and slaughtered in the Lombardy and Emilia-Romagna regions. They must be at least 18 months old at slaughter. The production of the hams is done by a total of eleven companies in the municipalities of Busseto, Roccabianca, Polesine Parmense, San Secondo, Zibello, Sissa, Soragna and Colorno.

This ham is made from the thick butt and the bottom nut and is distinguished by a deep ruby-red colour. The two parts of the ham, 4.5 to 5.5 kg, are enriched with salt, pepper, garlic and red or white wine. The salting time is about 6 days and a mixture of sea salt and table salt is used. The hams are then salted through for a period of 18 to 21 days at a temperature between 0 and 5° C. After this, the hams are wrapped in a pig's bladder and ripen for a period of 14 to 18 months.

PROSCIUTTO DI CINTA SENESE

The pig from which this ham comes is characterized by a white band behind or on its shoulders. All production operations take place in the province of Tuscany. The ham is labelled PDO (Protected Designation of Origin). Most of the hams produced are consumed locally.

The animals weigh between 160 and 180 kg at slaughter and are 12 to 16 months old.

The hams are salted and rubbed with spices and herbs such as pepper, rosemary, sage, wild thyme and bay leaf. They ripen for a period of 18 to 24 months.

The hams eventually weigh between 13 and 15 kg.

PROSCIUTTO DI SUINO NERO DEI NEBRODI

Including birth, raising and slaughter, all stages of the manufacturing process of these hams must take place in Sicily. Other provisions state that the pigs must be at least 14 months old at slaughter and weigh at least 120 kg.

The salting period depends on the weight of the ham. The hams dry and ripen for at least 18 to 24 months, the process of flavouring and seasoning is done in two phases. The final hams weigh 12 to 14 kg with 2 to 4 cm of fat.

Cinta means belt or band in Italian, which refers to the white band on the pig. A Senese is a resident of Siena. The *Cinta Senese* pigs are mainly found around the city of Siena.

HAM AND THE FINANCIAL WORLD

In Italy there is a clear historical link between the financial world and ham. Ham has been considered a good form of investment, especially in Parma, and the banks responded to this. At certain times ham was even more popular as an investment product than gold. Ham has played an important role in the history of a number of banks in Parma.

That link is still retained today. For example, the Italian Minister of Agriculture recently supported a plan to accept expensive ham as collateral for a loan. The idea comes from a wealthy bank director and gourmet who wants to support ham producers whose turnover has dropped recently.

SPAIN

There are two types of dried ham in Spain: Serrano ham and Iberico ham. A number of variations fall under each category, each with a verified designation of origin. They can be clearly distinguished from each other. Serrano ham comes from a white domestic pig, Iberico ham from a dark Iberian pig.

SERRANO HAM

Originally, every ham that was produced in Spain, regardless of the breed, was a Serrano ham. The name refers to the mountainous areas (Sierras) in the north and the south of Spain that are characterized by dry, fresh mountain air.

Now the name is only reserved for dried hams from white pigs produced on Spanish territory.

According to historical Roman sources, the Serrano ham from Hispania goes back to the late 2nd century BC.

Jamón Serrano is produced according to legal requirements from Spanish pigs of at least 110 kg, produced in Spain and dried for at least 9 months. In addition, the ham must meet a number of technical requirements. The hams must have at least 1 cm of fat cover, lose 34% of moisture compared to fresh ham, and undergo permanent quality checks from the Consorcio del Jamón Serrano Español. Each Serrano ham has a label with a control number and can be recognized by the large letter S with the name Serrano underneath.

Serrano ham is rubbed with sea salt and stacked for 2 weeks. Afterwards the hams are washed and piled up for 6 weeks in drying rooms. They are then aged 6 to 16 months in drying rooms. The minimum weight of the hams is 6.1 to 6.3 kg.

There are three classifications, depending on the ripening process:
- **Serrano Bodega:** with a ripening time of 10 to 12 months.
- **Serrano Reserva:** with a ripening time of 12 to 15 months.
- **Serrano Gran Reserva:** with a ripening time of more than 15 months.

The colour of Serrano ham varies from pink to purple, the taste goes from mild to slightly salted. In comparison with the Iberico ham, the taste, aroma and structure are slightly softer.

JAMÓN SERRANO

WITH PROVENANCE

- **Jamón Trevélez:** from an area 1,200 metres above sea level in the province of Granada, including the municipalities of Trevélez, Portugos, Capileira, Berchules, La Taha Juviles, Busquistar and Bubión.
- **Jamón de Teruel:** from the area south of Aragon, where most ripening buildings are located around 800 metres above sea level.

IBERICO HAM

The pig breed that supplies these hams comes from the Iberian Peninsula and consists of registered sows and boars. The hooves of these animals are usually black, hence the name 'pata negra' (black leg). The colour of the Iberico ham varies from pink to deep red. The ham has a light fibrous structure that is subtly interlaced with fat, light in colour and mild in taste.

The Iberico ham is produced in the southwestern provinces of Salamanca, Caceres, Badajoz, Huelva, Cordoba, Seville, Malaga and Cádiz. Some have the Protected Designation of Origin.

The official classification of Iberico hams is determined by the type of food and the amount of acorns that the animal has eaten:

- **Ibérico Pata Negra Bellota** (bellota = acorn): from pigs kept on a farm with free range on land with many cork oaks. The diet consists of acorns from these trees. They are clearly the number one in taste with a maturation of 36 months or more.
- **Ibérico Bellota Cebo de Campo:** from pigs living in the countryside where they eat grass supplemented with natural compound feed such as vegetables and grain products. In season they also get acorns.
- **Ibérico Cebo:** from pigs kept on a farm and that receive compound feed only.

LABELS WITH VARIOUS COLOURS

Recently, Ibérico hams have begun to be labelled with various colours to protect the quality of the real Ibérico Pata Negra.

- **Black:** 100% Ibérico Bellota ham. This ham comes from pigs that are fed only with acorns and grasses and that enjoy free range. This is the only type that can carry the name Pata Negra.
- **Red:** Ibérico Bellota ham. This ham comes from pigs fed with acorns and grasses, but the pigs are not 100% Iberico purebred (50 to 75%). The pigs did enjoy free range during their life.
- **Green:** Ibérico Cebo de Campo ham. This ham comes from pigs that are fed grasses and mixed food. The pigs are not purebred and they have a partially free range.
- **White:** Ibérico Cebo ham. This ham comes from pigs that are fed mixed food. The animals are not purebred and did not enjoy free range.

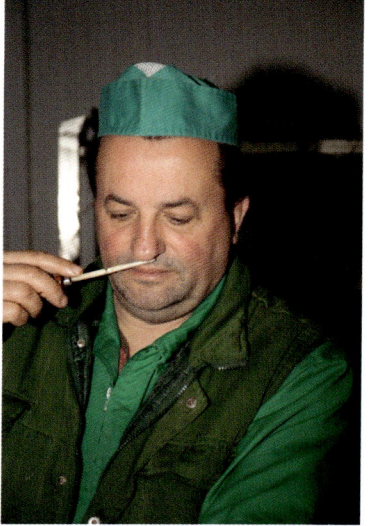

After curing for a few months – usually 6 months – and then every month after that, the ham master uses a piece of bone (made from the tibia of a horse's leg) to test the odour at five designated points on the ham. He 'smells' to make sure the meat has not gone sour. If that happens, the ham is automatically rejected for consumption.

To prevent the hams from drying out, they are coated with olive oil from the region. Here you see shoulder hams from Huelva.

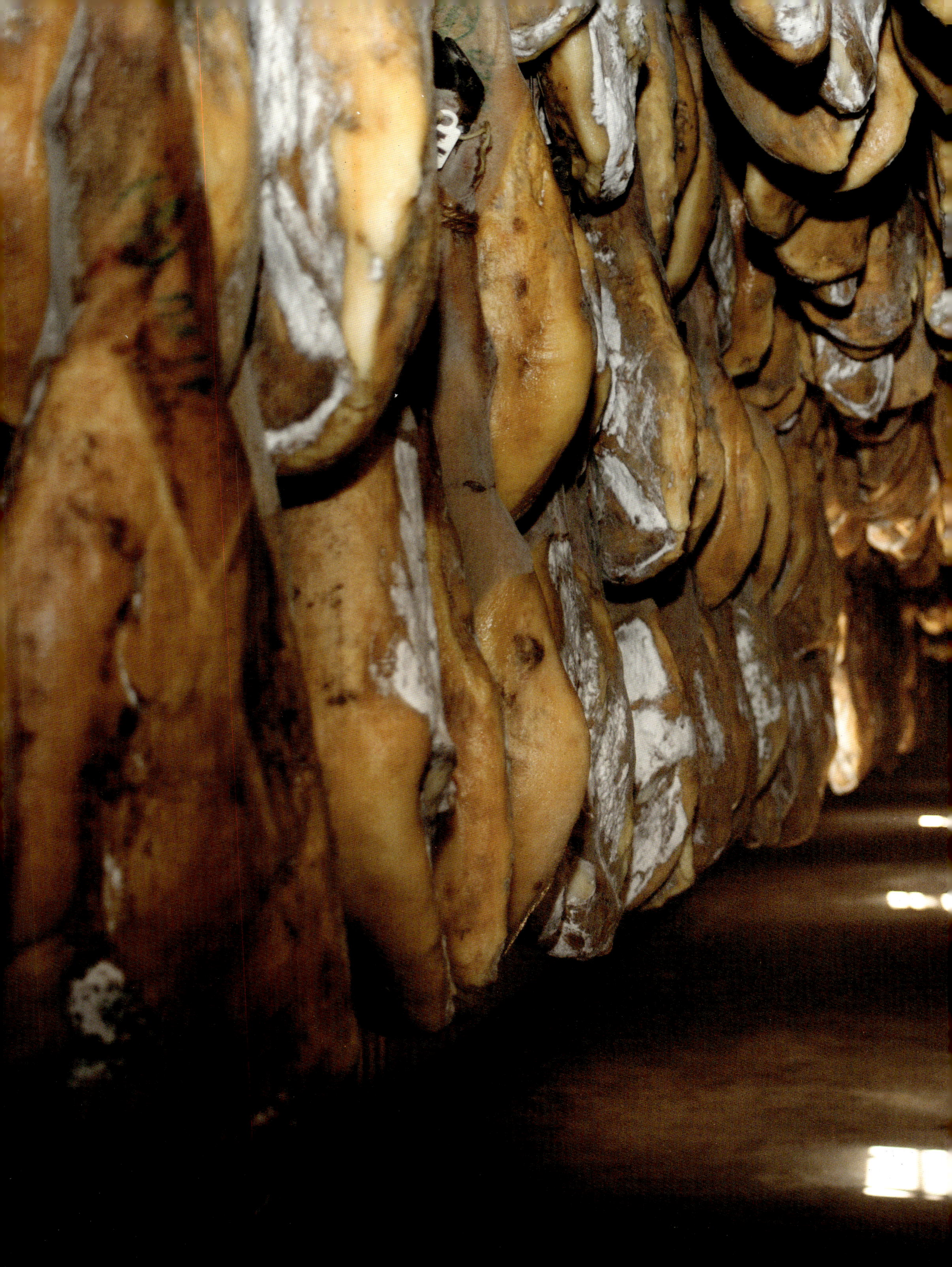

THE MOST EXPENSIVE HAM IN THE WORLD

The honorary title for the most expensive ham in the world goes to a Manchado de Jabugo that went for 4,100 euros in 2016 at a trade fair. The ham comes from ham producer Eduardo Donato. Although originally a Catalan, he has lived for the greater part of his life in Cortegana in the province of Huelva. This producer supplies only 80 hams per year from the endangered Manchado de Jabugo pigs. This pure Iberian spotted pig was almost completely destroyed by a swine fever plague and the large-scale industrialization of the sector. Some small pig farmers have managed to save the animal by raising some animals for their own use. The hams of these pigs are considered the best in the world.

The animals are cultivated strictly ecologically and run freely among streams, waterfalls and oak forests. It takes at least 3 to 5 years for the animal to reach its ideal weight. Getting such a ham is an exquisite privilege because the producer refuses to sell them digitally despite applications from all over the world. He insists on taking his hams to the buyer personally.

WHY DO YOU SOMETIMES FIND WHITE DOTS ON RAW HAM?

The presence of white dots on ham may seem like a defect to some, but nothing is farther from the truth. These dots are the crystallization of tyrosine, an amino acid that is regarded by experts as a sign of quality. The dots are the result of the free range of the pigs during their lifetime and a long, continuous maturation period of the hams in the cellars.

OTHER COUNTRIES

In addition to the five large ham-producing countries, Portugal and Hungary also supply two renowned hams from improved pig breeds.

PORTUGAL

PRESUNTO DE BARRANCOS

Portugal produces quality ham, including Presunto.

The Alentejano breed (named after the province of the same name) is unique and appreciated for its authenticity all over the world. These pigs walk around freely for 14 to 16 months and eat acorns and grass.

The most famous ham of this animal is the Presunto de Barrancos. Like Iberico ham, this ham has fine fatty veins and a rich, full-bodied flavour with nutty accents.

Alentejano hams are covered with sea salt for a week at a temperature between 1 and 6° C with an air humidity of 80 to 90%. In the following days the salt is removed and the meat is resalted. This gives the hams more consistency.

The hams are then dried at a temperature between 30 and 35° C. The ripening benefits from the favourable microclimate of Barrancos. The winters are wet and the summers are hot, which ensures the right cold and dryness. This ripening process lasts between 24 and 30 months.

The annual production is about 2,500 hams.

HUNGARY

MANGALICA HAM

The Mangalica is an authentic historic Hungarian pig that is a first-line descendant of the Serbian Sumadija pig. This type of pig is known as the progenitor of all pig breeds and is related to the Iberico pig.

The Mangalica pig has thick, long hair that is reminiscent of woollen fur. In spring, the dark hair turns into blond, shiny and upright curly hair.

Because these animals move a lot, they only slowly increase in weight and height. In the 1990s, Mangalicas almost completely disappeared, but an extensive study and breeding program saved the animal from extinction.

In line with tradition, these pigs are bred in the Hungarian steppes where they can feed on corn, grains and grass. After slaughter, the meat is brought to Spain (due to climatic conditions) to dry there.

Mangalica ham is known as an exclusive high-quality dried ham. After salting, during which the salt infiltrates the fat in the meat, the hams undergo a long, slow ripening of 28 months.

THE ART OF SLICING HAM

The next step after ripening is slicing the ham perfectly. This is a real craft and it requires skill and experience to master this technique. Hand-slicing can really increase the value of a ham.

Nowhere in the world is the profession of 'ham slicer' as highly regarded as in Spain. There, the profession of cortador de jamón is a highly respected profession that, according to some, even borders on art. To have Spanish ham sliced in perfect slices on the spot, combined with information about the origin, the breeding of the pigs and the wide range of flavours, and then, often in combination with the matching wine … That's an experience in itself.

Ham, cut on the spot by a maestro cortador tastes distinctly different from pre-cut and vacuum-packed ham, that's for sure. The real professional did not just learn this art on his own, but followed training in a specialized institute such as the Escuela Internacional de Cortadores de Jamón in Barcelona. Here the students learn everything about ham, how to cut it, sell it and present it.

For hams with a bone, it is important to work with a good machine with a sharp blade. Slicing hams with a bone requires much more skill, and a collection of essential tools is also required. A good ham clamp is at the top of the list. This is the basic requirement for holding the ham in a safe position in an easy way. We distinguish two types of clamps: the Italian ham clamp, which holds the ham horizontally, and the typical Spanish ham clamp, which holds the ham more at an angle. The most important thing about a ham clamp is its base: it must be sturdy and heavy enough so the ham can be sliced as stably as possible.

In addition, you need three types of knives to cut well and get a nice return from the ham: a sturdy knife with a wide blade that is used to start the ham; a second, very sharp and flexible ham knife with a long and narrow blade, called the 'tranche lard', with or without notches, perfect for cutting very thin slices; and finally a boning knife, a fairly narrow and sturdy knife with a short blade, which is used to loosen the ham meat from the bone and to cut slices in the most difficult corners.

Finally, a good sharpening steel is essential for the regular maintenance of the knives.

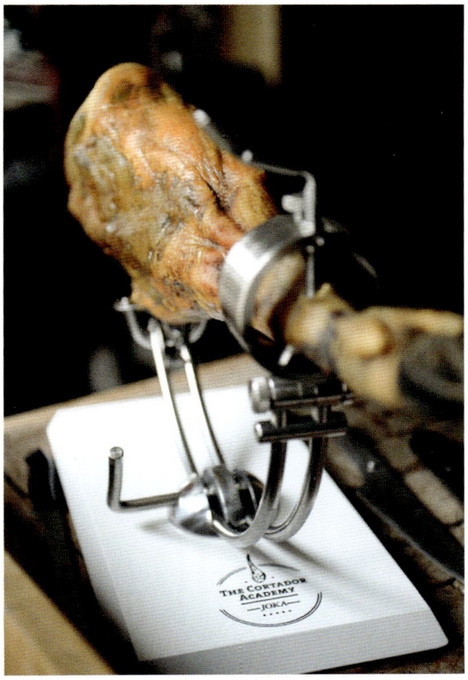
THE CORTADOR ACADEMY
JOKA

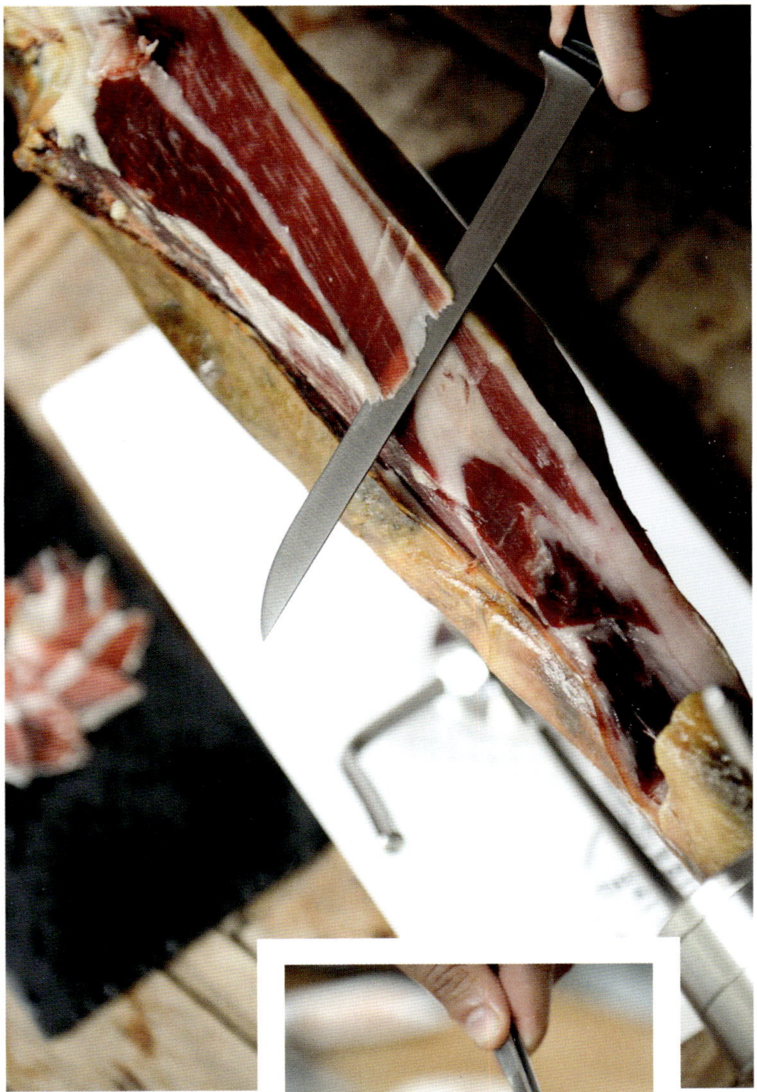

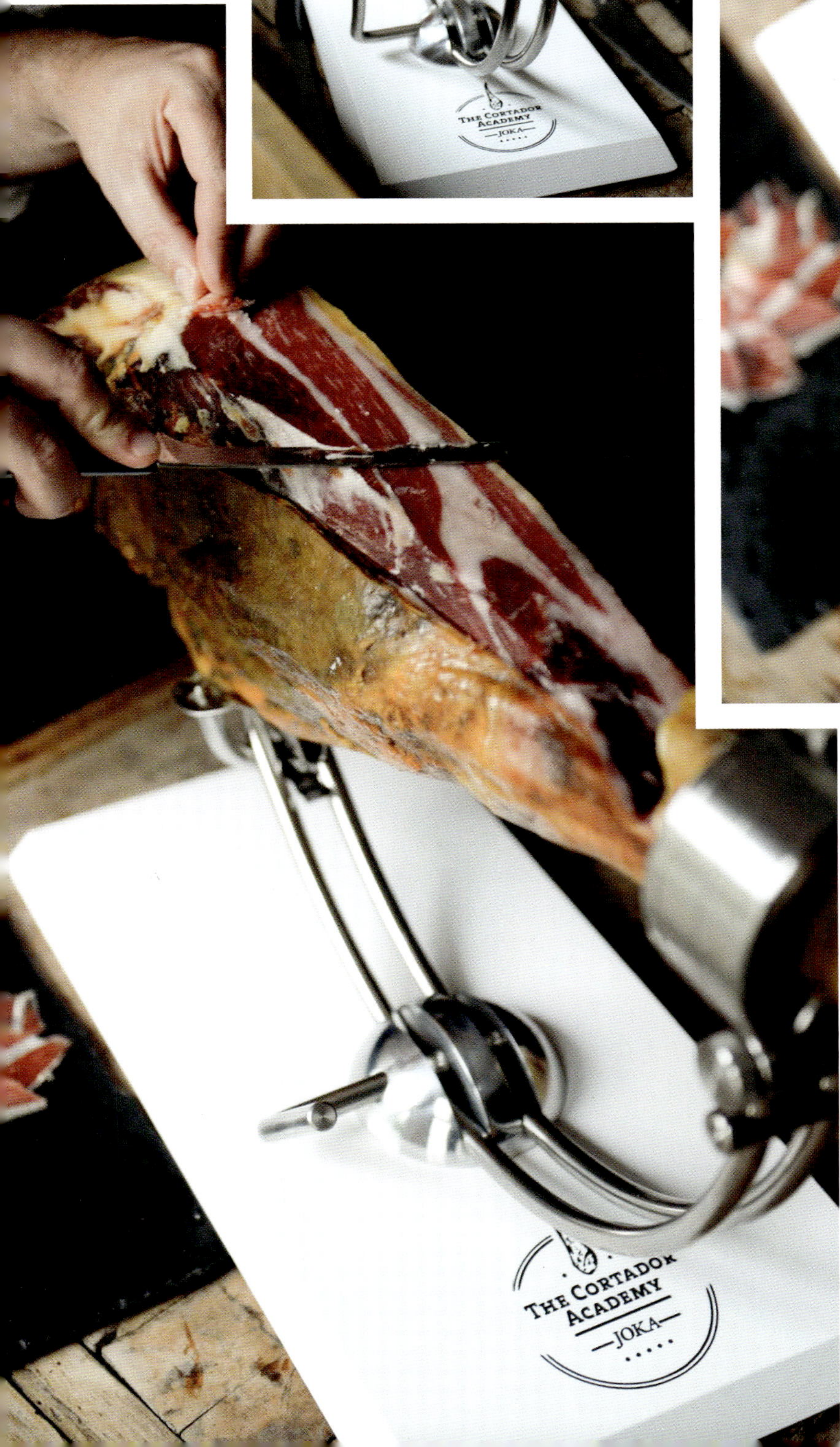
THE CORTADOR ACADEMY
JOKA

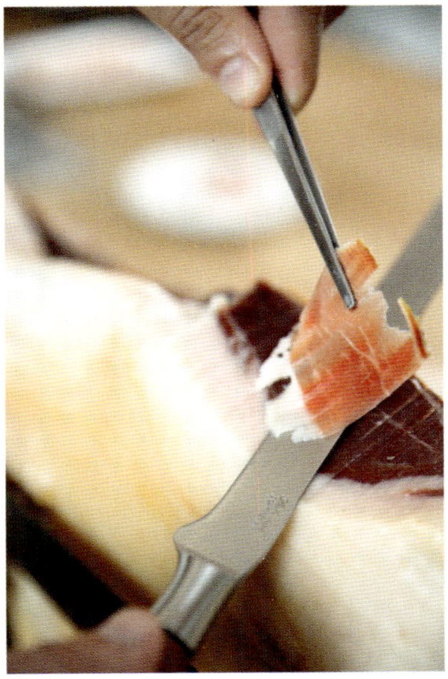

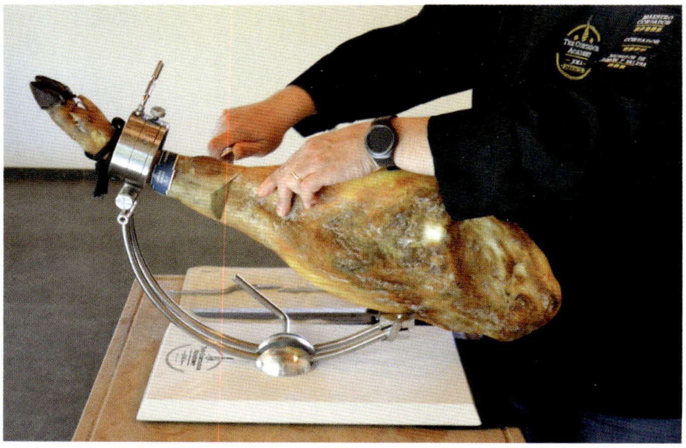
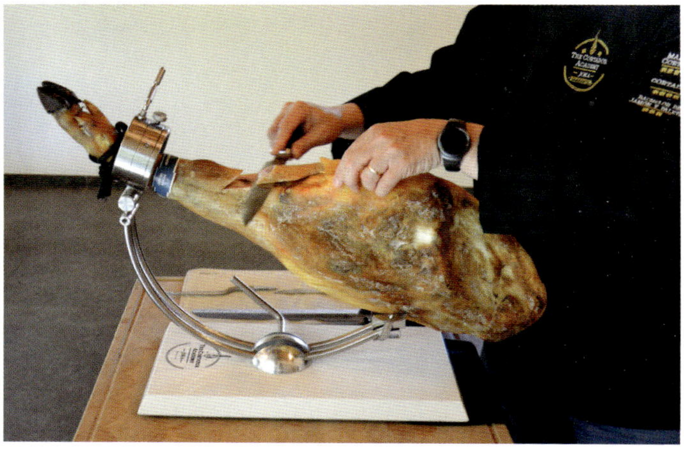
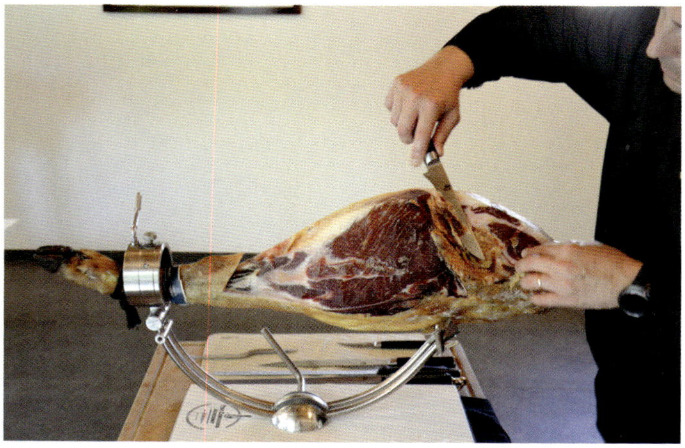
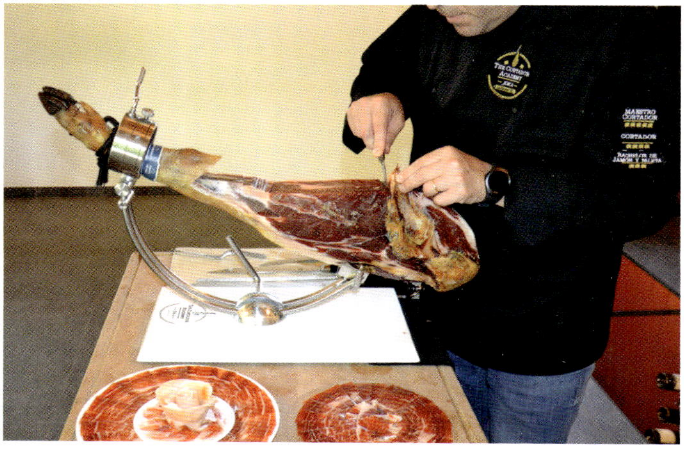
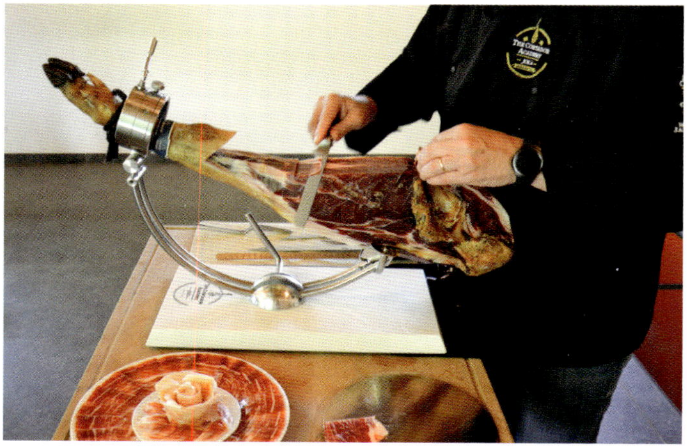
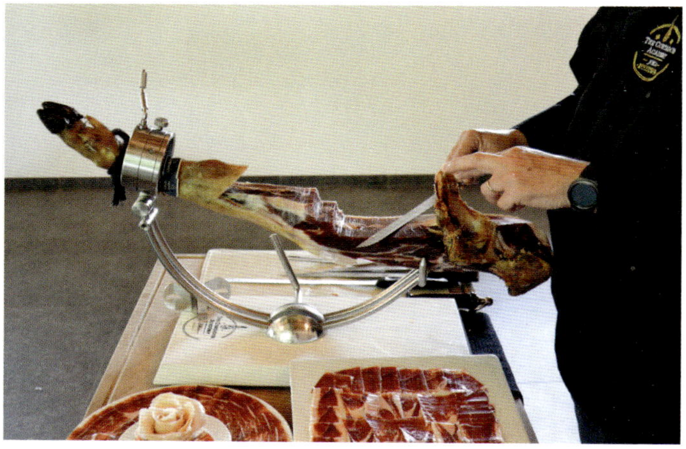
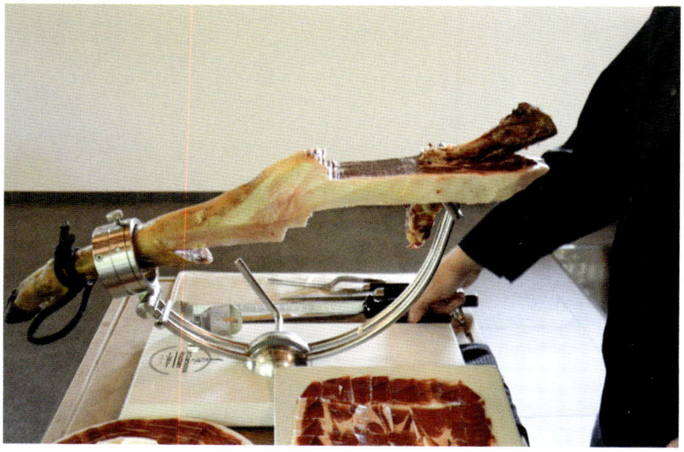
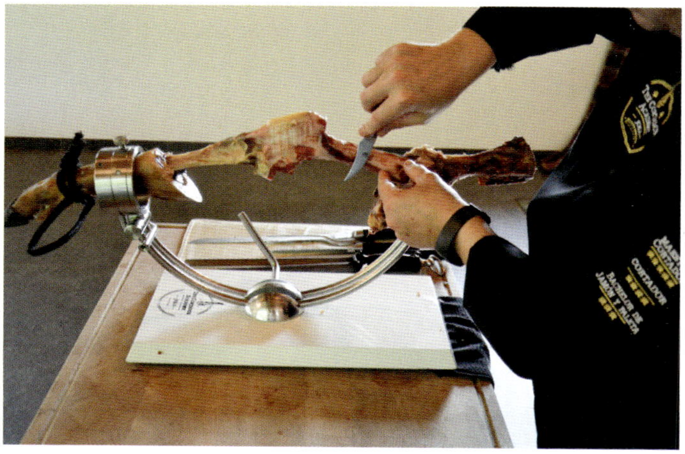

The position in which the ham is placed depends on the timespan in which the ham will be sliced and the number of slices you want to cut. When the hoof or shank is positioned up, you start with the thickest part of the ham, the cobourg. This is the best position if the ham is to be sliced completely right away. If the ham will be sliced over a period of several weeks, place the ham with the hoof or shank down. That way the butt is at the top. When cutting the ham, make a notch on the shank. The skin and the yellowish fat are then removed from the ham. Cut away the white fat as little as possible, because this gives the delicious taste to the ham. During the ripening process, natural fungi can form that can be simply cut away. If the ham is not to be sliced completely, only the part to be sliced is set ready for cutting.

Now the cutting area can be exposed by removing the top layer of fat (about 3 cm / 1 inch) in thin slices until the ham becomes visible. Save this cut away fat to put on the exposed area if you keep the ham for several weeks, in order to reduce dehydration.

Then we can start cutting slices of about 5 cm [2 inches] long. When slicing, we always start at the hoof or the shank, and slice toward the butt. Repeat this as horizontally as possible until you get to the bone and then turn the ham. Keep the knife as flat as possible, so that each slice is thin and seems transparent. Do not push the knife, but let the razor-sharp knife do its job. The texture and taste of each slice depend on the part from which the slice is cut, so it is wonderful to combine it each time.

During slicing it is important that you use the boning knife to separate the meat from the leg and thus slice the ham to the last piece. When both sides of the ham are cut (the butt and the thigh), you can make delicious soups or broth from the bones, which can also be the basis for original croquettes. Pre-cut the remaining meat into small pieces (tacos) to mix with the dough made with the delicious stock. Coat the preparation with bread crumbs and make surprising croquettes from Iberico, Mangalica, Serrano, Noir de Bigorre, etc.

To slice a front leg (paleta / spalla) you follow the same procedure as for the hind leg above, except that it does not matter which way you start.

With thanks to The Cortador Academy by Joka. For more info: JokaJoka.be

DIFFERENT TYPES OF PACKAGING

Dried ham can be made available in various ways.

In accordance with traditional Flemish custom, artisanal hams with bone and rind were hung in a dry place. As a tribute to this, a number of manufacturers adopt this form. You can place such hams in a ham clamp as a whole and cut off slices at will. Nothing else is needed other than a slice of farm bread and a bit of mustard for a delicious snack.

With some hams, the producers go a step further and also retain the hoof.

Most hams are either deboned, tied or pressed.

Another possibility is a block of ham.

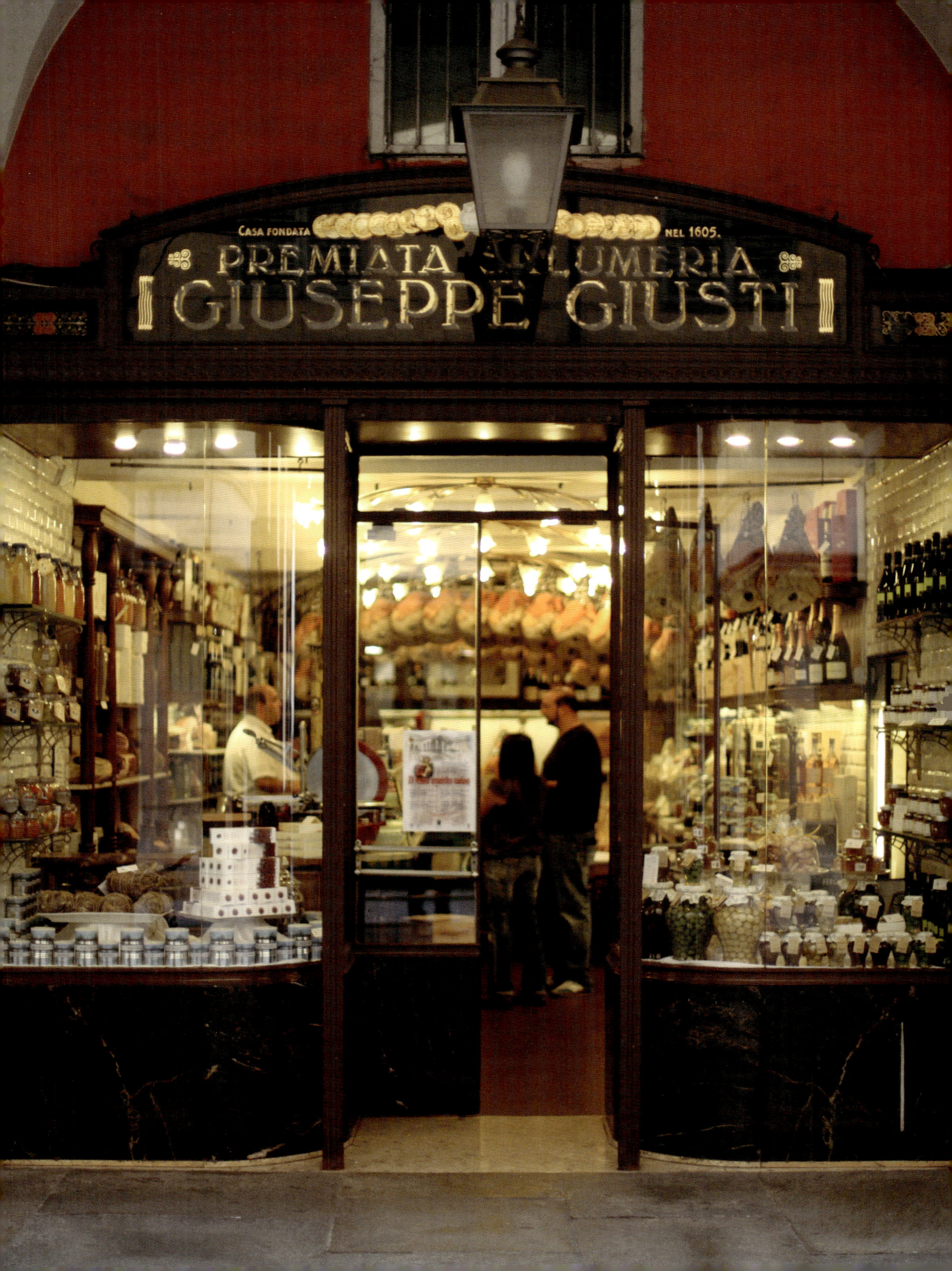
CASA FONDATA
NEL 1605.
PREMIATA
GIUSEPPE GIUSTI

THE CHOICE OF TOP CHEFS

That pure ham is delicious is denied by no one. But also as an ingredient, raw ham is an undeniably tasty part of many dishes. Top houses like to use ham in their kitchen. Two of those top chefs – Geert Van Hecke from Belgium and Massimo Bottura from Italy – are happy to share their recipes as well as their view of and experience with raw ham. Piet Huysentruyt also gives his organoleptic verdict on raw ham.

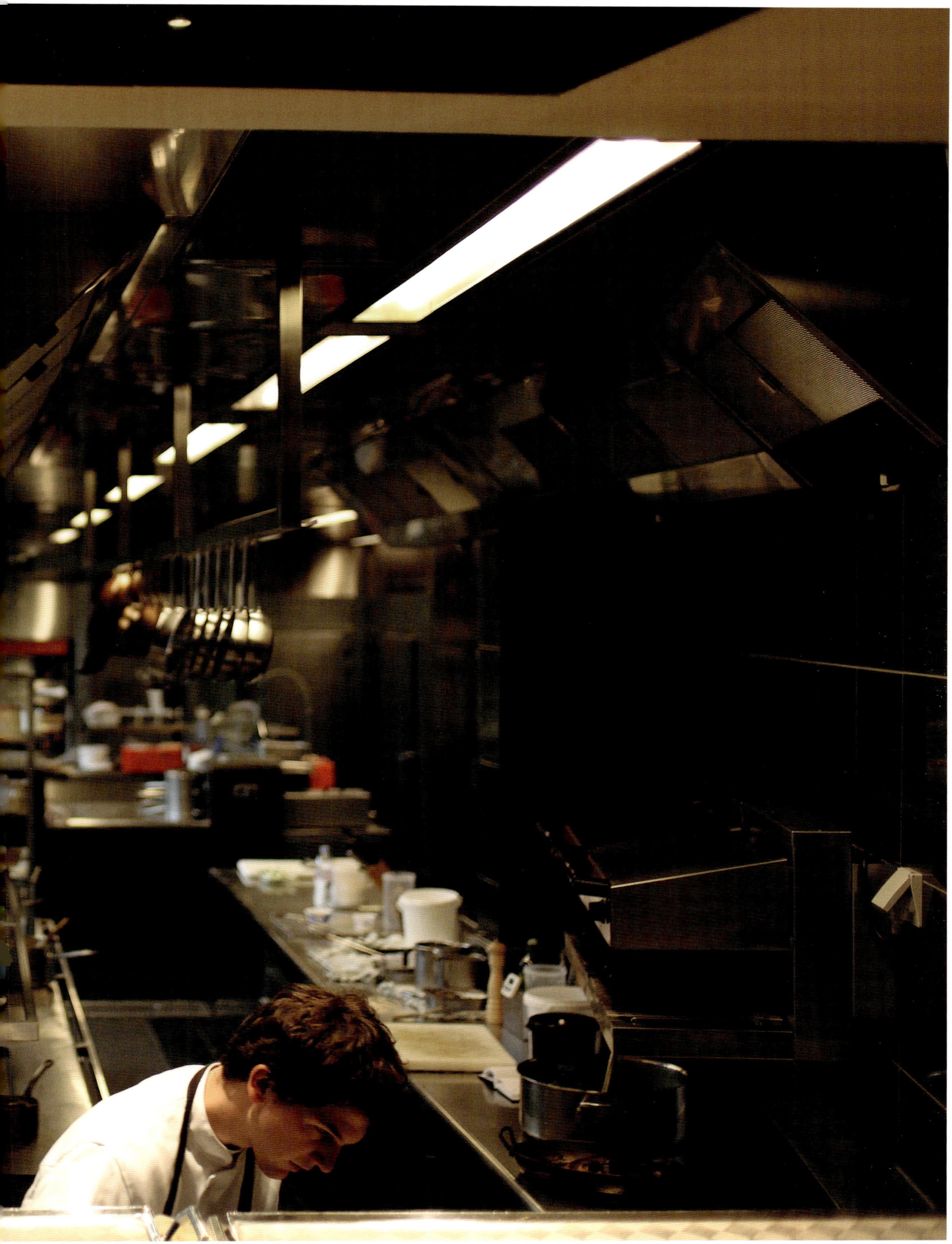

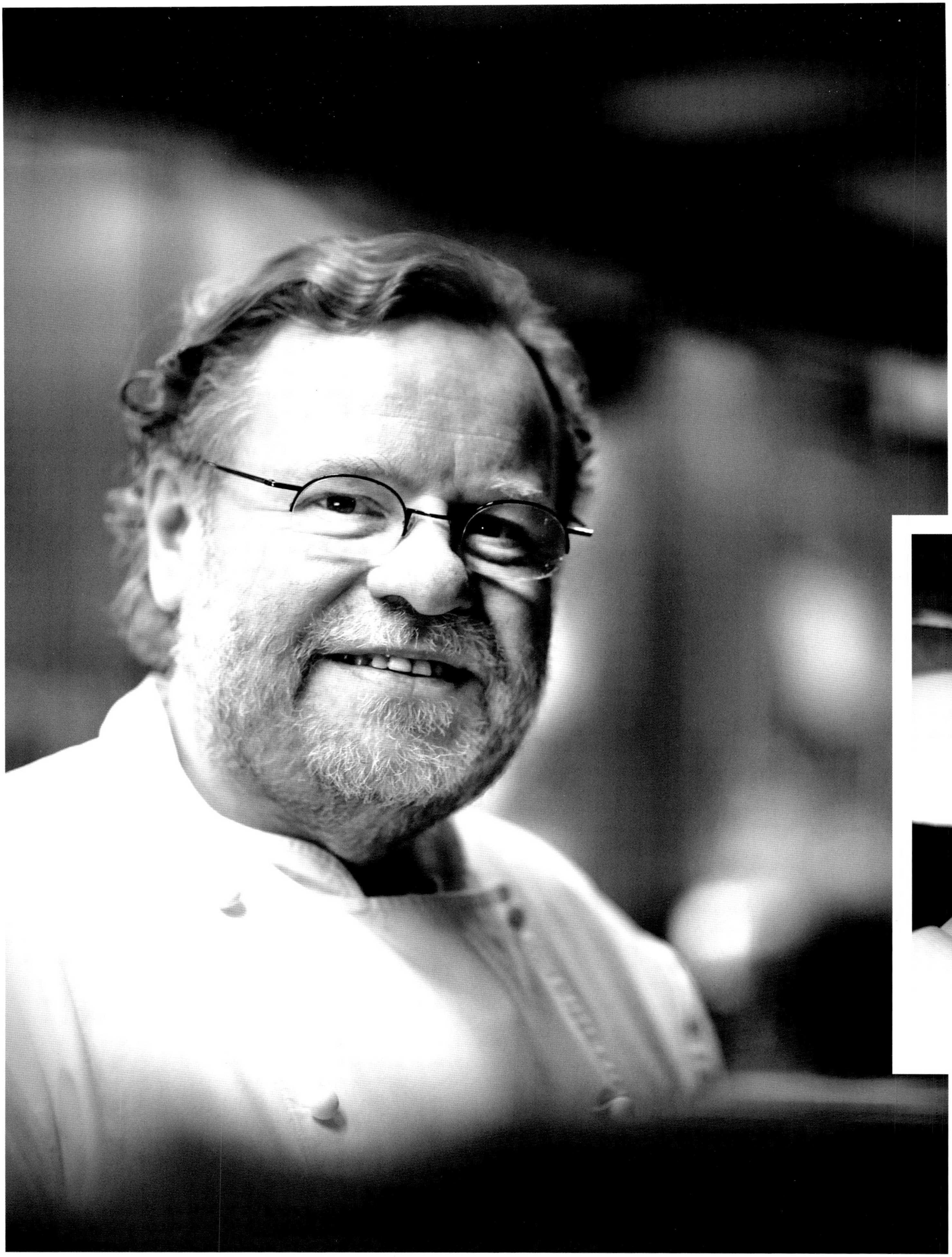

GEERT VAN HECKE
HAM: A CULINARY MAINSTAY, IDEAL INGREDIENT AND TASTY CONDIMENT

De Karmeliet***, Bruges, Belgium
Zet'joe*, Langestraat 11, 8000 Bruges, Belgium

A few months after Geert Van Hecke discontinued his life's work, the three-star restaurant De Karmeliet in Bruges, the chef wanted something else to do. So he launched Restaurant Zet'joe, also in Bruges, on a smaller scale, but with an equally tasty cuisine. Since then it has also become equally renowned.

'I am true to my principles,' Geert says about his cuisine. 'I work exclusively with top-quality products without making any concessions. I respect classic techniques and serve products the way they ought to taste. No compromises are allowed. Raw ham is one of these quality products. A plate of ham from different countries is an adventure of flavours. I never say no to that!

A piece of pork with a noble heritage, sea salt and nature: these factors make quality raw ham a unique experience, with a slightly different character each time but again and again oh so tasty.

'What is raw ham for me? Ham is a flavouring, a natural flavouring. In my kitchen I usually use raw ham as one of the ingredients. I love the combination of fish and shellfish with raw ham. Hams are salted with sea salt, that is the link with the fish. I savour it in the tastiest combinations.

'In my cuisine, ham is used mainly to support flavour. Cod, turbot and brill, for example, are all types of fish that "come to life" taste-wise when you combine them with ham.

'Raw ham and the saltiness of a Zeeland oyster in combination with a delicious egg or in a unique combination with the best cheeses. You can do all kinds of things with this prime product.

'For me, ham is an ideal local product. In my own region you have Duke of Berkshire and Ganda Ham, two ingredients that are always at the top of my list as I develop new dishes.

'I notice that colleagues abroad also use and serve their local ham types as a perfect ingredient, whether it is in France, Spain or Italy. We can be rightly proud of our ham.

'I am elated when I consider the skill required. It seems simple, but much is required before prime ham can be served at the table. The salting process, the drying process, it all has to be just right.

'As a chef, I am happy that I have access to such quality ingredients for my cuisine.'

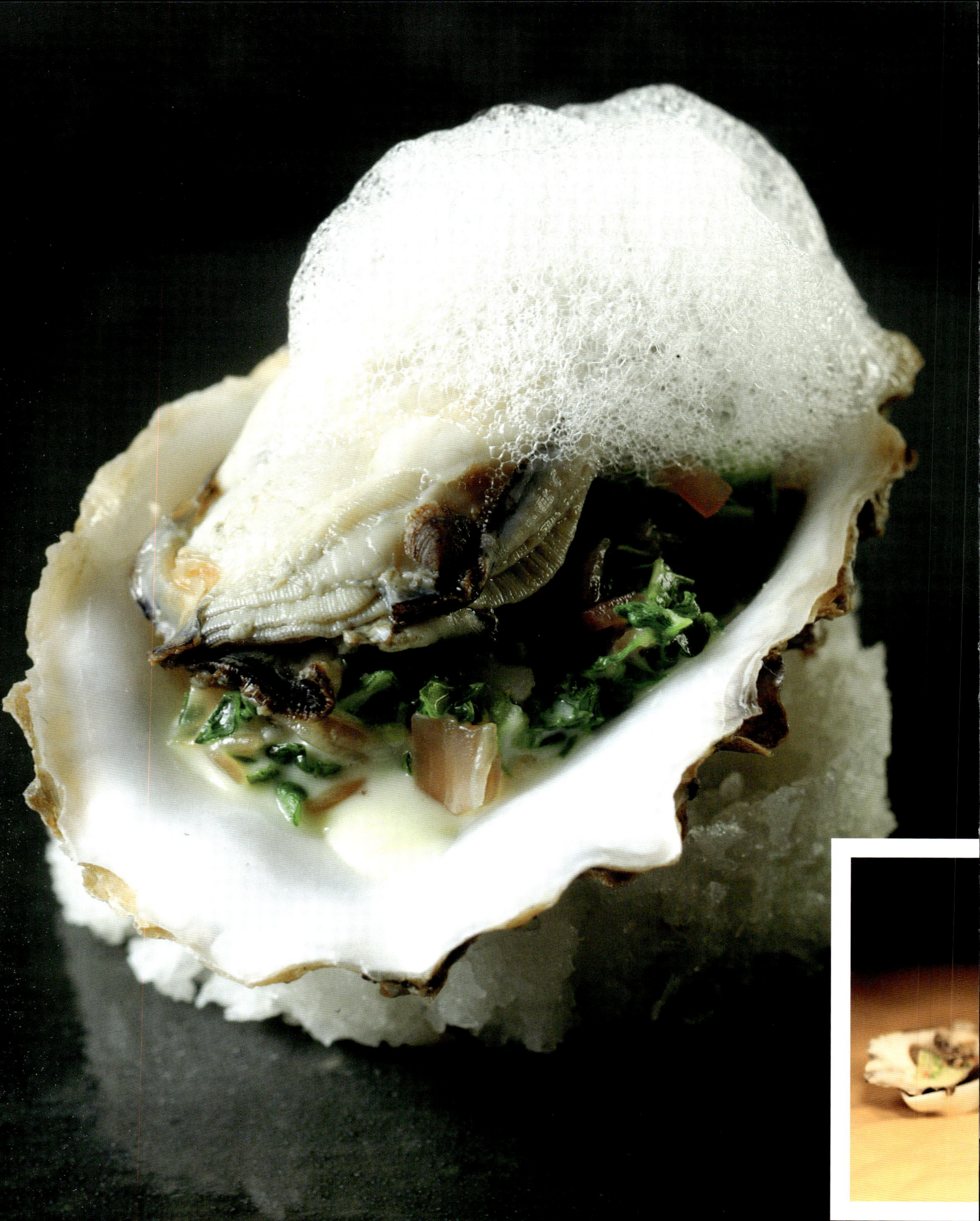

GANDA HAM WITH OYSTERS

INGREDIENTS

- 12 Zeeland Crassostrea oysters, size 3
- 400 g [14 oz] green cabbage with ribs removed
- 2 shallots
- 2 slices of Ganda Ham (12 months)
- 20 g [¾ oz] butter
- 1 dl [½ cup] dry white wine
- 100 g [3 ½ oz] butter

PREPARATION

- Open the oyster shells and carefully remove the oysters. Strain the oyster liquor.
- Clean the empty shells well and boil them briefly in water. Allow to cool and dry.
- In plenty of salted water, poach the green cabbage until tender. Shock in ice water. Drain well and dry on a kitchen towel. Cut into thin strips.
- Clean the shallots and cut very fine.
- Cut the Ganda Ham into small cubes.
- Heat the butter and sauté the shallots in it at a low temperature. Mix in the green cabbage and the Ganda Ham and stew warm.
- Add the white wine to the oyster liquor, bring to a boil and remove from the heat. Dip the oyster meat in the liquid for 10 seconds and then take it out.
- Finish the oyster liquor by stirring in small blocks of cold butter.

SERVING INSTRUCTIONS

- Arrange the oyster shells with the Ganda Ham stew in them.
- Place the oysters on top of each shell.
- Mix the sauce until it is frothy.
- Coat the oysters with a thin layer of froth.

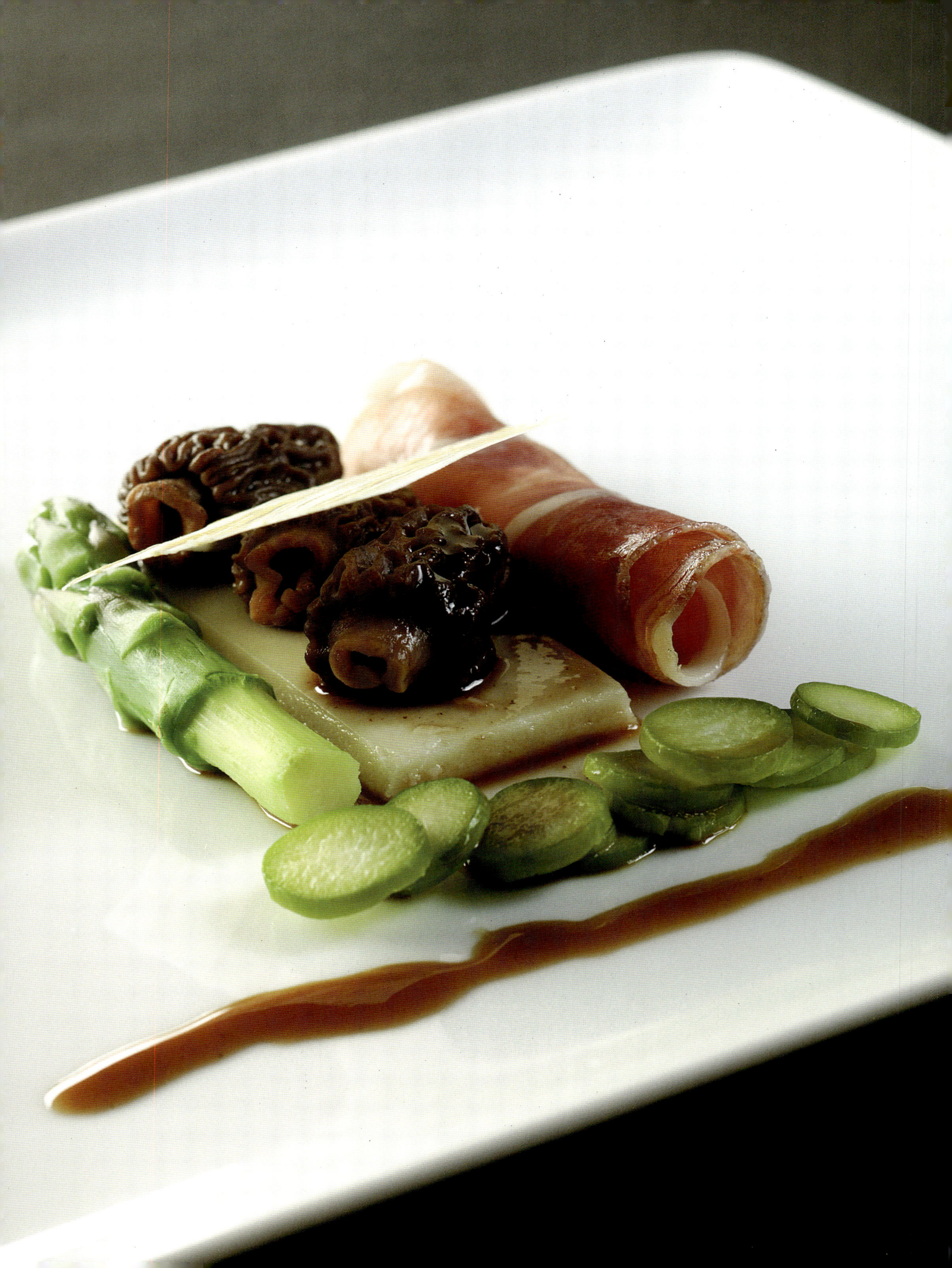

FINE CREAM OF GREEN ASPARAGUS WITH GANDA HAM AND MOREL MUSHROOMS

INGREDIENTS

- 4 large Belgian green thin asparagus spears
- 4 slices of Ganda Ham (12 months), rolled up

FOR THE FINE CREAM OF GREEN ASPARAGUS

- 150 g [5 oz] cooked green asparagus spears
- 50 g [2 oz] Ganda Ham fat scraps, cut into pieces and dried for 20 minutes in a preheated oven at 80° C.
- 1 egg and 4 yolks
- 1 dl [½ cup] whole milk
- 1 dl [½ cup] cream
- 1 knife point of grated nutmeg, cayenne pepper and coarse salt

FOR THE SAUCE

- 12 beautiful morel mushrooms, perfectly washed and trimmed
- 50 g [2 oz] butter
- 6 cl [¼ cup] Madeira wine
- 1 dl [½ cup] poultry stock
- 5 cl [¼ cup] soft whipped cream

PREPARATION

- Place all ingredients for the fine cream of asparagus in a blender and mix finely. Pass through a fine sieve and spread out in a fireproof dish. Place in a bain-marie for 30 minutes in a preheated oven at 170° C [340° F]. Let cool and put in the refrigerator for at least 2 hours.
- Peel the green asparagus spears and cook them in plenty of salted water until they are tender. Shock in ice water.
- Make the sauce: Melt the butter and heat the mushrooms in it. Do not fry. Deglaze with the Madeira and the stock, simmer for 3 minutes. Remove the mushrooms and let it reduce for a while. Finish with the cream.

SERVING INSTRUCTIONS

- Warm the asparagus and the fine cream briefly in a steam oven.
- Serve a thick layer of fine cream with a green asparagus spear and a roll of Ganda Ham.
- Finish with the mushrooms and a dash of sauce.

WILD SALMON TOPPED WITH GANDA HAM, POIVRADE ARTICHOKE AND WILD GARLIC SAUCE

INGREDIENTS

- 4 portions of 120g [4 oz] of wild salmon fillet
- 4 slices of Ganda Ham (12 months)
- 1 dl [½ cup] olive oil
- lemon, pepper and salt
- 6 poivrade artichokes
- 12 wedges of dried tomato

FOR THE SAUCE

- 2 dl [1 cup] poultry stock
- 5 cl [¼ cup] dry white wine
- 1 shallot
- 20 g [½ oz] garlic and flat parsley

PREPARATION

- Arrange the Ganda Ham on the salmon fillets.
- Heat the olive oil and poach the salmon in it briefly.
- Clean the artichokes and cook them in water with lemon, pepper and salt until done. Halve carefully.
- Make the sauce: Bring the white wine with the stock and a shredded shallot to a boil. Pour into a blender with the garlic and parsley and puree. Pour through a fine sieve.

SERVING INSTRUCTIONS

- Serve each piece of salmon with three artichoke halves and a dried tomato.
- Finish with the wild garlic sauce.

TIP Put a few garlic leaves in the warm oil of the salmon and let them drain. Use these as a garnish.

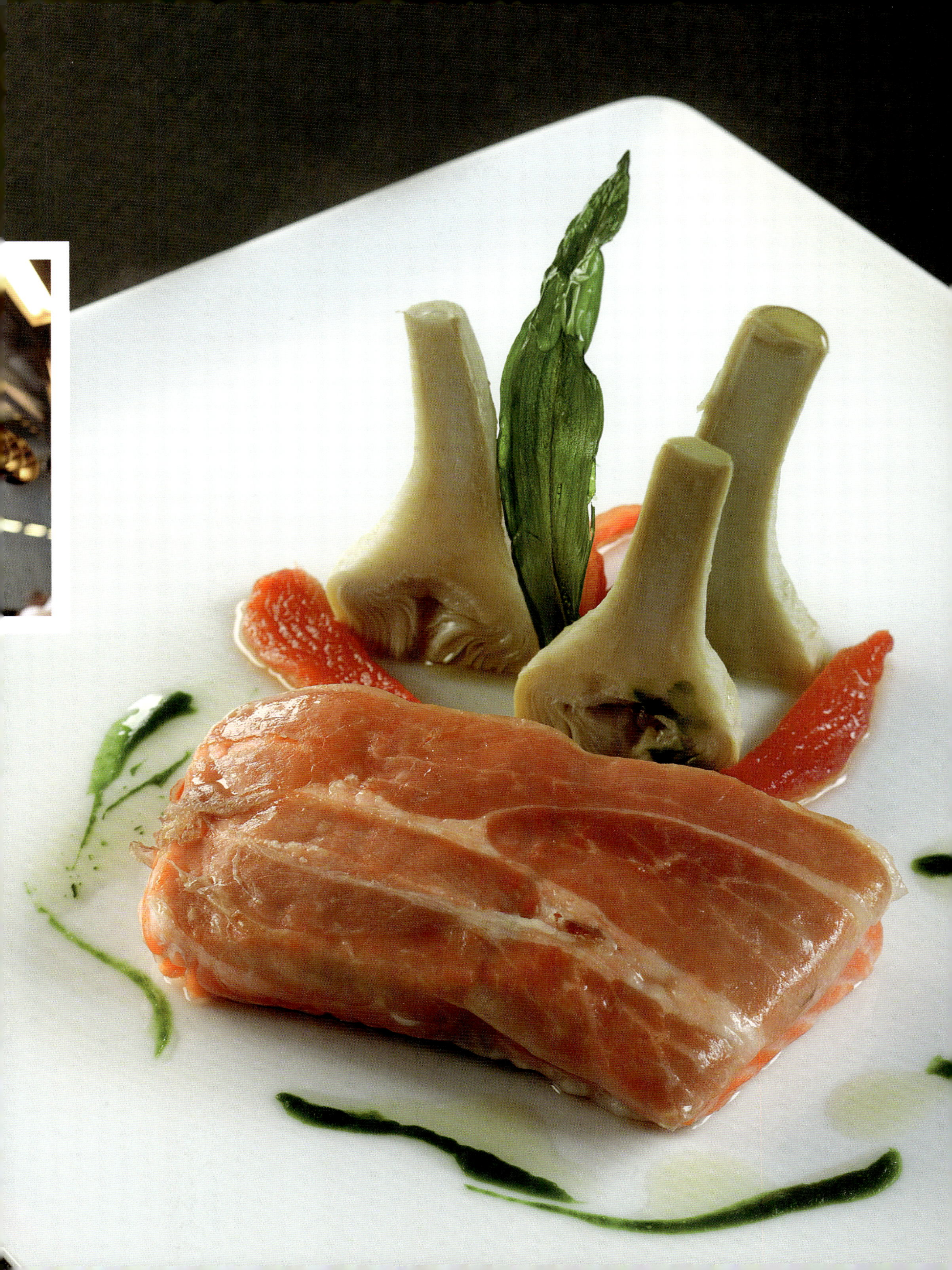

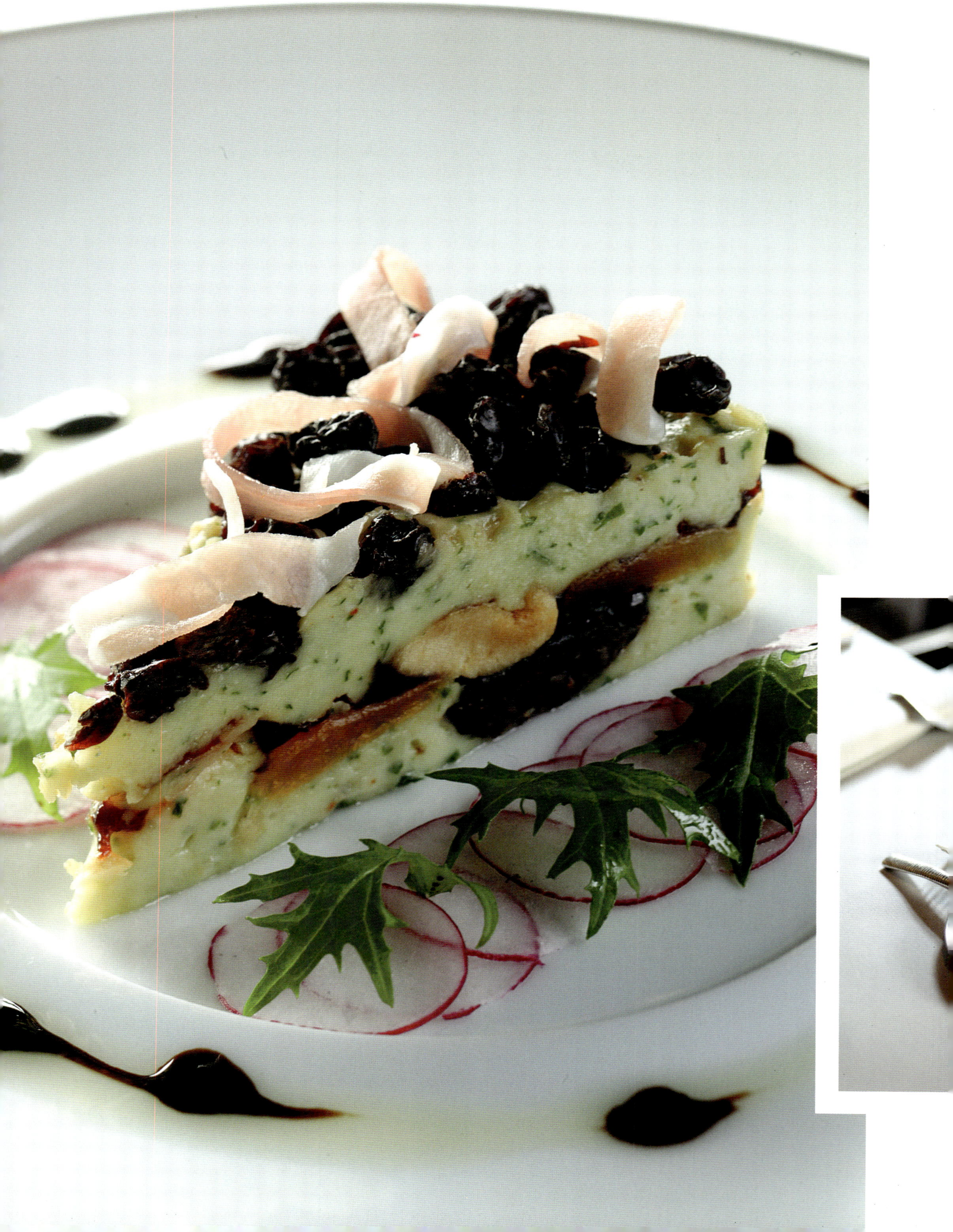

CHEESE TERRINE WITH GANDA HAM AND RAISINS

INGREDIENTS

- 8 radishes
- arugula
- 1 dl [½ cup] olive oil
- 5 cl [¼ cup] balsamic vinegar
- 50 g [2 oz] raisins in sweet white wine
- 2 slices of Ganda Ham (9 months), wafer thin

FOR THE TERRINE

- 300 g [11 oz] cheese mix (blue, brie and Munster)
- 50 g [2 oz] butter
- 10 g [⅓ oz] mixed green herbs (chives, tarragon, sage)
- knife point of Piment d'Espelette
- 2 shallots, shredded
- 4 slices of Ganda Ham (12 months)
- 100 g [3 ½ oz] dried fruit (dates, raisins, apricots)

PREPARATION

- Add the three cheeses, the butter, the mixed herbs, a knife point of Piment d'Espelette and the shallots together in the food processor and knead nicely together.
- Line a cake mould with plastic foil and cover with a layer of cheese mixture. Arrange the slices of Ganda Ham and distribute the dried fruit (some chopped). Distribute the rest of the cheese mixture over and cover with plastic foil. Place overnight in the refrigerator, minimum 5 hours.
- Slice the radishes very thinly and lay them together with leaves of rocket in ice water.
- Mix the olive oil with the balsamic vinegar.

SERVING INSTRUCTIONS

- Serve the cheese terrine and finish with raisins and fine strips of Ganda Ham.
- Arrange the slices of radish and salad leaves.
- Finish with vinaigrette.

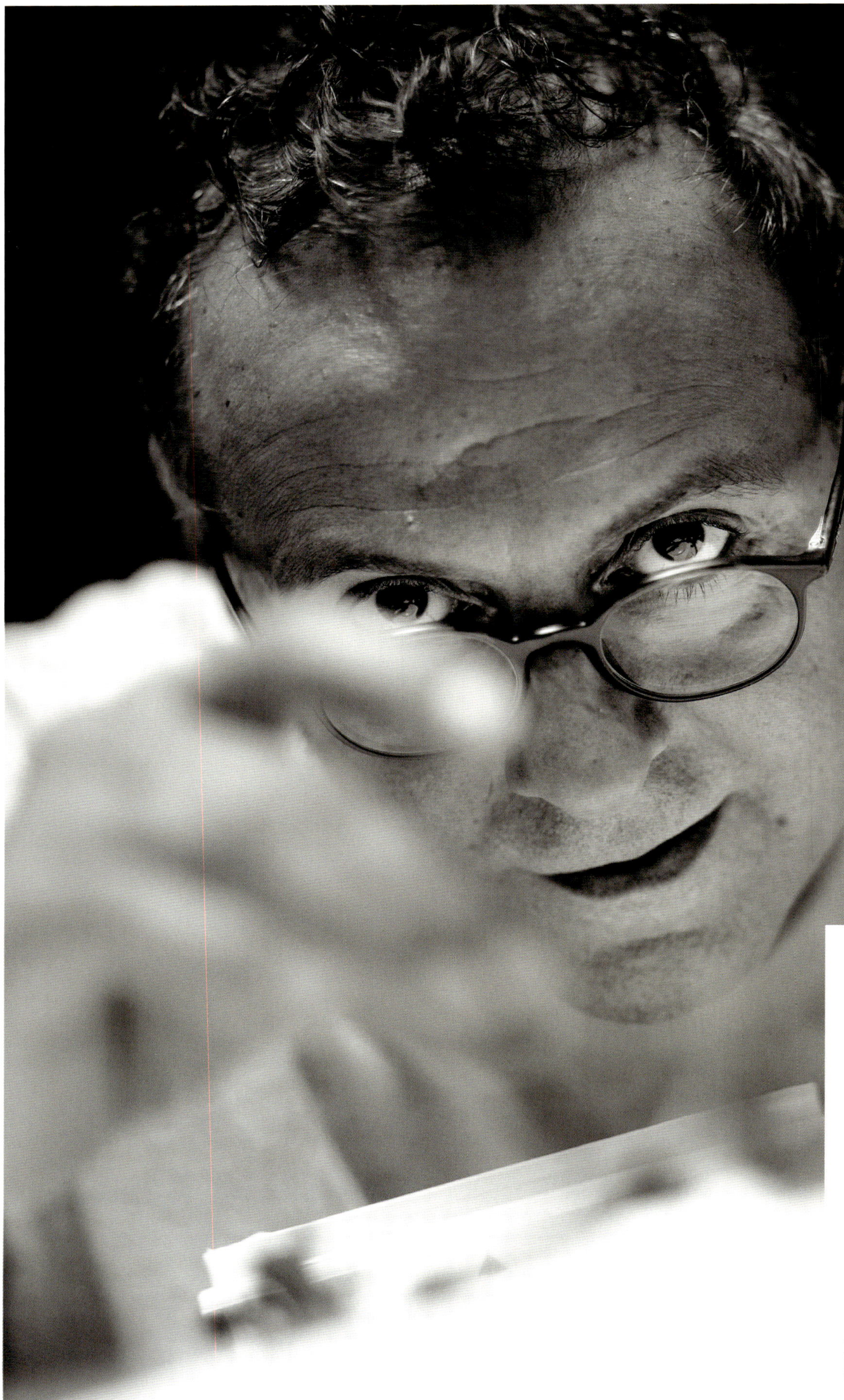

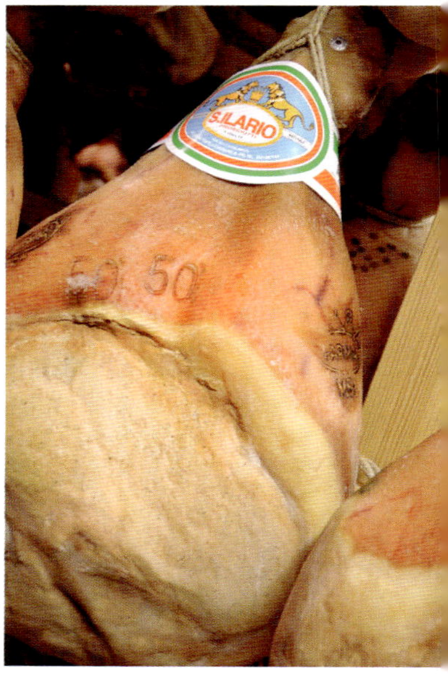

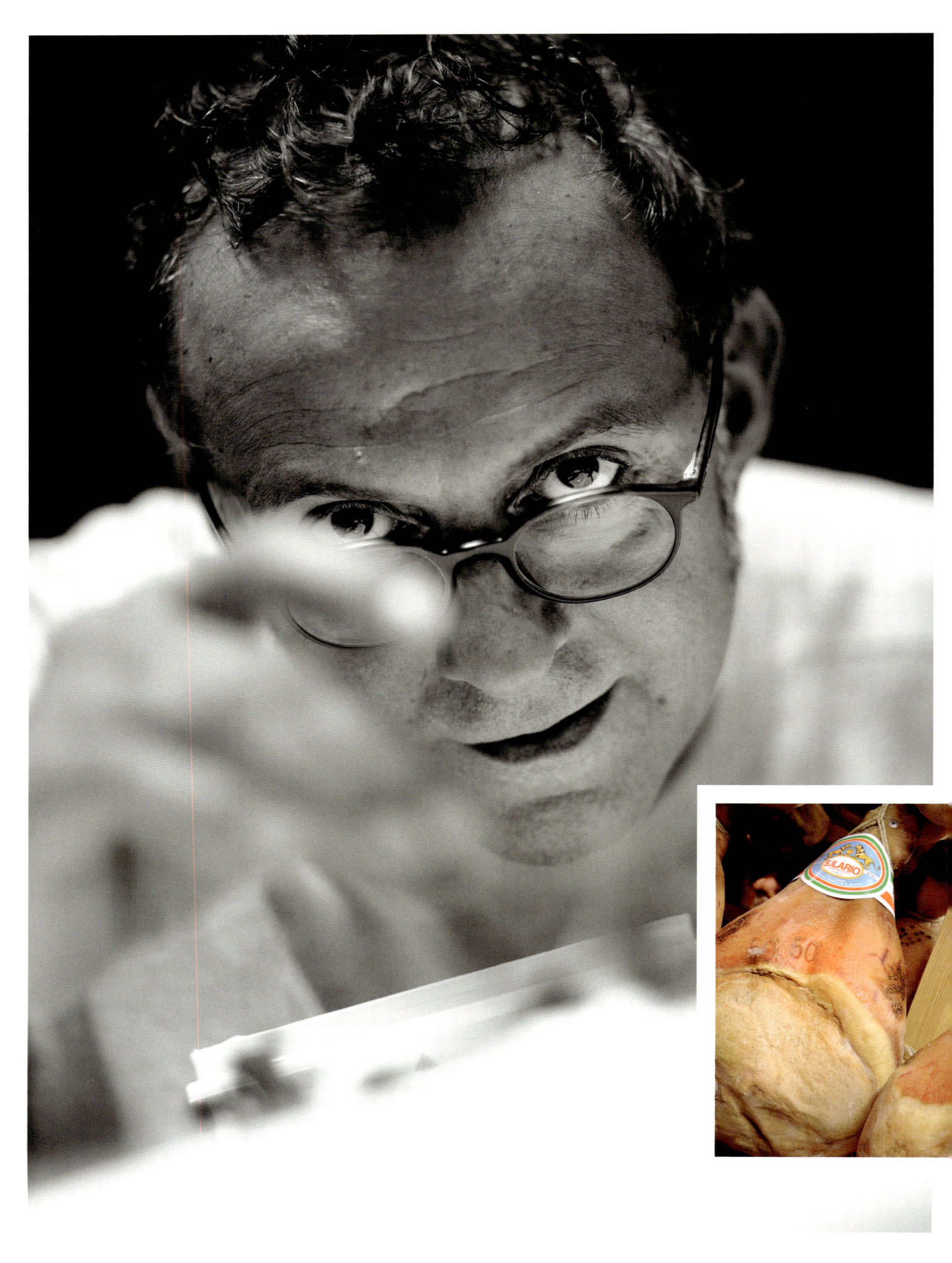

MASSIMO BOTTURA
COME WITH ME TO ITALY

I arrived at Parma, Italy for some appointments with chefs, but they all had forgotten our appointment. I had no program, no hotel, niente. I had only one more number, that of Massimo Bottura, world-renowned chef in Modena. I had an appointment, but not until two days later. It had been difficult for me to make contact with him, but thanks to Peter Goossens (for which I am grateful) and after sending a few of my cookbooks, I had succeeded.

I took the plunge, made use of my best Italian (limited to buongiorno and grazie) and rang his number. Massimo was extremely friendly and brief: 'Come to Modena, to the restaurant and we will solve your problem. I am busy but come on anyway, you are welcome …'

At 11 o'clock I was in Modena, standing in front of the entrance to Osteria Francescana.

Is Massimo here?

Yes, but he is busy with an interview for the RAI.

Could you please tell him that Stefaan from Belgium is here?

Two minutes later, a jovial Italian stood before me … 'Sono Massimo'. The RAI would have to wait, the Belgian chef came first … Typical. When Massimo promises something, he does it.

Thanks to Massimo I was able to fill in my Italian program perfectly. He took me to his favourite market in Modena, the 'Mercato Albinelli', told me about hams, art and jazz, the most beautiful combination ever. Thanks to him, I also visited three excellent ham firms: Galloni in Langhirano, San Giacomo Sala Baganza, and not to be overlooked, the exclusive S.Ilario in Ponte-Langhirano.

Twice I had the privilege of enjoying a meal in Massimo's restaurant, Osteria Francescana, which I consider to be one of the best restaurants in the world, and Massimo, full of enthusiasm, also told me what food, ham and life (love) mean to him.

Massimo: 'I am a think tank. When I see something, when I hear something, when I smell or feel something, my senses stimulate my brain and

Osteria Francescana ***
Via Stelle 22, 41121 Modena, Italy
World's Best Restaurant 2018

I have to create something! Then I think of the next step, dishes must evolve. Take for example raw ham, sorry Parma ham, the best ham in the world by the way!

What is Parma ham to me? I think of mist, the rising mist above the Parma river and the fields around it. I think of silence, the silence of nature. I think about history, the history of the Italian people, Modena, Parma. I taste the salt, the salt of the Parma river. I smell nature, the trees, the drying rooms for Parma ham …

Then comes the creation of the recipe: haze and mist above the Parma river, it could be a work of art, a poem, a piece of music …'

Prosiutto di Parma is, along with Parmigiano Reggiano cheese and the balsamic vinegar of Modena, one of the best ingredients a cook can desire. And when all three are produced in your own region, you are on top of the world! What could be better?

I watch and listen: 'Say yes to your eyes, experience what you see, the whole world is your window, and experience every taste. That is why traveling is so important to me.'

We taste raw ham, supplied by the S.Ilario firm that matures hams especially for Massimo (dried and ripened for 30 months). I taste sweet-and-sour as well as salt in the ham, giving me a minimalistic experience. After a long pause, Massimo continues. 'I get emotional, my palate unites with my soul and I enjoy …'

Music by Thelonious Monk is playing in the background. Massimo mentions his favourite artists: Joseph Beuys, Andy Warhol, Damien Hurst, Maurizio Cattelan, Carlo Benvenuto.

Thus a dish is born.

Thanks, Massimo!

TARTAR OF CHIANINA, PARMA HAM FOAM

or Morning landscape with mist and fog

- Chianina beef fillet flavoured with black truffle, Villa Manodori extra virgin olive oil and a few pieces of Sichuan buds (a yellow flower of the Brazilian jambu plant, which causes a cold, almost electrifying sensation in your mouth).
- Sorbet of Parmesan cheese.
- Foam of S.Ilario Parma ham bouillon.
- Sauce of traditional demi-glace stewed from a S.Ilario Parma ham bone and finished with Villa Manodori extra matured balsamic vinegar.

ICE COD, KATSUOBUSHI BROTH, PARMA HAM

- Ice cod with the skin baked crisp in olive oil and Villa Manodori lemon oil, then cooked until done in fish stock without the liquid touching the skin.
- Katsuobushi broth. Katsuobushi are dried, fermented and lightly smoked pieces of tuna (preferably Skipjack Tuna), made in combination with trimmings of dried S.Ilario Parma ham (30 months).
- Squid ink, soy sauce and sugar to finish the stock.
- White celery, spring onion and daikon supplemented with candied ginger, oyster leaf and slices of Buddha's hand citrus fruit.
- For the powder: powder of dried S.Ilario Parma ham (30 months) mixed with sea urchin powder and vegetable ash (carrot, white celery, parsley, thyme, sage, rosemary and basil dried and baked in the oven at 220 °C until they are 'blackened'; then ground fine and sieved.)

RAVIOLI BATHED IN TOMATO SAUCE

- Ravioli made from Italian oo flour with eggs and egg yolks.
- Filling of traditional cotechino (Italian traditional pork sausage, steamed in red Lambrusco wine), dried S.Ilario Parma ham (30 months), mixed breadcrumbs of white and wholemeal bread.
- Tomato sauce with Lambrusco wine and Piennolo tomatoes (tomatoes grown on the flanks of Mount Vesuvius).

ASPARAGUS, PARMA HAM, PARMESAN CHEESE

- Green wild asparagus, steamed briefly
- Chlorophyll (from herbs, parsley and lemongrass) together with Villa Manodori balsamic vinegar.
- Dried S.Ilario Parma ham (30 months).
- Milk skin made from Parma ham brodo (broth), Parmesan cheese aged for 50 months (cheese crusts and grated cheese) and whole cow's milk from Parma.
- Bottarga made from egg yolk, original Sicilian salt used to dry the Parma ham and caster sugar.

These recipes are indicative and can be found in detail in the book: Massimo Bottura, Never trust a skinny Italian chef, published by Phaidon
With thanks to S. Ilario Prosciutti, Via Ponticella 18 – 43037 Mulazzano Ponte, Villa Manodori, Via Galliana 4 – 41051 Montale

S.ILARIO HAM

The hams of S.Ilario are not only a concept within the Italian 'Parma ham scene', but according to experts they are the absolute world top.

In Mulazzano Ponte next to the Parma river, the hams of the Montali family dry in the authentic way. All operations are done manually without using modern technologies such as machines, fans and computers. The extremely carefully selected hams, from Large White pigs from Mantua in Lombardy, are first given a flat rest and are salted with exclusive salt from Puglia. After 70 days they are given their distinctive round S.Ilario cut, the so-called toelettatura.

The ham gets its special taste, the profumo, from the muffa, a natural fungus that grows through the supply and removal of air from coniferous and deciduous trees that blow into the drying chambers via the Parma river. The ventilation is also manually operated several times a day according to the family's Parma scheduling booklet.

The hams of S.Ilario, which dry for at least 24 months, are a real delicacy. Only selected star restaurants, including Osteria Francescana, and some delicacy stores have the honour of processing or selling these hams. So if you ever have the chance to taste this ham …

THE TASTE OF THE RIVER
or Parma ham with Parma shrimp

- Sheets of crispy, translucent gelatine made from broth of S.Ilario Parma ham and Parma ham bone together with fine, clarified fish stock.
- Filled with raw shrimp from the Parma river, fresh and caught wild.

THE GARDEN OF ITALY, THE BEST OF FRUITS AND VEGETABLES

- Dried S.Ilario Parma ham (30 months).
- Combination of powder, ice powder, dried, crispy and fresh.
- Vegetables: asparagus, carrots, broad beans, chickpeas, beetroot.
- Fruits: strawberry, melon, pomegranate.

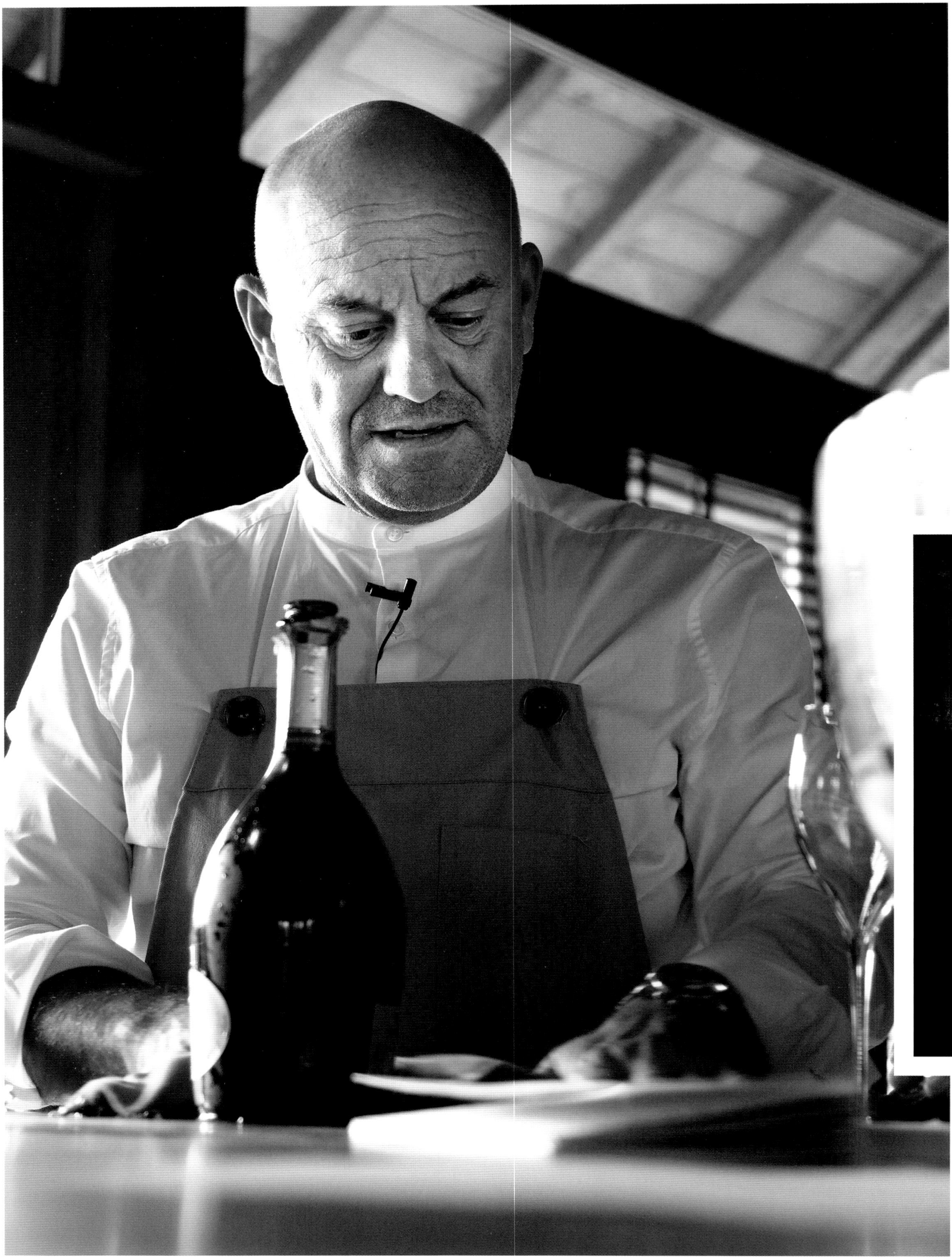

PIET HUYSENTRUYT
'WITH A DISH, NOT ONLY THE TASTE AND THE APPEARANCE ARE IMPORTANT, BUT ALSO THE AROMA.'

Restaurant Likoké*
7 Route de Païolive, 07140 Les Vans, France

I quote Piet from his cult book *Eigentijds en Eigenzinnig* (1997) [*Contemporary and Opinionated*].

Although his book is almost thirty years old, each of its recipes are gems from the 'Gastronomic Champions League'. The book has been in my extensive cookbook library for years.

As someone from West Flanders, I admire what Piet has accomplished and felt that this book would not be complete without a tribute to him. Piet introduced us to Ganda Ham and taught us how to eat it. He did this in his restaurant, and on TV it was also a recurring ingredient. A good example is found in *Eigentijds en Eigenzinnig*: an open sandwich with Ganda Ham, a bit of lard and grain mustard.

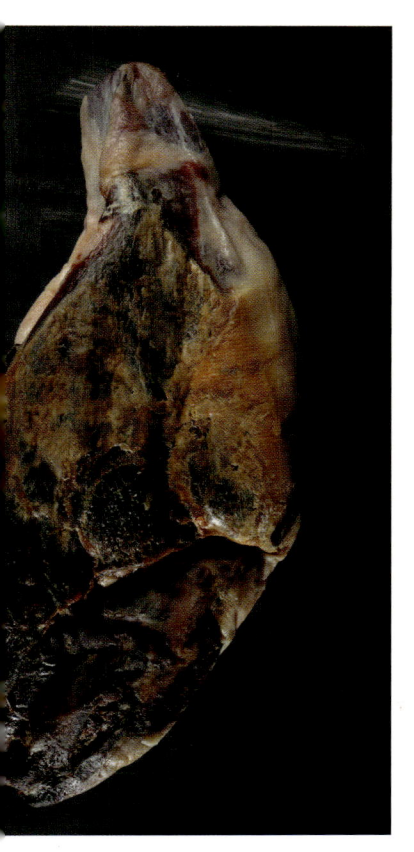

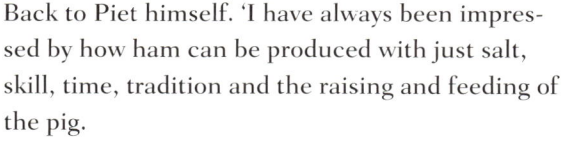

Piet's explanation with a distinctly West Flemish accent: 'Well now, an open sandwich with raw ham, lard and a bit of mustard.' A sandwich from my youth, the way we used to eat ham. Simple and good! I made my own version and added blood sausage. If you read my preface, you will know why.

Back to Piet himself. 'I have always been impressed by how ham can be produced with just salt, skill, time, tradition and the raising and feeding of the pig.

It still amazes me how our ancestors arrived at their ideal recipe. Each had his own preparation method and drying process. I remember how different butchers from my childhood fiercely discussed who had the best raw ham. *My maturing cellar is the best cellar, I have the best natural ventilation …* I continue to be intrigued and those conversations stay with me, they were so beautiful and imaginative.

For me, ham is part of our culture, who we are, what we do. Ham belongs to our flavour tradition. It is significant that Spain and Italy also have this culture.

We like our local customs. I still make my own dried ham, coppa, pancetta and dried sausages, and I'm quite proud of that!'

AN OPEN SANDWICH FROM FLANDERS

My tribute to Piet Huysentruyt

INGREDIENTS

- 1 loaf of Flemish hearth bread, white
- 120 g [4 oz] lard
- fresh rosemary leaves, finely chopped
- 10 slices of Ganda Ham
- 50 g [2 oz] butter
- 2 blood sausages
- 50 g [2 oz] grain mustard

PREPARATION

- Remove the sides of the bread and cut into it. Brush with the lard, sprinkle with rosemary and place slices of Ganda Ham on it. Close it back into a loaf.
- Heat the butter until it turns light brown and fry slices of blood sausage in it.

SERVING INSTRUCTIONS

- Cut slices of bread of about 2 cm [1 inch] thick and arrange on a dish.
- Finish with tufts of grain mustard and a slice of blood sausage.

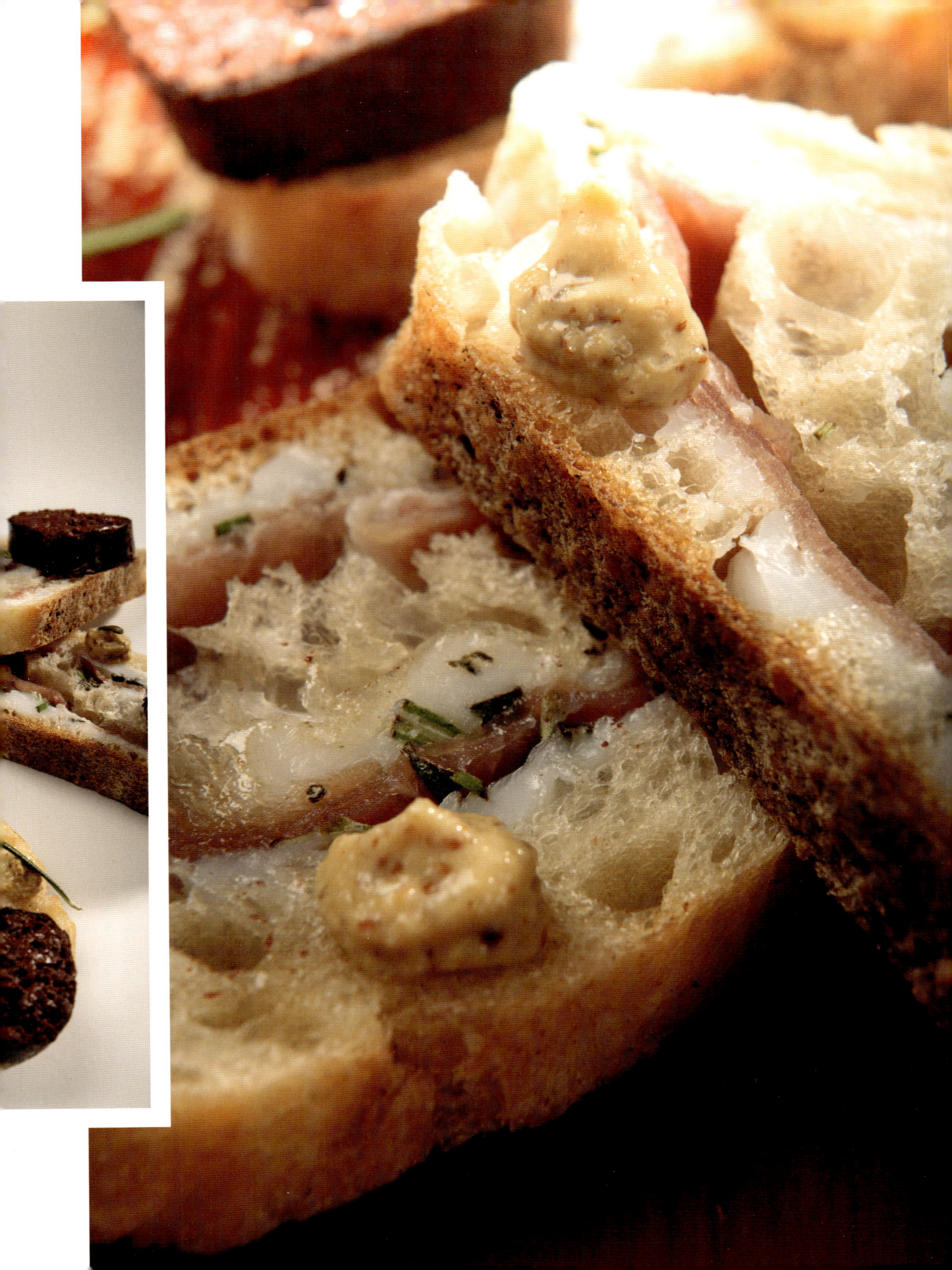

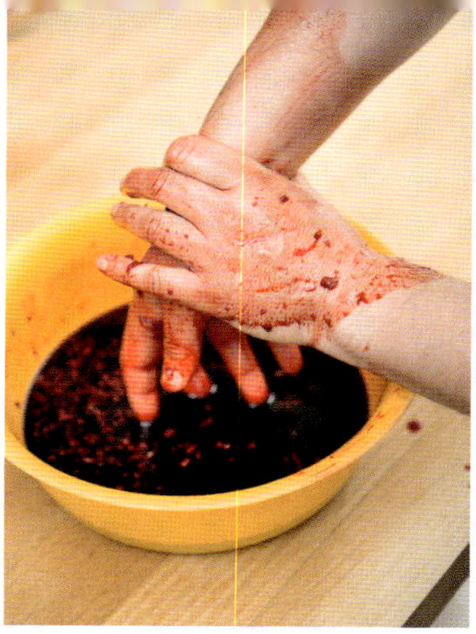
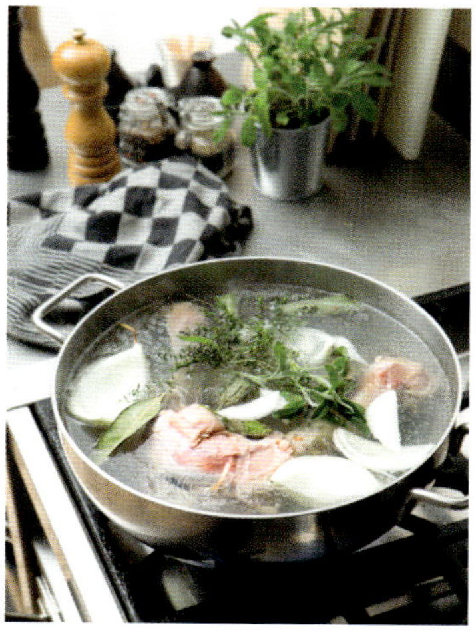
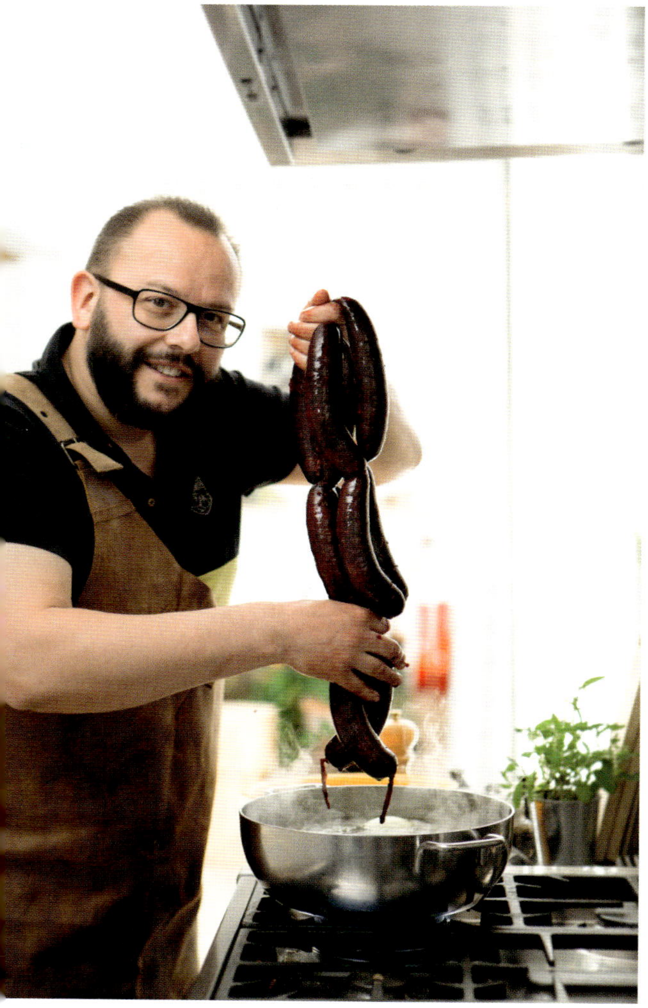
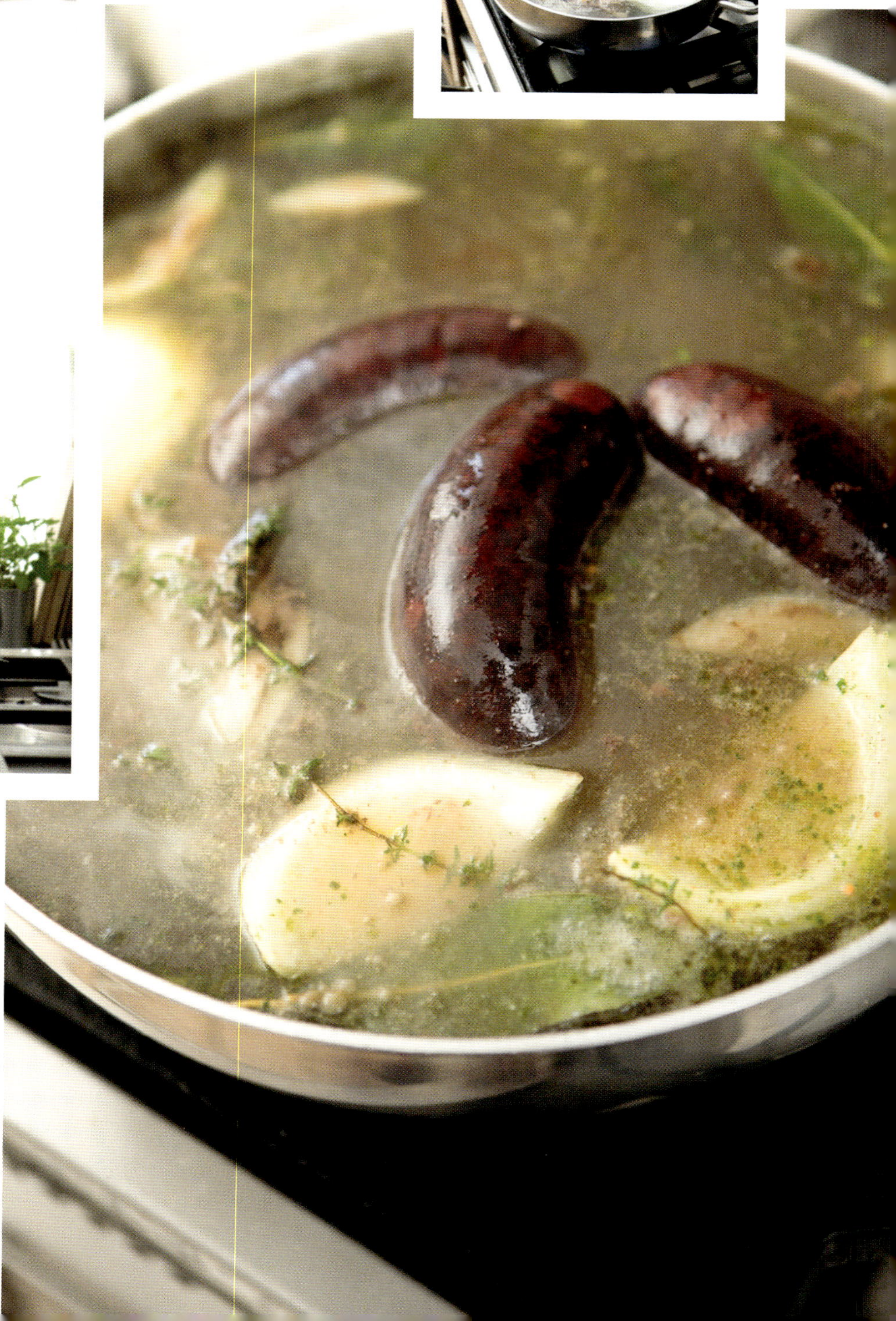

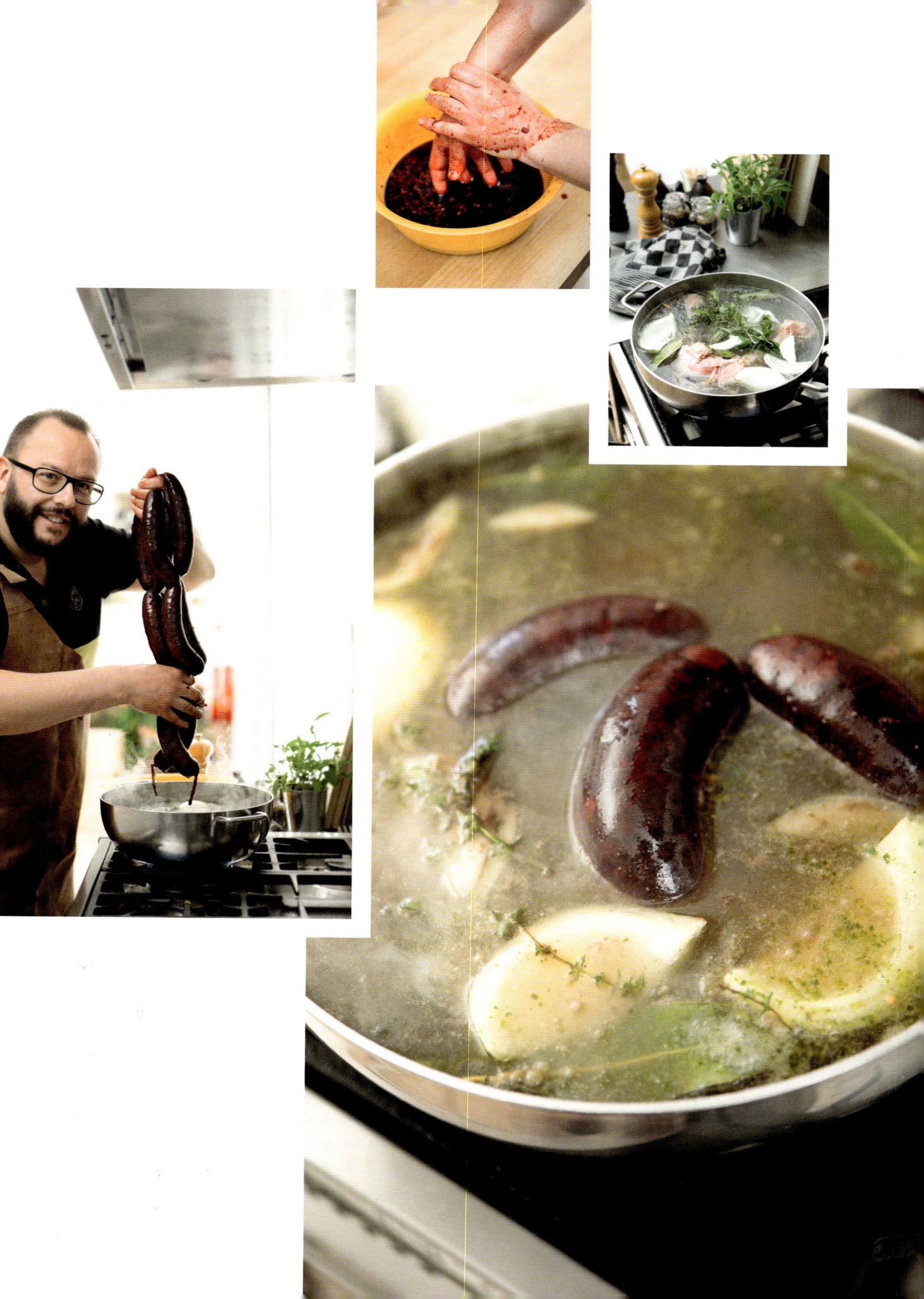

MY BLOOD SAUSAGE

INGREDIENTS

- 1.3 kg [2.8 lbs] of sweet onions
- 2 Jonagold apples
- 500 g [18 oz] Ganda Ham fat in small cubes or finely ground
- 500 g [18 oz] jowl bacon in small cubes or finely ground
- 1.5 litres [1.6 US quarts] fresh, pure pigs' blood
- 3 dl [1 ¼ US cups] cream 35%
- 3 eggs
- 1 ham bone
- sage, thyme, laurel

FOR THE HERB MIX

- 40 g [1 ½ oz] finely ground coarse sea salt
- 8 g [¼ oz] finely ground black muntok pepper
- 2 g [1 tsp] finely grated nutmeg
- 4 g [2 tsp] finely ground fennel seed
- 3 g [1 ½ tsp] finely ground cayenne pepper
- 3 g [1 ½ tsp] finely ground cinnamon
- 30 g [1 oz] brown sugar

FOR THE SAUSAGE CASING

- pig casing, cleaned and rinsed, size 3.6-3.8

PREPARATION

- Peel the onions and chop them very fine.
- Peel the apples, remove the cores and chop the apples very fine.
- Heat a pan and melt the Ganda Ham fat in it. Add the onion, apple cubes, spice mix and jowl bacon and leave on a low heat so it does not discolour.
- Warm the blood without bringing it to a boil (best on induction burner or in a au bain-marie). Keep stirring so that no binding or coagulation occurs.
- Mix the eggs with the cream and make a liaison.
- Remove the blood and the cream mixture from the burner and mix everything carefully. Add the liaison and taste. If necessary, season with extra sea salt and black pepper.
- Pull the sausage casing onto a funnel. Do not forget to tie the end of the casing. Fill by repeatedly pouring a dash of the filling into the casing. Avoid getting air in the casing.
- Tie off equal sized sausages and let rest for a while.
- Bring a large pan of water to a boil with the ham, the herbs and the onion in it, leave to soak for 30 minutes and then remove the bone.
- Bring the stock almost to the boiling point (80 to 90° C / 175 to 200° F) and poach (do not allow to boil) the sausages for about 30 minutes.
- Prick each sausage carefully with a skewer to check the doneness. If no more blood drips out, the sausage is cooked.

TIP Shock the hot blood sausage in ice water, so that it retains its beautiful blood-red colour.

CULINARY HAM

For the professional chef and the passionate amateur chef, raw dried ham is an ideal ingredient that you can use in limitless ways, and throughout the day, from breakfast to evening snack in front of the television, from the daily kitchen to the festive menu.

You can start the day with dried ham. It is also the ideal filling for sandwiches. Many like to add a bit of mustard. For this, select a quality mustard such as Tierenteyn with a good mixture of spices. Together with the ham, this can provide a wonderful balance of flavours that you can enjoy for a long time.

Ham also scores high for classic appetizers and snacks. The specific taste and structure of quality raw ham needs few extras. Ham is able to play a leading role according to the motto 'less is more'. Careful use of ham with an appetizer stimulates the taste buds so your guests are eagerly waiting for what comes next.

It is no accident that raw ham with melon is a classic combination. For many it is an indispensable refreshing appetizer or it can even serve as a light lunch on sunny days. Others might select something more adventurous and creative. Why not experiment with mango, fresh figs, pomegranate, passion fruit …

Raw ham also forms a successful marriage with olive oil. A slice of prime ham, a few drops of extra virgin olive oil with some grated cheese, shreds of garlic and roasted pine nuts: life can be simple but oh so delicious …

Ham can also feature in salads. For example, raw ham does fine with exotic fruit, soft cheeses and savoury salads such as arugula. Because of the salt in the raw ham, no added salt is needed.

Ham must always be served with tapas. Ham can easily be combined with cheese, fruits, vegetables and even fish. Ham also provides a nice colour accent. Do you want to abide by the rules of the art? Then on your tapas plate serve a selection of quality raw ham varieties, so everyone can taste and compare them to their heart's content. If desired, serve with some crunchy bruschetta or toast.

When using raw ham for warm dishes and casseroles, add the ham after cooking. Of course you can also choose to wrap ham around your preparation and heat it. This ensures a delicious crunchy crust.

Do you have some raw ham that is too dry to use? Do not throw it away! You can finely shred the ham and use it to season a dish.

You can also dry ham yourself. Place thin slices of raw ham on a baking sheet covered with parchment paper. Set the oven to hot air function at 80 to 90° C and let the ham dry for an hour until the slices are completely hard. Break the ham into pieces or crumble them. Ideal to add to your preparations!

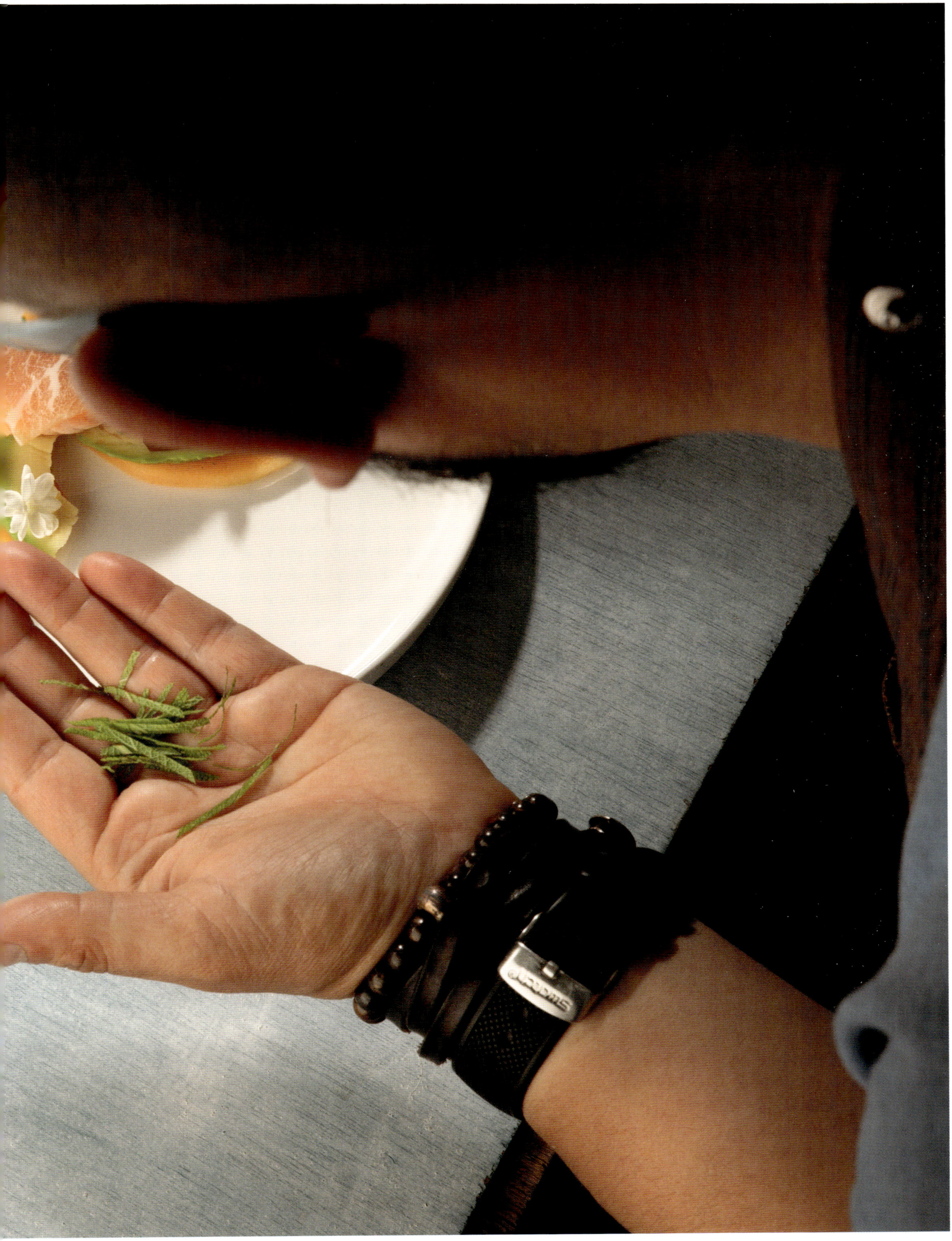

BREAKFAST

INGREDIENTS

- baguette
- olive oil
- tomato, type Toma'Chef
- Ganda Ham

PREPARATION AND SERVING INSTRUCTIONS

- Cut the bread in half and rub it with olive oil, place the tomato between the pieces of bread and press them together to press the tomato into the bread.
- Finish with slices of raw ham.

BREAKFAST NEW STYLE

INGREDIENTS

- ciabatta or Spanish baguette
- olive oil
- tomato, type Toma'Chef
- slices of Serrano ham
- Prince de Bretagne tomatoes in different colours: yellow, orange, green, red
- tapenade of paprika
- shallot, in fine rings
- asparagus shoots
- curls of Manchego cheese
- white pepper from the mill

PREPARATION AND SERVING INSTRUCTIONS

- Cut the bread into the desired shape, sprinkle with olive oil and grill briefly.
- Cut the tomatoes into slices.
- Arrange the bread on the plate and garnish with the various ingredients.

TIP For the tapenade: fresh cream cheese, red pepper, conserved piquillo (peeled Spanish mini peppers preserved in olive oil), shallot and olive oil. Mix everything in the blender until smooth. Finish with pepper and salt, and for those who like it, some pimento sauce.

APPLE CUCUMBER SHOT WITH BLACK FOREST HAM

INGREDIENTS

- 1 cucumber
- 1 stick of white celery
- 1 Granny Smith apple and 1 Jonagold apple
- 2 sage leaves and some sage flowers
- juice of 1 lemon or 3 cl [2 US tbsp] cucumber vinaigrette
- black pepper

FOR THE BREADSTICKS
- 1 baguette
- olive oil
- 8 slices of Black Forest ham

PREPARATION

- Peel and cut the cucumber and celery into large pieces.
- Remove the cores from the apples.
- Blend the apples together with the celery and the cucumber, the sage and the lemon juice. Press through a fine sieve.
- Cut the baguette into equal, long strips and fry them crispy in hot olive oil. Drain.
- Wrap them with the slices of raw Black Forest ham.

SERVING INSTRUCTIONS

- Serve the apple-cucumber drink in shot glasses and finish with sage flowers and some black pepper.
- Arrange the ham sticks.

TIP Cucumber vinaigrette: juice of cucumber mixed with apple juice, lime juice and white balsamic vinegar

BELL PEPPER GAZPACHO WITH SERRANO HAM

INGREDIENTS

- 4 slices of Serrano ham
- 2 small cherry tomatoes, type Toma'Dor
- 1 piquillo pepper
- 100 g [3 ½ oz] ham crunch (see tip)
- fennel seed and fennel plumes
- olive oil

FOR THE GAZPACHO

- 1 small fennel
- 8 dl [3 ⅓ cups] vegetable stock
- 1 tomato
- 2 red peppers
- 2 piquillo peppers
- 2 slices of raw ham
- 5 cl [¼ cup] olive oil

PREPARATION

- Clean the fennel and cut into equal cubes, laying the tufts aside for the garnish.
- Cook the fennel cubes al dente in the stock. Remove them and let them drain. Do not throw away the broth.
- Remove the seeds from the red peppers and cut them together with the tomato and the piquillo peppers into pieces. Stew together with the ham in the olive oil and moisten with the stock. Let it simmer for about 5 minutes and remove from the heat. Allow to cool. Mix everything well and pour through a sieve.
- Roll up the ham and cut into little rolls, cut the tomato into thin slices and the piquillo into strips.

SERVING INSTRUCTIONS

- Serve the little rolls of ham, the fine slices of tomato with ham crunch along with the fennel cubes, fennel seeds and the tufts.
- Finish with the gazpacho and a few drops of olive oil.

TIP Ham crunch: Take 100 grams [3 ½ oz] of raw ham pieces and fry them in a frying pan on a low heat until crispy..
Rub 100 grams [3 ½ oz] of bread with olive oil and paprika powder and bake in the oven until crispy. Let the bread and ham cool down and grind both in the blender.

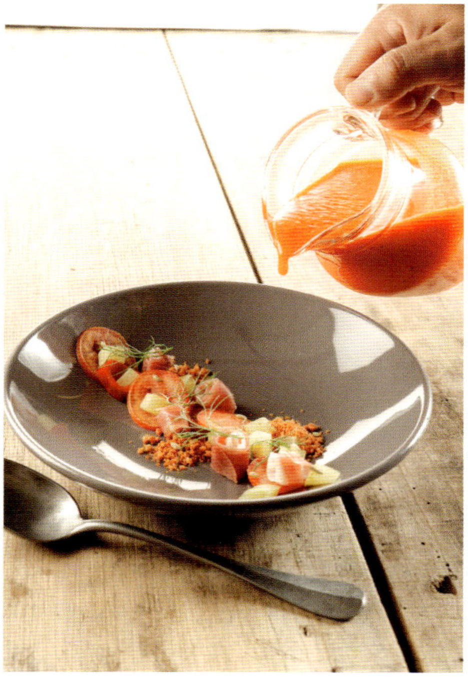

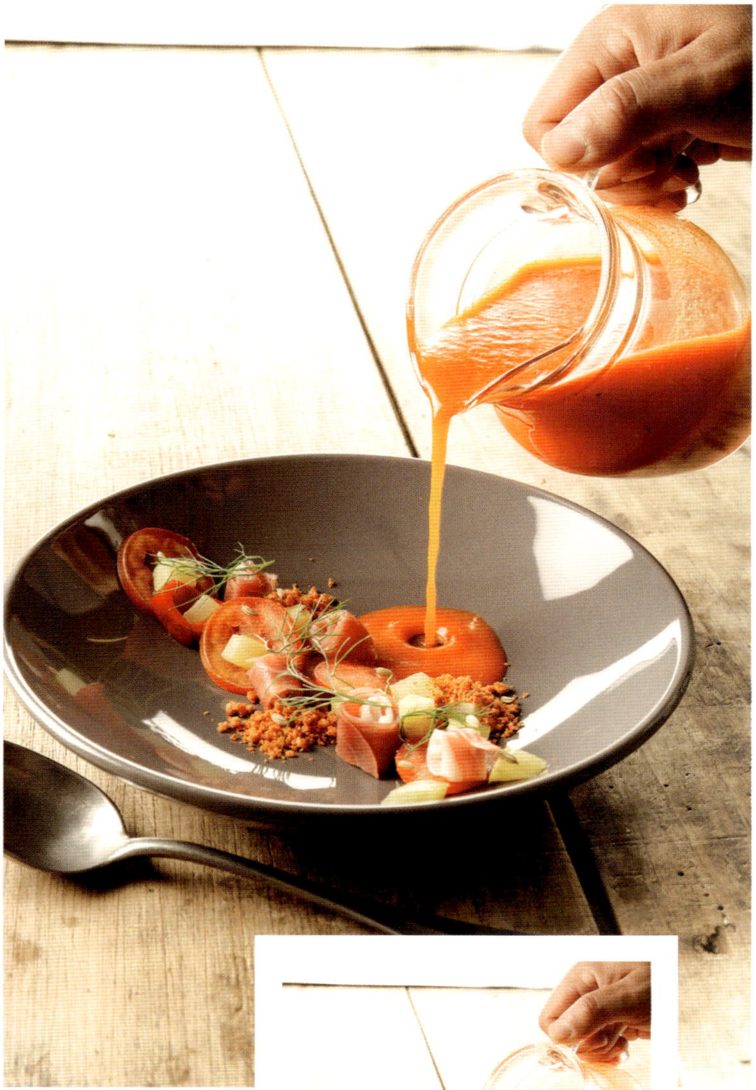

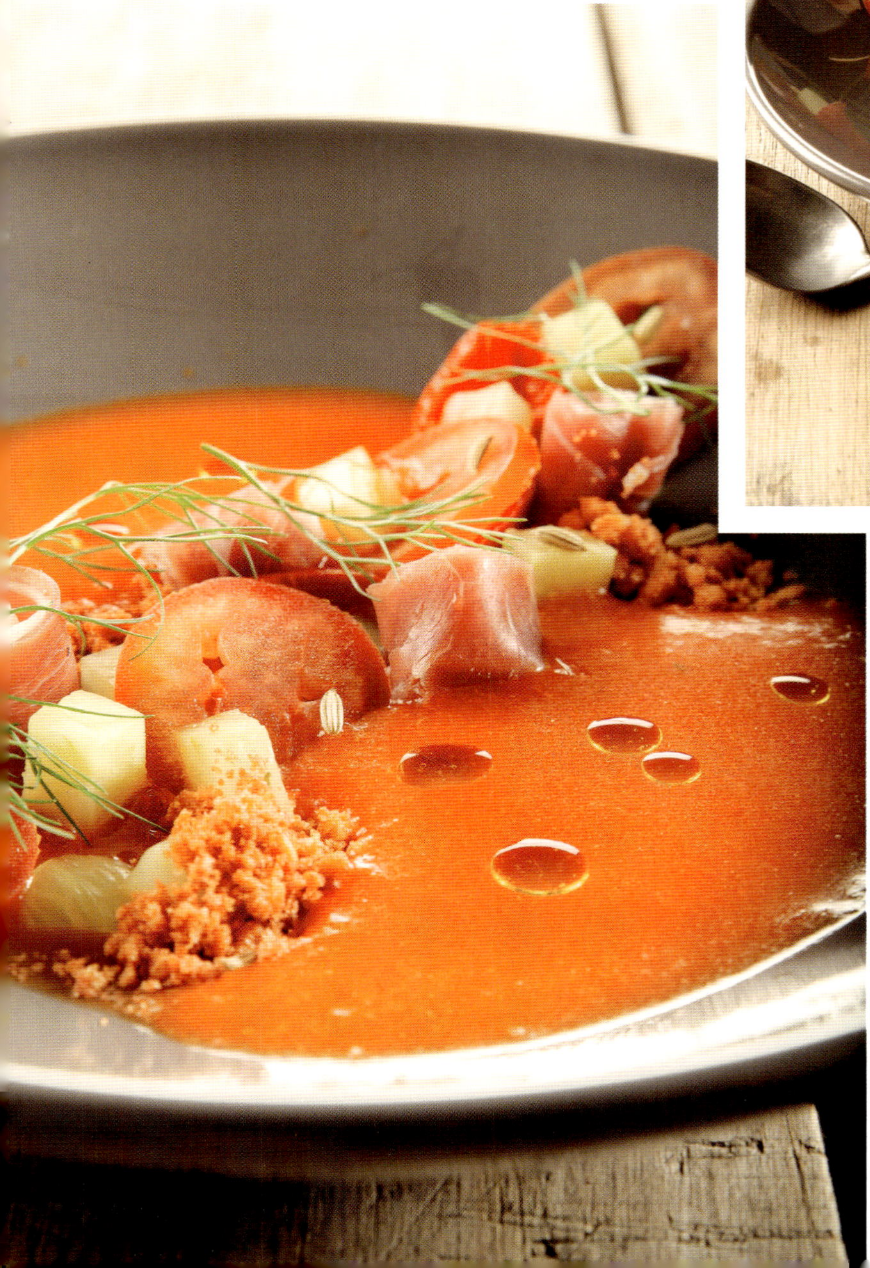

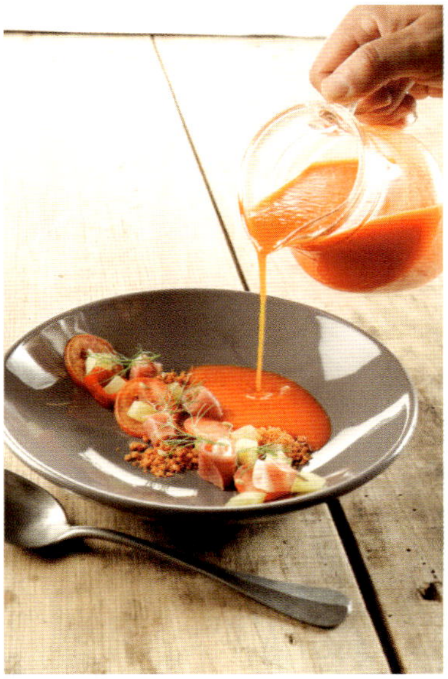

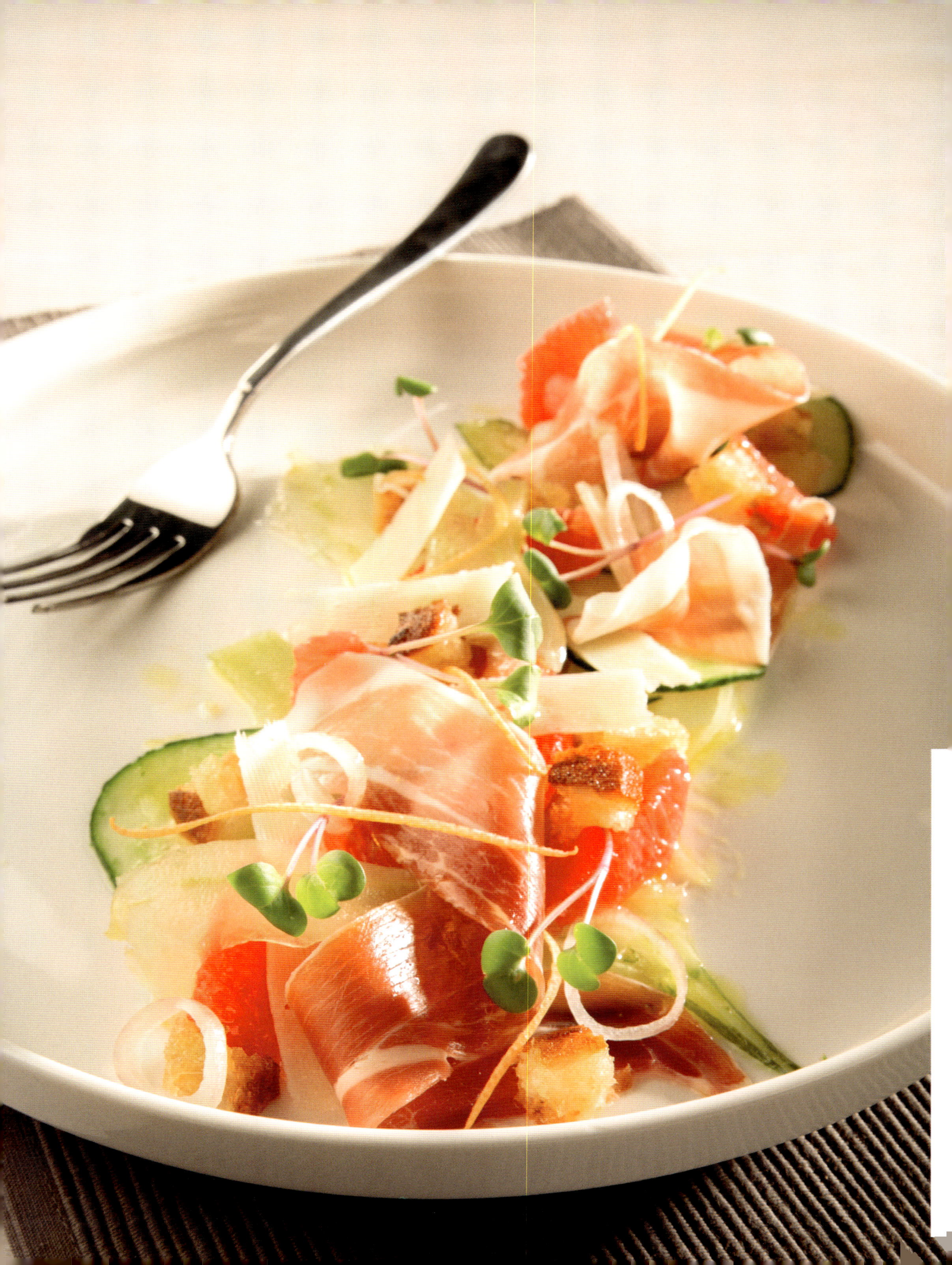

FENNEL BAYONNE HAM SALAD, THE SUN ON YOUR PLATE

INGREDIENTS

- 4 slices of Bayonne ham
- ½ cucumber
- 1 pink grapefruit
- curls of pecorino
- adji cress

FOR THE CANDIED FENNEL
- 1 large fennel
- 1 banana shallot
- 4 dl [1 ⅔ cups] chicken broth
- juice of 1 orange
- 5 cl [¼ cup] olive oil
- 1 cl [2 tsp] sesame oil
- 3 cl [2 US tbsp] absinthe or anise drink

FOR THE CROUTONS
- baguette
- olive oil

PREPARATION

- Clean and cut the fennel and shallot into fine slices. Cut the cucumber into fine slices.
- Moisten the fennel and the shallot slices with stock, orange juice, olive oil, sesame oil and absinthe. Bring to a boil and let it cook until al dente. Remove from the heat and add slices of cucumber.
- Cut the baguette into small cubes and cook crispy in olive oil. Let drain.
- Remove the zest from the grapefruit and cut it very fine.
- Cut off the peel and white pith from the grapefruit.

SERVING INSTRUCTIONS

- Arrange the fennel slices and cucumber slices on a plate.
- Arrange grapefruit wedges, Bayonne ham, shallots and pecorino curls.
- Finish with meat jus, croutons and cress.

MY FAVOURITE BRUSCHETTA

INGREDIENTS

- ciabatta
- olive oil
- Parma ham
- buffalo mozzarella

FOR THE TOMATO SALSA

- various tomatoes, type Toma'Chef
- shallot
- mini basil leaves or cress

PREPARATION AND SERVING INSTRUCTIONS

- Make the tomato salsa: Cut the tomatoes into small cubes and the shallot ultrafine. Mix together with the small basil leaves.
- Cut the ciabatta into equal slices. Fry crispy in hot olive oil.
- Place a slice of Parma ham on each piece of ciabatta.
- Serve together with the tomato salsa and buffalo mozzarella.

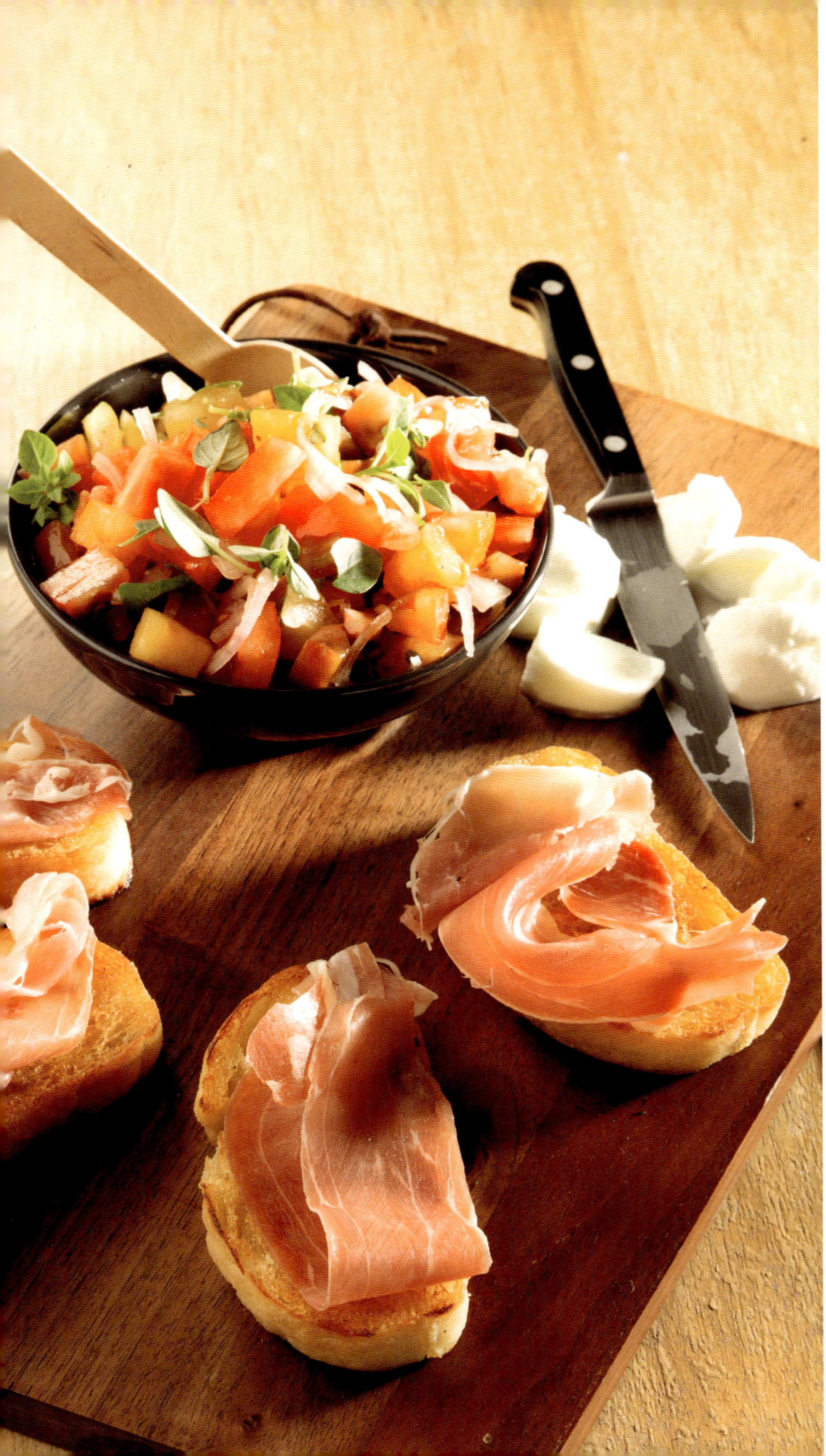
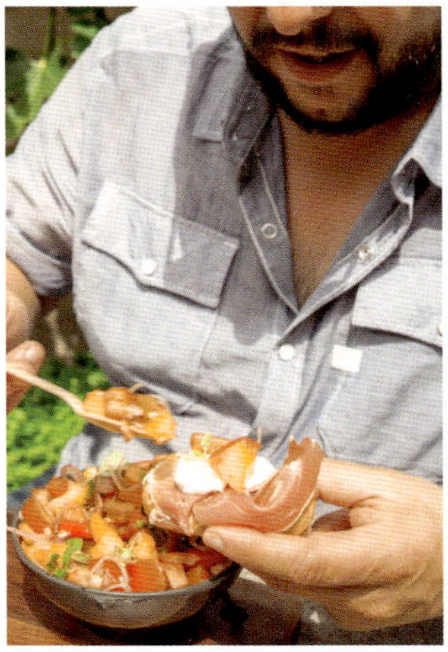
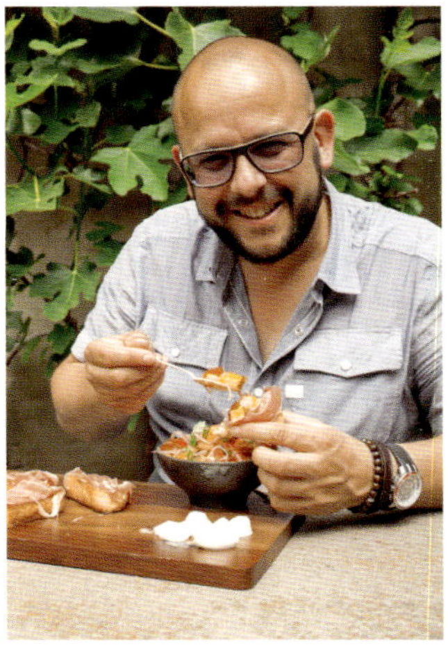
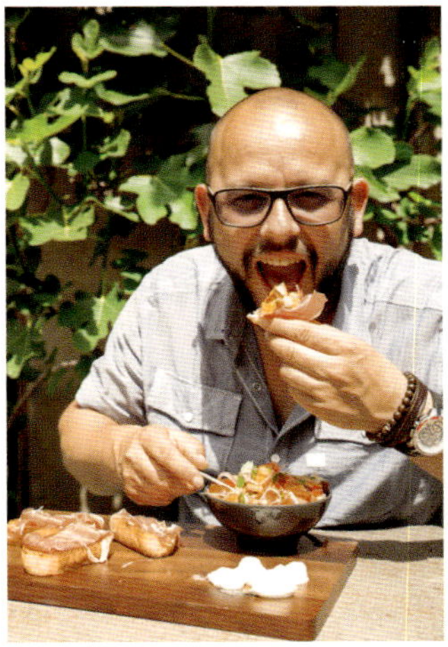
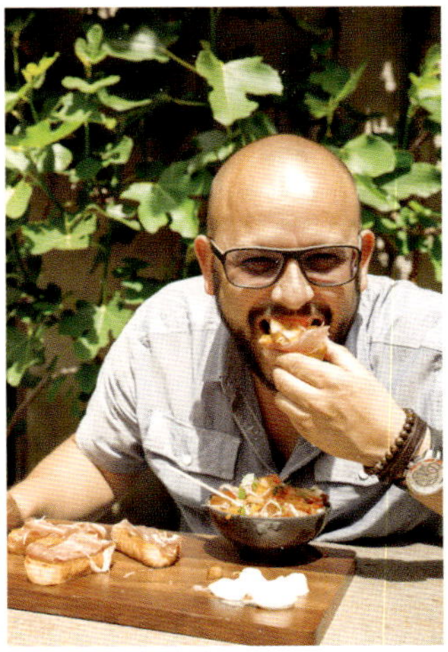

GREEN ASPARAGUS, CHEESE SAUCE AND MANGALICA HAM

INGREDIENTS

- 20 green asparagus
- 4 slices of Mangalica ham
- 10 g [⅓ oz] roasted ciabatta crunch
- black poppy seeds
- asparagus shoots
- coriander leaves

FOR THE CHEESE SAUCE

- 6 dl [2 ½ cups] whole milk
- 2 dl [1 cup] vegetable stock
- 50 g [2 oz] butter
- 50 g [2 oz] flour
- 3 cl [2 US tbsp] lemon juice
- 150 g [5 oz] mixture of grated Grana Padano and Emmentaler cheese
- pepper, salt and nutmeg

PREPARATION

- Peel the green asparagus and cook them until al dente. Shock them in ice water, so they keep their beautiful green colour. Drain.
- Make the cheese sauce: Bring the milk to a boil with the stock. In the meantime, melt the butter and stir in the flour to make a roux. Allow to dry briefly and then pour in the warm milk while stirring. Let it boil briefly until it becomes a smooth sauce. Remove from the heat and finish with the cheese mixture. Season with pepper, salt and nutmeg.

SERVING INSTRUCTIONS

- Serve a slice of Mangalica ham and then arrange the green asparagus on it. Finish with the cheese sauce, crunch of ciabatta and poppy seeds.
- Arrange the fresh herbs.

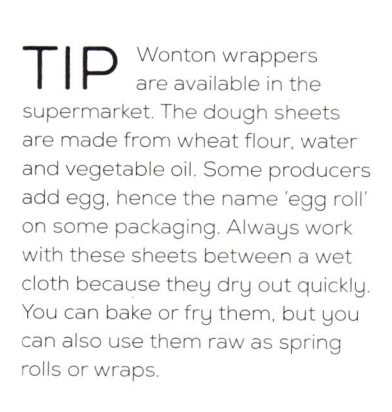

TIP Wonton wrappers are available in the supermarket. The dough sheets are made from wheat flour, water and vegetable oil. Some producers add egg, hence the name 'egg roll' on some packaging. Always work with these sheets between a wet cloth because they dry out quickly. You can bake or fry them, but you can also use them raw as spring rolls or wraps.

126

SPRING ROLLS

INGREDIENTS

- 1 ripe mango
- 10 slices of Ganda Ham
- 20 mini wanton wrappers
- chives
- 200 g [7 oz] Enoki mushrooms

FOR THE MANGO SAUCE

- 1 ripe mango
- 5 cl [¼ cup] olive oil
- 3 cl [2 US tbsp] white wine vinegar, type Chardonnay
- juice of ½ lemon
- olive oil
- pepper from the mill
- a few drops of pimento sauce (optional)

PREPARATION

- Peel and cut the mango into fine strips.
- Arrange half a slice of ham on each wonton wrapper.
- Then place on each a piece of mango, a few sprigs of chives and a bunch of Enoki mushrooms. Roll up tightly.
- Make the mango sauce: Peel the mango and remove the meat from the pit. Add all ingredients together in a blender and mix into a nice smooth sauce. Season with pepper from the mill and possibly a few drops of pimento sauce for the fanciers.

SERVING INSTRUCTIONS

- Serve a spot of mango sauce and arrange the rolls beside it.

BOUILLON OF MUSHROOMS WITH COURGETTE AND SAN DANIELE HAM

INGREDIENTS

- ½ courgette
- 100 g [3 ½ oz] Parisian miniature mushrooms
- 200 g [7 oz] Enoki mushrooms
- 4 slices of San Daniele ham
- black sesame seeds
- red cabbage shoots

FOR THE BROTH
- 2 shallots
- 500 g [18 oz] mixed mushrooms (Parisian mushrooms, chestnut mushrooms, oyster mushrooms)
- 5 cl [¼ cup] olive oil
- 8 dl [3 ⅓ cups] vegetable stock

PREPARATION

- Make the broth: Clean the shallots and cut finely. Clean the mushrooms and cut them fine. Fry together for 5 minutes in the olive oil (do not let them discolour). Moisten with the stock and simmer for 30 minutes. Arrange a kitchen towel in a sieve and pour through.
- Cut the courgette into wafer-thin slices and the mushrooms into quarters. Allow the Enoki to boil briefly in the broth.

TIP Enoki: this protein-rich miniature mushroom is a Japanese mushroom variety that has recently conquered our kitchens. It is harvested young and in bunches and thrives in dark, damp spaces. You can find them in white or dark brown, they taste like nuts and are best used raw or slightly warmed.

SERVING INSTRUCTIONS

- Serve the broth with the various garnishes and finish with strips of San Daniele ham, black sesame seeds and red cabbage shoots.

HAM WITH CAULIFLOWER

INGREDIENTS

- 1 cauliflower
- 2 litres [4 ¼ US pints] chicken broth
- 8 Parisian mushrooms
- 5 cl [3 US tbsp] olive oil
- 8 slices of Black Forest ham

FOR THE CAULIFLOWER PUREE

- 400 g [14 oz] cooked cauliflower
- 5 cl [3 US tbsp] chicken stock
- 20 g [½ oz] butter
- fresh thyme leaves
- pepper and salt

PREPARATION

- Clean the cauliflower and cut into florets. Lay 1 floret aside and cook the rest in the chicken stock. Drain, lay 3 cooked florets aside and place the rest in a blender with some stock, the butter and some of the thyme leaves. Puree into a smooth mass and season with salt and pepper. Divide into a piping bag.
- Cut one floret into thin slices and store in ice water.
- Cut the cooked florets into smaller pieces and the mushrooms into equal slices. Fry both crispy in hot olive oil.
- Lay the slices of Black Forest ham flat and squirt the cauliflower puree on them. Roll up into beautiful cannelloni.

SERVING INSTRUCTIONS

- Serve the slices of raw cauliflower and fried mushrooms, place with each of them 2 cannelloni and a few fried cauliflower florets.
- Finish with thyme leaves and some pepper from the mill.

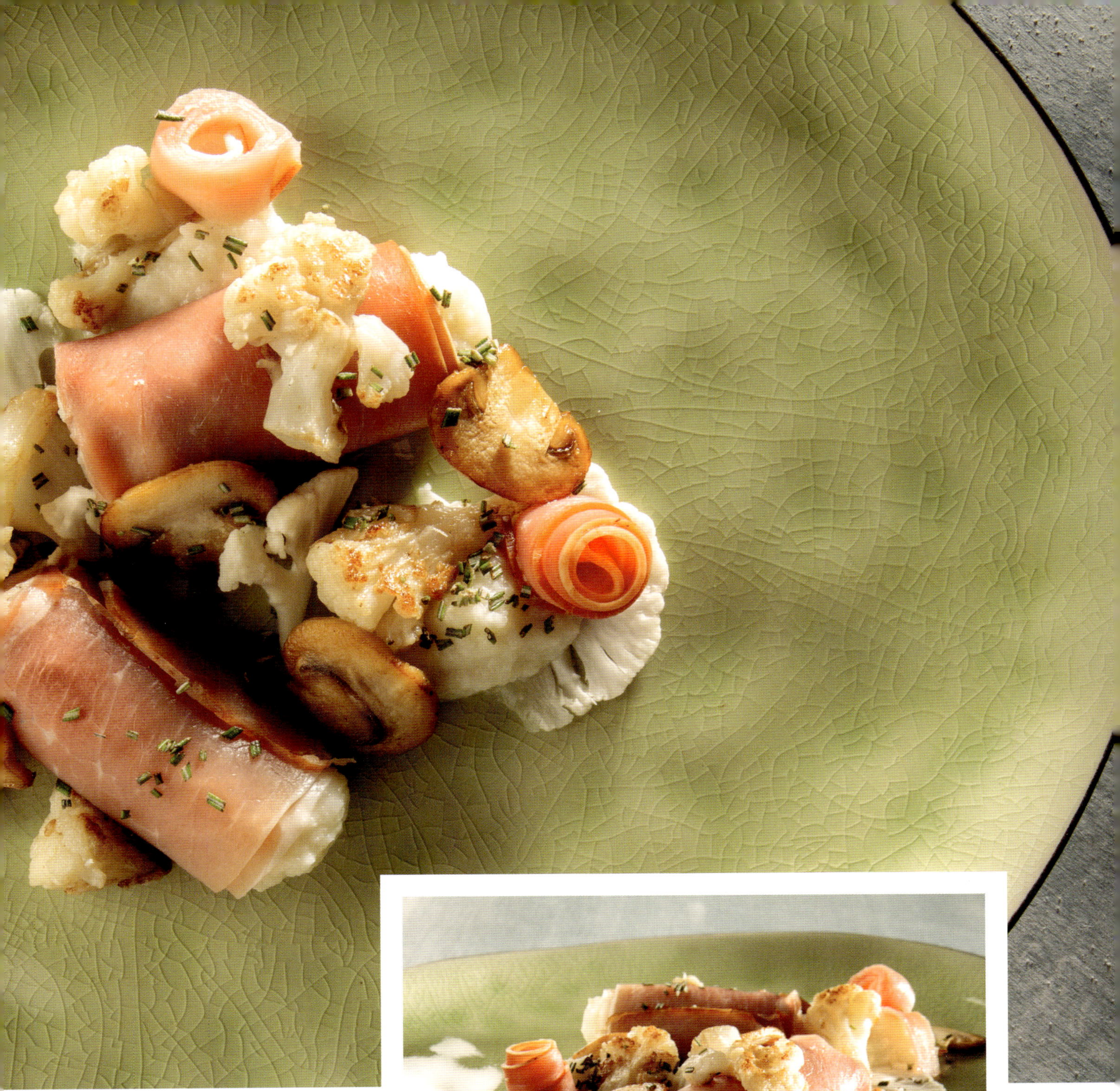

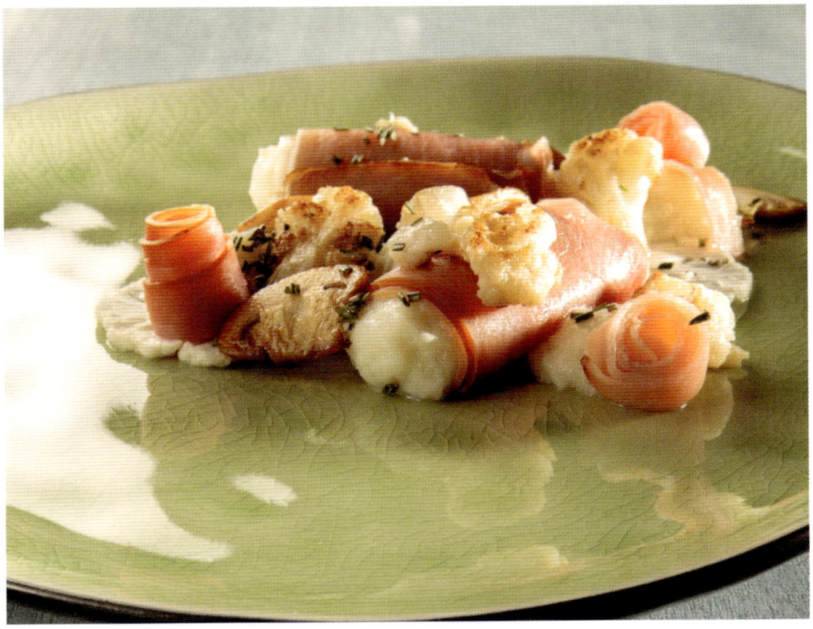

PLATE OF IBERICO HAM WITH GUACAMOLE AND SAGE

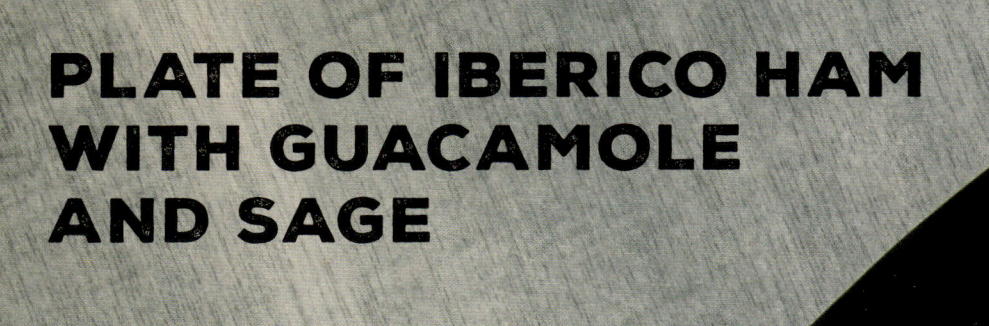

INGREDIENTS

- 8 slices of Iberico ham
- Spanish baguette
- 1 small red onion
- 2 piquillo peppers
- 1 dl [½ US cup] olive oil
- fresh sage leaves
- some sage flowers

FOR THE GUACAMOLE
- 1 shallot
- 10 g [⅓ oz] red peppers
- 2 ripe avocados
- 1 dl [½ US cup] Greek yogurt
- 3 cl [2 US tbsp] olive oil
- 3 cl [2 US tbsp] lime juice
- pepper and salt

PREPARATION

- Make the guacamole: Clean the shallot and, together with the paprika, cut into small pieces. Peel the avocados and remove the pits. Put the avocados and all the other ingredients in a blender and mix into a smooth mass. Season to taste with pepper and a little salt.
- Grill the baguette until crispy and cut into the desired shape.
- Clean the red onion and, together with the piquillo peppers, cut into thin rings.
- Warm the olive oil and fry the sage leaves until crispy. Allow to drain on a kitchen towel.

TIP Guacamole: If you want to make a mousse, you can add a soaked and melted leaf of gelatine to the preparation and allow it to cool for at least 2 hours.

SERVING INSTRUCTIONS

- Serve the guacamole and arrange the rest of the garnishes, the onion, piquillo pepper, grilled baguette, fried sage leaves with it. Finish with the Iberico ham and sage flowers.

TIP Serve on a large plate and eat all together from one plate, that is *sharing*.

TOMATO CARPACCIO WITH BURRATA AND SERRANO HAM

INGREDIENTS

- 4 tomatoes, type Toma'Chef, yellow, orange, green, black
- 1 large red onion
- 1 burrata mozzarella
- 8 slices Serrano ham
- mini basil leaves
- black pepper from the mill
- ciabatta or baguette

FOR THE VINAIGRETTE

- 5 cl [3 US tbsp] olive oil
- 3 cl [2 US tbsp] xeres vinegar
- 2 cl [4 tsp] tomato vinegar

PREPARATION AND SERVING INSTRUCTIONS

- Make the vinaigrette by combining all of its ingredients and beating them into an airy sauce.
- Cut the various tomatoes into thin slices and arrange on the plate. Cut the cleaned onion into thin rings.
- Distribute the burrata, torn into pieces, on top together with the Serrano ham and onion rings. Finish with mini basil leaves and pepper from the mill.
- Serve with ciabatta or baguette.

PEA SOUP WITH HAM FROTH

INGREDIENTS

- 8 slices of Ganda Ham
- a few peas
- tarragon leaves

FOR THE PEA SOUP

- 1 large shallot
- butter
- 400 g [14 oz] frozen peas
- 4 dl [1 ⅔ US cups] vegetable stock
- 4 dl [1 ⅔ US cups] chicken broth
- 8 mint leaves
- leaves of 1 large branch of tarragon
- pepper from the mill

FOR THE FROTH

- 2 dl [1 US cup] whole milk
- 100 g [3 ½ oz] paring scraps of raw ham

PREPARATION

- Make the pea soup: Clean the shallot and cut into small pieces. Lightly fry them in the butter until glazed and then add the peas, the mint and the tarragon leaves. Allow to continue cooking briefly, but do not fry. Moisten with the stock and simmer for 10 minutes. Mix until smooth in the blender and pass through a fine sieve. Season with pepper from the mill. Do not add salt, the ham and the froth are the flavours here.
- Bring the milk to a boil with the ham scraps and simmer for 5 minutes. Pour through a fine sieve.
- Cut the ham slices into strips.

SERVING INSTRUCTIONS

- Serve the ham with some peas and tarragon leaves.
- Make froth from the ham milk with a froth beater.
- Put froth on the ham.
- Add the pea soup.

TIP In the summer, the soup can be served perfectly cold. Small ice cubes with tarragon leaves and peas make it something special.

PARMA ROLLS, PESTO GENOVESE AND GRANA PADANO CHEESE

INGREDIENTS

- 12 slices of Parma ham
- 4 tomatoes, type Toma'Gusto
- 100 g [3 ½ oz] rocket
- 16 slices of Grana Padano cheese, very thin
- 50 g [2 oz] of roasted pine nuts

FOR THE PESTO

- 100 g [3 ½ oz] Grana Padano cheese
- 80 g [3 oz] small basil leaves
- 100 g [3 ½ oz] roasted pine nuts
- 1 dl [½ US cup] olive oil
- pepper from the mill

PREPARATION

- Make the pesto: Combine all the pesto ingredients except the olive oil. Mix smooth in a blender and add the olive oil by squirting it in. Season with pepper from the mill. Do not use salt.
- Make the rolls: Lay a slice of Parma ham flat and top with a quarter tomato, a few arugula leaves and 2 slices of Grana Padano cheese. Roll up and cut in two.

TIP For a red pesto, use the same base but add 50 grams [2 oz] of concentrated tomato passata and 100 grams [3 ½ oz] of sun-dried tomatoes. Finish with 50 grams [2 oz] of basil.

SERVING INSTRUCTIONS

- Serve a spot of pesto and the Parma ham rolls with it. Finish with arugula and roasted pine nuts.

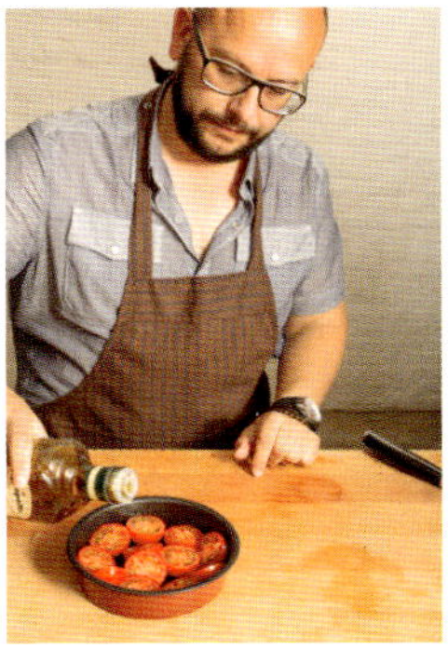

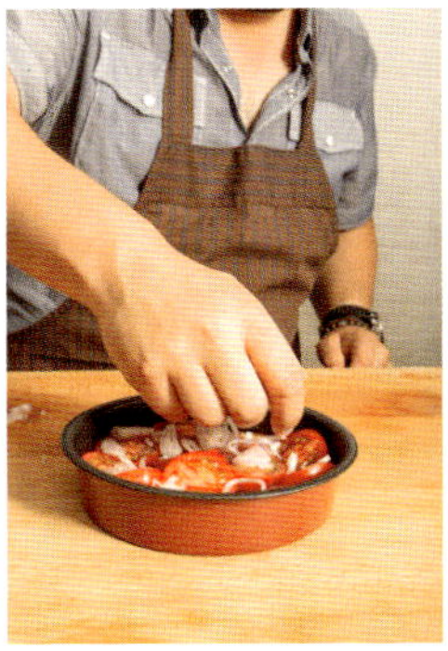

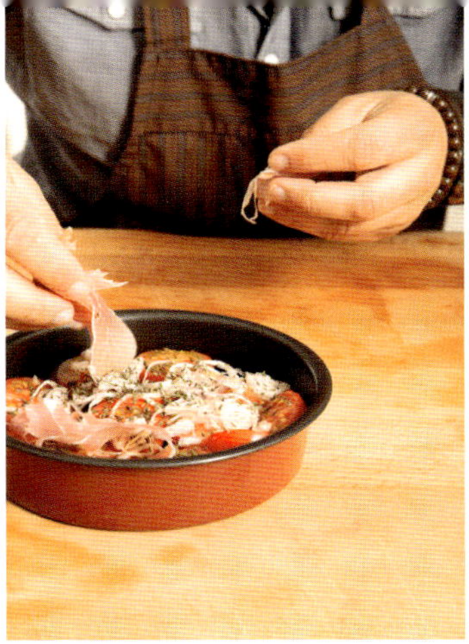

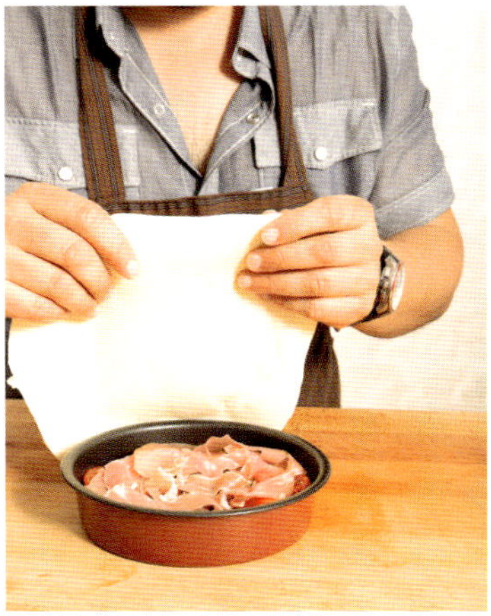

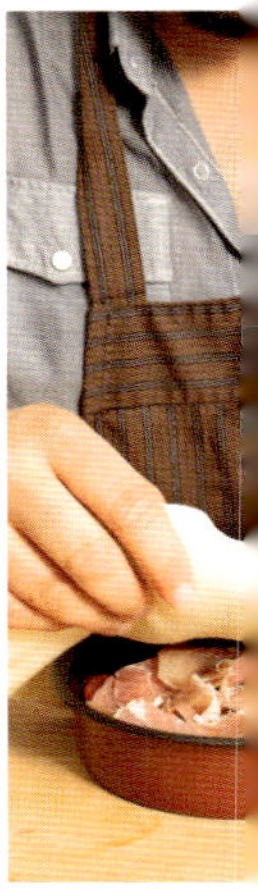

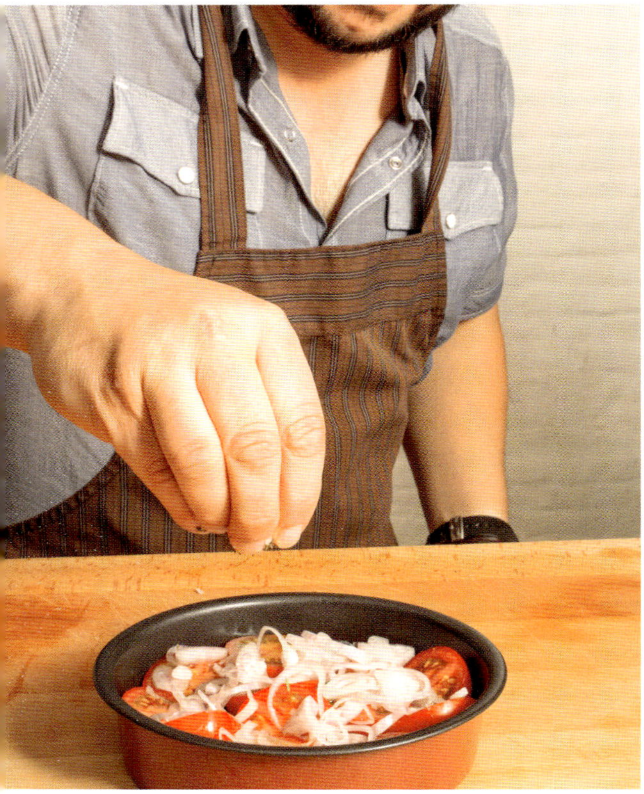

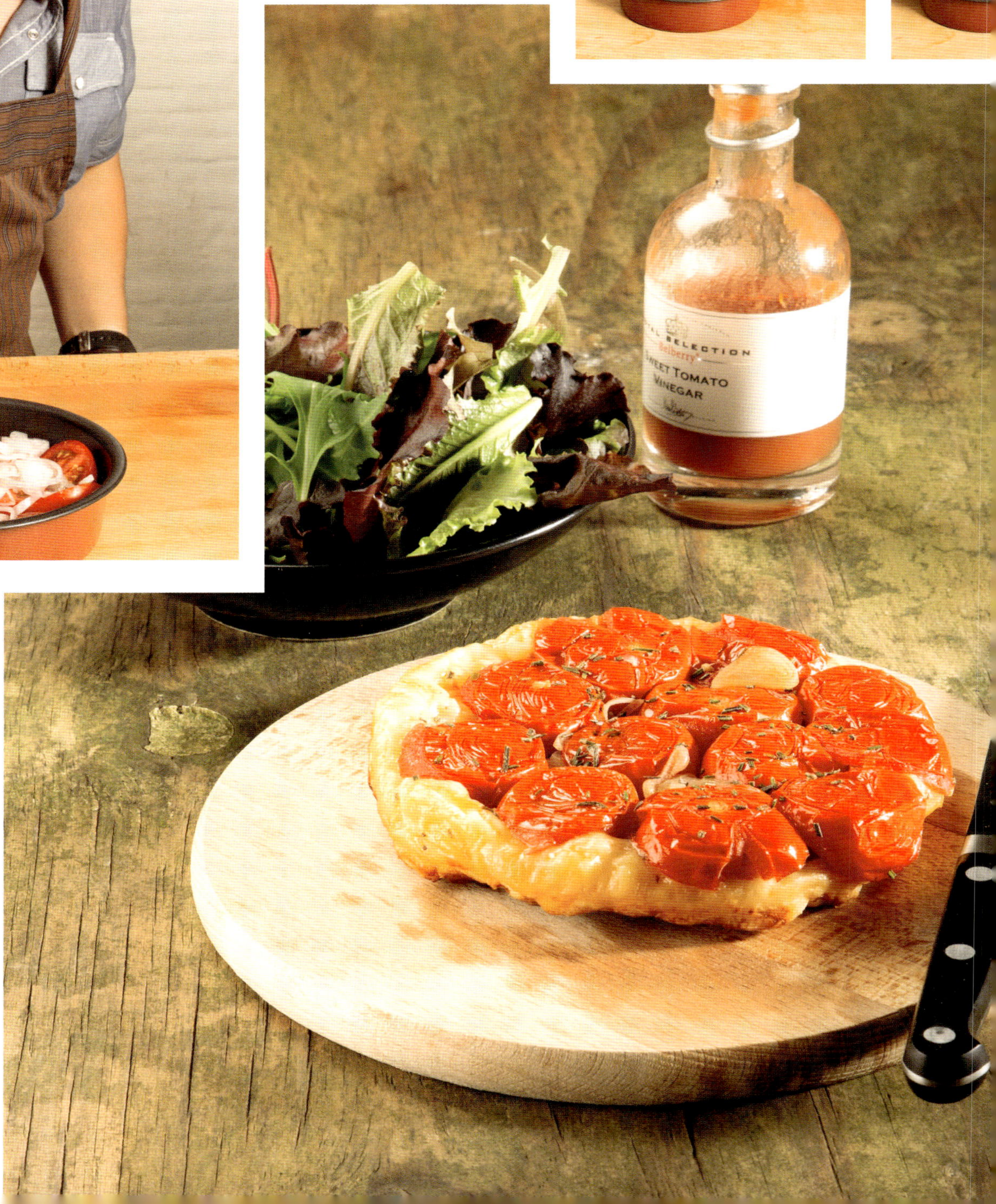
SELECTION
TOMATO
VINEGAR

TARTE TATIN WITH TOMATO AND BAYONNE HAM

INGREDIENTS

- 100 g [3 ½ oz] young lettuce shoots
- 1 dl [½ US cup] tomato vinaigrette

FOR THE TARTE TATIN
- 2 large banana shallots
- 2 sprigs of rosemary
- 2 cloves of garlic
- 1 dl [½ US cup] olive oil
- 20 g [½ oz] butter
- 12 tomatoes, type Toma'Rito (a type of tomato between the classic and the cherry tomato)
- 8 slices of Bayonne ham
- 2 sheets of puff pastry of 20 × 20 cm

PREPARATION

- Preheat the oven to 150° C [300° F].
- Clean and cut the shallots in thin rings, remove the leaves of rosemary from the sprig and finely chop them. Peel and crush the garlic and chop very fine.
- Heat the oil and the butter and briefly simmer the shallot, garlic and rosemary. Pour into a pie dish and arrange the halved tomatoes. Place in the oven for 5 minutes.
- Increase the temperature of the oven to 190° C [375° F].
- Arrange the Bayonne ham on the tomatoes and lay a sheet of puff pastry on top. Press gently and gently fold in the sides. Brush the dough with some olive oil.
- Place in the oven for 15 minutes until the dough is a nice golden brown.
- Remove the tart from the oven, place a plate or board over the tart pan and turn over in one smooth movement.

SERVING INSTRUCTIONS

- Serve the Tarte Tatin with a side order of mixed young lettuce and some tomato vinaigrette.

GAZPACHO FULL OF FLAVOUR

INGREDIENTS

FOR THE GAZPACHO
- 1 red onion
- 2 cloves of garlic
- 6 ripe tomatoes, type Toma'Gusto
- 4 piquillo peppers
- 1 small fennel
- ½ cucumber
- 2 slices of white bread, without crusts or 'mie de pain'
- 2 dl [1 US cup] vegetable stock
- a few drops of pimento sauce to taste, type tabasco

FOR THE GARNISHES
- ½ cucumber
- 1 red pepper
- 1 red onion
- 2 spring onions
- 4 slices of Black Forest ham

FOR THE CROUTONS
- 4 slices of white bread, without crusts or 'mie de pain'
- 20 g [½ oz] butter
- 1 small box of Atsina® cress (it has an anise flavour)

PREPARATION

- Make the gazpacho: Clean the various vegetables for the gazpacho and put them in the blender. Mix the whole and pour through a sieve. Place in the refrigerator.
- Clean and cut the vegetables for the garnish into small cubes, the ham into fine strings.
- Cut the bread into small cubes and bake golden brown in frothy butter in the pan.

SERVING INSTRUCTIONS

- Serve the gazpacho with the croutons and some leaves of Atsina® cress.
- Serve with the crispy vegetables and the tasty Black Forest ham.

143

GRILLED SCALLOPS WITH DRIED HAM

INGREDIENTS

- 4 slices of Bayonne ham
- 12 scallops
- 50 g [2 oz] coconut oil
- 200 g [7 oz] paprika tapenade

FOR THE GARNISHES

- 1 cucumber
- 1 Jonagold apple
- 1 dl [½ US cup] cucumber vinegar
- 20 g [½ oz] sunflower seeds
- fresh dill plumes

PREPARATION

- Preheat the oven to 100° C [210° F].
- Arrange the ham on butter paper and place in the oven. Allow to dry for 1 hour.
- Rub the scallops with the coconut oil and grill them in a hot grill pan for 1 minute on each side.
- Cut the cucumber in half and remove the seeds, remove the core from the apple. Cut both into fine cubes. Moisten with the vinegar and mix in the sunflower seeds and dill.

SERVING INSTRUCTIONS

- Form a strip of paprika tapenade and place the brunoise of vegetables on it.
- Serve three scallops with slices of dried ham in between.

TIP Paprika tapenade: Cut 2 large red peppers (with skin and seeds removed), 1 tomato (with skin and seeds removed) and 1 shallot into cubes. Braise in 5 cl [3 US tbsp] of olive oil and 1 gram of oregano. Let it simmer for 5 minutes and mix until smooth in a blender.

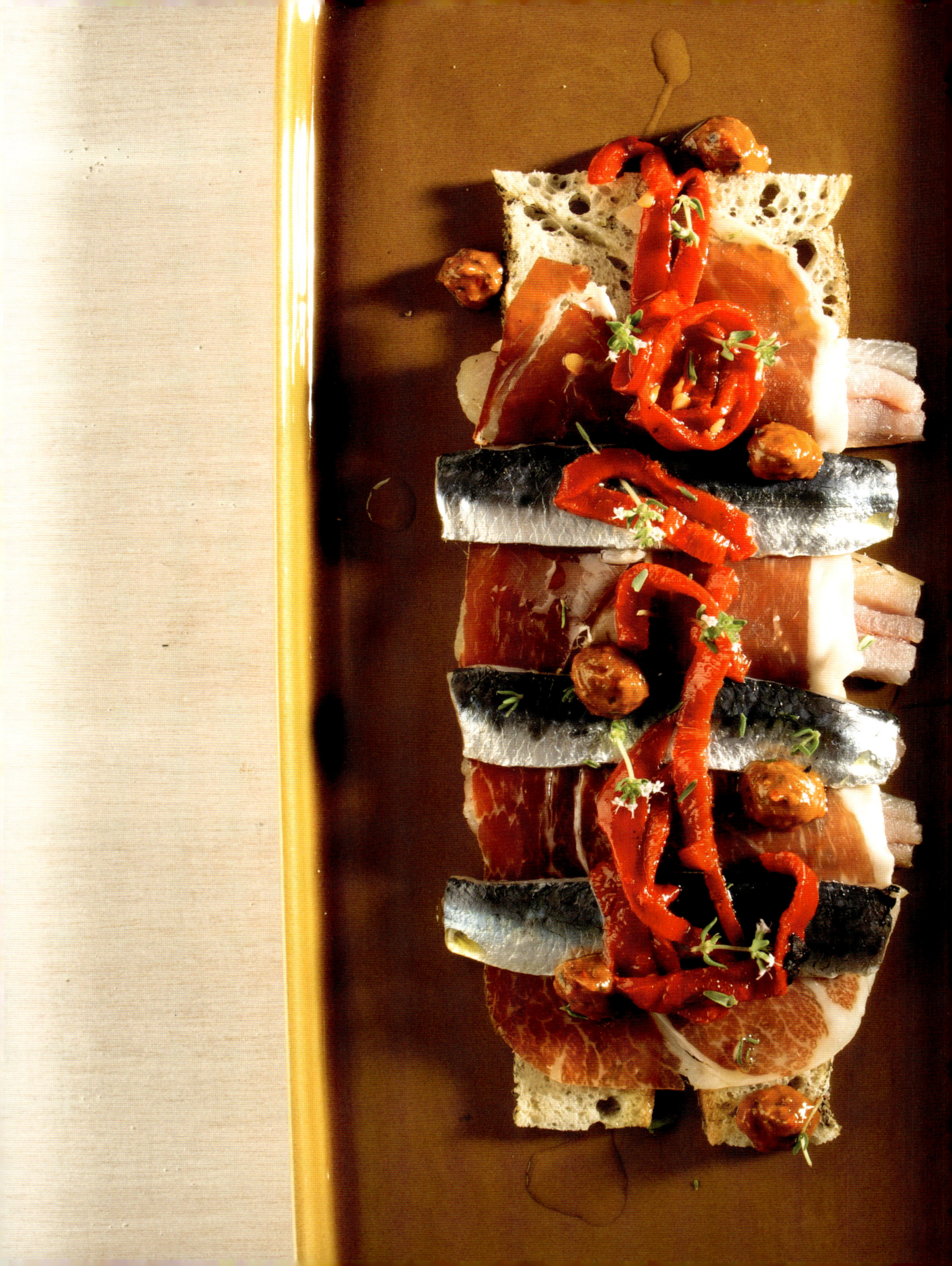

SPANISH SARDINES WITH SERRANO HAM

INGREDIENTS

- 12 sardines, bones and scales removed
- 1 dl [½ US cup] olive oil
- 2 cloves of garlic
- pepper from the mill
- 1 plain focaccia bread
- 4 slices of Serrano ham
- 4 piquillo peppers
- lemon thyme

TAPENADE FROM SUN-DRIED TOMATOES AND OLIVES

- 100 g [3 ½ oz] sun-dried tomatoes
- 100 g [3 ½ oz] green olives
- 5 g [⅕ oz] small oregano leaves
- 5 cl [3 US tbsp] chicken broth

PREPARATION

- Preheat the oven to 65° C [150° F].
- Brush a griddle with the olive oil mixed with the cloves of garlic. Pepper slightly. Arrange the sardine fillets with the skin side up. Put in the oven for ten minutes.
- Cut the focaccia bread into thin slices and grill until crispy.
- Make the tapenade by mixing all the ingredients in a blender until smooth.

SERVING INSTRUCTIONS

- Serve the toast with the sardine fillets and ham on top.
- Finish with the peppers and tufts of tapenade.
- As a finishing touch, add a spoonful of oil and some leaves of lemon thyme.

STEWED SCALLOPS, BEETROOT, SAN DANIELE HAM

INGREDIENTS

- 12 scallops
- 2 red beets, cooked
- 200 g [7 oz] of red beet tapenade
- 200 g [7 oz] red beets, cooked (parings)
- 20 g [½ oz] green olives
- 50 g [2 oz] sesame paste
- 3 g [¾ tsp] honey
- 4 slices of San Daniele ham
- 2 salt biscuits, crumbled, type TUC biscuits
- 1 bowl of chilli cress

FOR THE VINAIGRETTE

- 1 dl [½ US cup] olive oil
- 1 dl [½ US cup] sushi vinegar
- 5 cl [3 US tbsp] red beet juice
- 3 g [¾ tsp] acacia honey

PREPARATION

- Cut each scallop into three equal slices.
- Mix all ingredients for the vinaigrette.
- Cut the red beet into cylinders and then into slices the size of a scallop. Marinate them for 20 minutes in the vinaigrette.
- Mix the ingredients for the tapenade in a blender until smooth and put in a piping bag.

SERVING INSTRUCTIONS

- Make a ring of the scallops and the beetroot slices.
- Place the strips of ham on top and squirt tufts of beetroot tapenade around it. Finish with the crumble of salt biscuits and a few sprigs of chilli cress.
- Serve the vinaigrette with it and finish with a spoonful of vinaigrette just before serving.

SCAMPI, HAM AND CHICORY

INGREDIENTS

- 16 scampi 16/20, peeled and gutted
- 8 slices of Jambon d'Ardenne
- 5 cl [3 US tbsp] olive oil
- 4 heads of chicory and 2 extra for the garnish
- 2 Jonagold apples and 1 extra for the garnish

FOR THE VINAIGRETTE
- 3 cl [2 US tbsp] olive oil
- 3 cl [2 US tbsp] Chardonnay wine vinegar
- 1 cl [2 tsp] lime juice
- fresh dill plumes
- apple blossom

FOR THE CURRY MAYONNAISE
- 2 dl [1 US cup] basic mayonnaise
- 2 cl [4 tsp] lime juice
- 2 g [½ tsp] yellow curry paste

PREPARATION

- Roll the scampi up in ½ slices of Jambon d'Ardenne (cut the slices in two lengthwise).
- Heat the oil in a pan and fry the scampi until crispy.
- Cut 4 stalks of chicory into thin strips, cut the Jonagold apples into fine cubes (brunoise) and mix everything together with the ingredients for the vinaigrette. Mix in chopped dill plumes.
- Make the curry mayonnaise by mixing all the ingredients. Put the mixture in a spray can.

SERVING INSTRUCTIONS

- Serve the chicory-apple salad with the fried scampi on it.
- Finish with tufts of curry mayonnaise, leaves of chicory, apple slices, a few apple blossoms and dill plumes.

TIP For the mayonnaise: Beat up 2 egg yolks with a teaspoon of mustard. While squirting in 5 dl [2 ¼ US cups] of peanut oil, whisk into a nice firm, bound mass. Finish with a squirt of vinegar, pepper and salt to taste

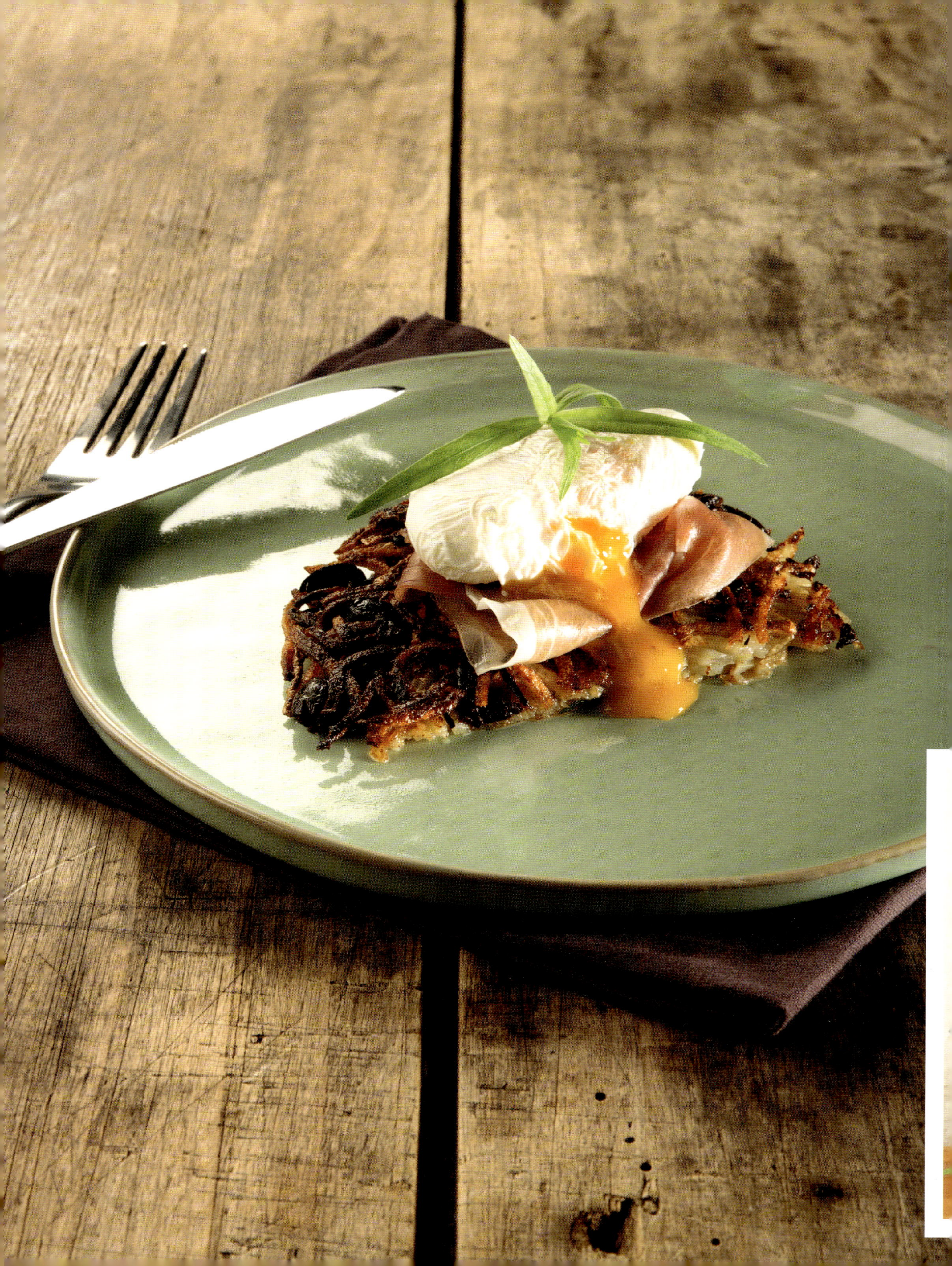

POTATO PIE WITH PARMA HAM AND POACHED EGG

INGREDIENTS

- 4 farm eggs
- 4 slices of Parma ham
- fresh tarragon

FOR THE PIE

- 400 g [14 oz] early summer potatoes, peeled and washed
- 40 g [1 ½ oz] black olive tapenade
- 16 black olives in rings
- black pepper from the mill
- fresh tarragon leaves
- 5 cl [3 US tbsp] olive oil

PREPARATION

- Preheat the oven to 160° C [320° F].
- Grate the potatoes with a potato grater or cut them with a mandoline slicer in fine strings. Mix with the tapenade, olive rings, black pepper and tarragon leaves.
- Heat the olive oil in a pan and spread the potato mass over it. Press well and let it cook crispy. Turn after about three minutes and fry the other side. Cook for 10 minutes in the preheated oven.
- Poach the eggs: carefully break each egg into a coffee cup first. Bring 1 litre [1 US quart + 5%] of water to a boil and add a little vinegar. Stir the water into a whirlpool with a whisk and pour in an egg. Let it poach for about 2 minutes and then remove the egg from the water. Repeat.

SERVING INSTRUCTIONS

- Arrange a pointed piece of potato tart on a plate and put a slice of Parma ham on it.
- Finish with the poached egg and tarragon leaves.

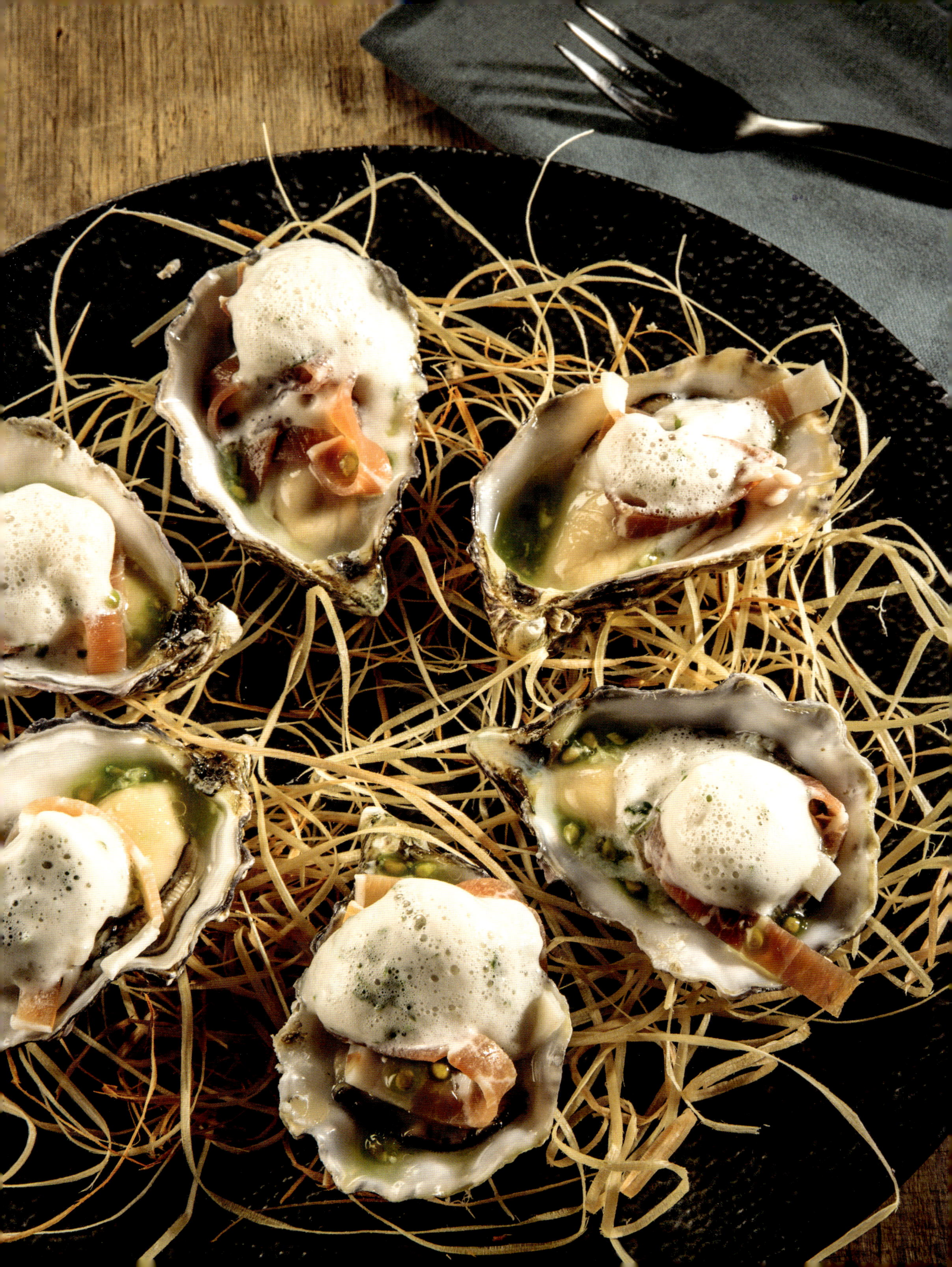

OYSTERS, BAYONNE HAM AND BASIL EMULSION

INGREDIENTS
FOR 12 OYSTERS

- 12 oysters, type Fines de Claire or Zeeuwse Creuses, size 3
- 4 yellow tomatoes, type Toma'Color
- 3 cl [2 US tbsp] white balsamic vinegar
- 4 slices of Bayonne ham, cut into strips

FOR THE BASIL / HAM EMULSION

- liquor from the oysters topped up with champagne to 1 dl [½ US cup]
- 20 g [½ oz] basil leaves
- 20 g [½ oz] trimmings from the Bayonne ham
- 1 dl [½ US cup] culinary cream
- black pepper from the mill

PREPARATION

- Open the shells carefully and remove the oysters. Strain the moisture.
- Bring the oyster liquor together with the basil leaves, the ham trimmings and the cream to a boil. Allow to stew for about three minutes, boil down and strain. Season with the pepper. Let cool until lukewarm.
- Cut the tomatoes into four and remove the seeds. Mix the pulp and press through a fine sieve. Add the seeds and mix with the white balsamic vinegar.

SERVING INSTRUCTIONS

- Place an oyster and a few strips of Bayonne ham in each shell. Spoon some tomato juice onto it.
- Whip the basil cream and top the oysters with it.

JAMBON D'ARDENNE, RED CHICORY, SQUASH AND RADICCHIO

INGREDIENTS

- 8 slices of butternut squash, each cut into 3 strips
- 8 leaves of radicchio
- 2 stalks of red chicory
- 8 slices of Jambon d'Ardenne
- leaves of spicy watercress (hippo tops)
- 10 g [⅓ oz] roasted pine nuts
- a few drops of lemon balsamic glaze

FOR THE VINAIGRETTE / MARINADE

- juice of 2 apples (Jonagold, ca. 2 dl [1 US cup])
- 5 cl [3 US tbsp] Chardonnay wine vinegar
- 5 cl [3 US tbsp] nut oil
- 10 g [⅓ oz] acacia honey

PREPARATION

- Mix the ingredients for the vinaigrette and marinate the strips of butternut squash in it for 20 minutes. Roll them up.

SERVING INSTRUCTIONS

- Serve a nice salad with the radicchio, leaves of red chicory, squash rolls and the slices of Jambon d'Ardenne.
- Finish with the watercress, squash seeds, drops of balsamic glaze and some vinaigrette.

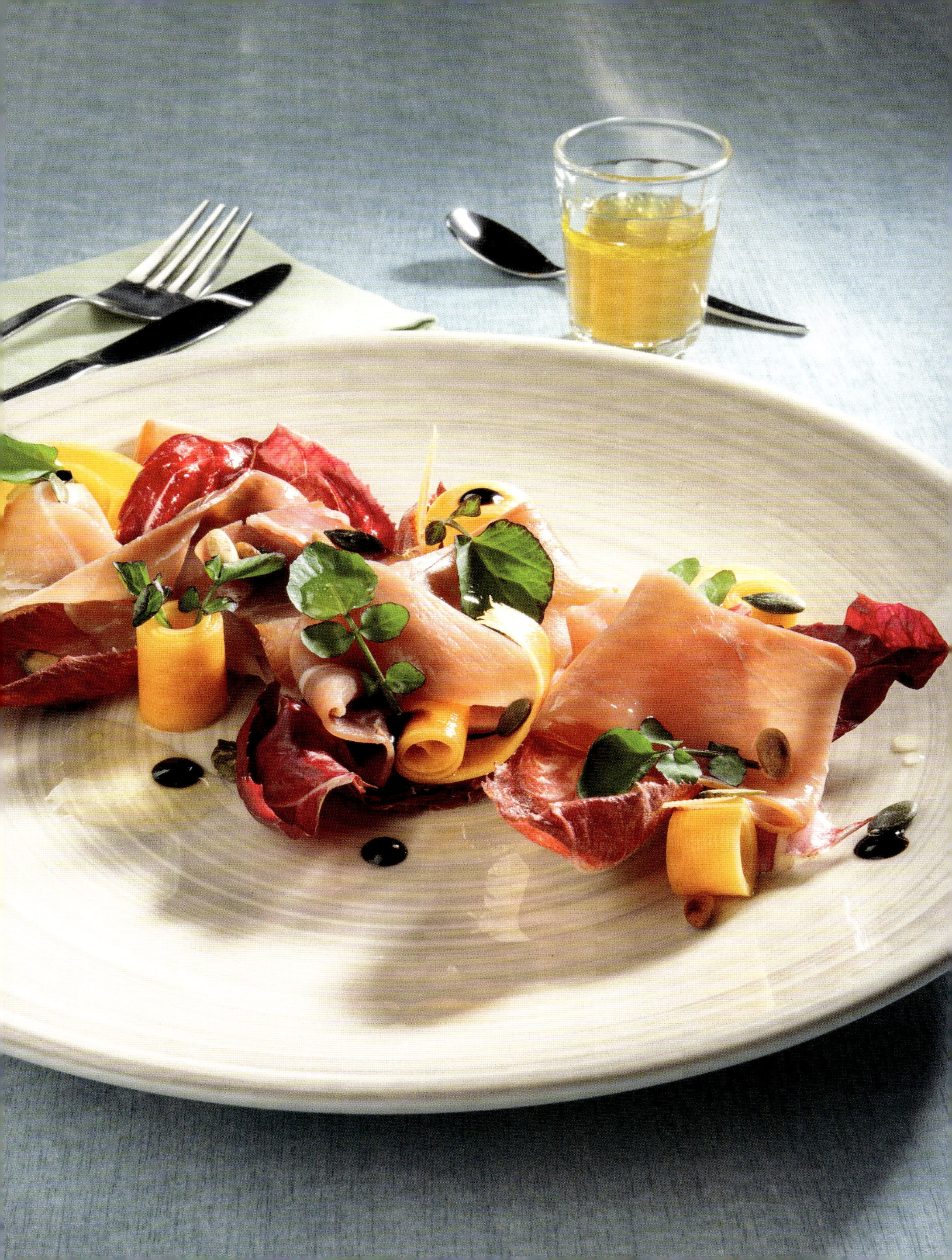

CARPACCIO MADE WITH OMEGA BASS, IBERICO HAM AND CAVAILLON MELON

INGREDIENTS

- 400 g [14 oz] omega bass fillet, deboned, skinned and degreased, in thin slices (carpaccio)
- 4 broccoli florets
- 10 g [⅓ oz] dried goji berries
- 160 g [5 ½ oz] Iberico ham, in wafer-thin slices
- 32 scoops of cavaillon melon
- 16 young lavender flower shoots

FOR THE VINAIGRETTE

- juice of 2 lemons
- juice of 1 white grapefruit
- 1 dl [½ US cup] sushi vinegar
- white pepper from the mill
- fleur de sel (special type of sea salt)

PREPARATION

- Combine the ingredients for the vinaigrette and mix lightly.
- Arrange the slices omega bass on a platter, spoon over the dressing and marinate for 10 minutes.
- Cut the flowers from the broccoli and finely chop the goji berries.

SERVING INSTRUCTIONS

- Arrange the omega bass with the slices of Iberico ham on top.
- Finish with the broccoli, the chopped goji berries, melon balls and lavender tufts.

TIP Omega bass: Belgian omega bass is raised in Kruishoutem and grows in purified and healthy rainwater. Its food consists of selected local vegetable materials enriched with seaweed. Thus no wild fish must be caught to feed the omega bass, which unfortunately is the case in traditional aquaculture. Moreover, there is a sustainable interaction with the neighbouring tomato nursery. Heat, energy and water are interchanged in the tomato cultivation, so nothing is lost. The delicious, boneless omega bass fillets, naturally rich in omega-3 fatty acids, are a joy for many chefs to use: fried, raw, smoked, sushi, tartar, etc. The applications are endless. The omega bass is a delicious fish for consumers and its production does not burden the environment.

INGREDIENTS

- wood shavings from an apple tree
- 4 slices of Bayonne ham
- 4 portions of 100 g [3 ½ oz] of salmon
- 2 small red onions
- 5 cl [3 US tbsp] olive oil
- fresh sage
- 12 young jasmine blossoms
- 1 avocado, peeled, in slices
- ½ cavaillon melon, peeled and pitted, in slices

FOR THE PORT GELATINE

- 5 cl [3 US tbsp] red port wine
- 3 cl [2 US tbsp] lemon juice
- 2 sheets of gelatine or 2 g [⅔ tsp] gelatine, soaked in cold water

FOR THE MELON SAUCE

- ½ cavaillon melon, peeled and pitted, cut into cubes
- 5 cl [3 US tbsp] red port wine
- 4 cl [2 ⅔ US tbsp] sherry vinegar
- white pepper and fennel seed from the mill
- fleur de sel

PREPARATION

- Warm and ignite the smoker with the wood shavings from an apple tree.
- Put the Bayonne ham slices on the skinned salmon fillet and place in the smoker for 4 to 5 minutes (depending on the smoke flavour you desire).
- Arrange on a platter and cover with foil. Let it cool down.
- Cut the red onions into slices and add them to the olive oil.
- Cut the sage into fine strips.
- For the gelatine: Bring the port wine to a boil and mix the lemon juice with it. Remove from the heat and mix in the crushed gelatine. Pour into a mould (ice cubes) and place in the refrigerator.
- Combine the ingredients for the melon sauce and mix. Season with the herbs.

SERVING INSTRUCTIONS

- Heat the salmon for 5 minutes in a preheated oven at 80° C [175° F].
- Place each time 2 slices of avocado and melon and arrange the salmon with Bayonne ham in between.
- Finish with the melon sauce, onion rings, port cubes, sage and some jasmine blossoms.

SEMI-COOKED SALMON AND BAYONNE HAM, AVOCADO, MELON AND PORT WINE

NEW POTATOES, FARM HAM AND FRIED EGGS, FARM STYLE

INGREDIENTS

- 16 small new potatoes
- 1 l [1 US quart + 5%] vegetable stock
- 4 sprigs of rosemary
- 50 g [2 oz] farm butter
- 4 farm eggs
- pepper
- fleur de sel
- 8 slices of farm ham

PREPARATION

- Bring the stock with the rosemary to a boil and cook the potatoes in it until done. Melt the butter into it. Cut the potatoes into equal slices.
- Fry the 4 eggs. Finish with some pepper and fleur de sel.

SERVING INSTRUCTIONS

- Serve a fried egg and around it arrange some potato slices and pieces of farm ham.
- Finish with leaves of rosemary and spoon the butter stock over it.

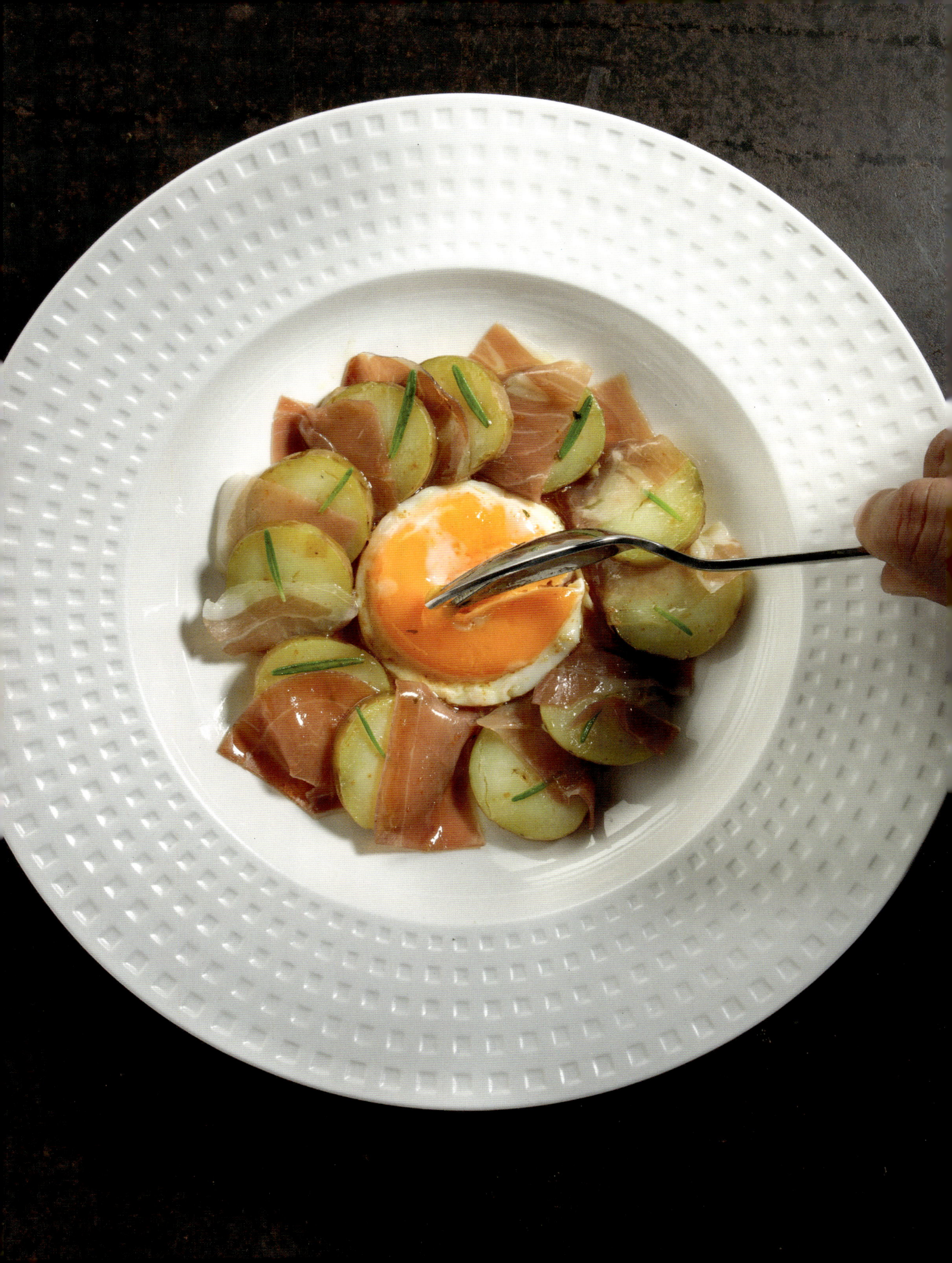

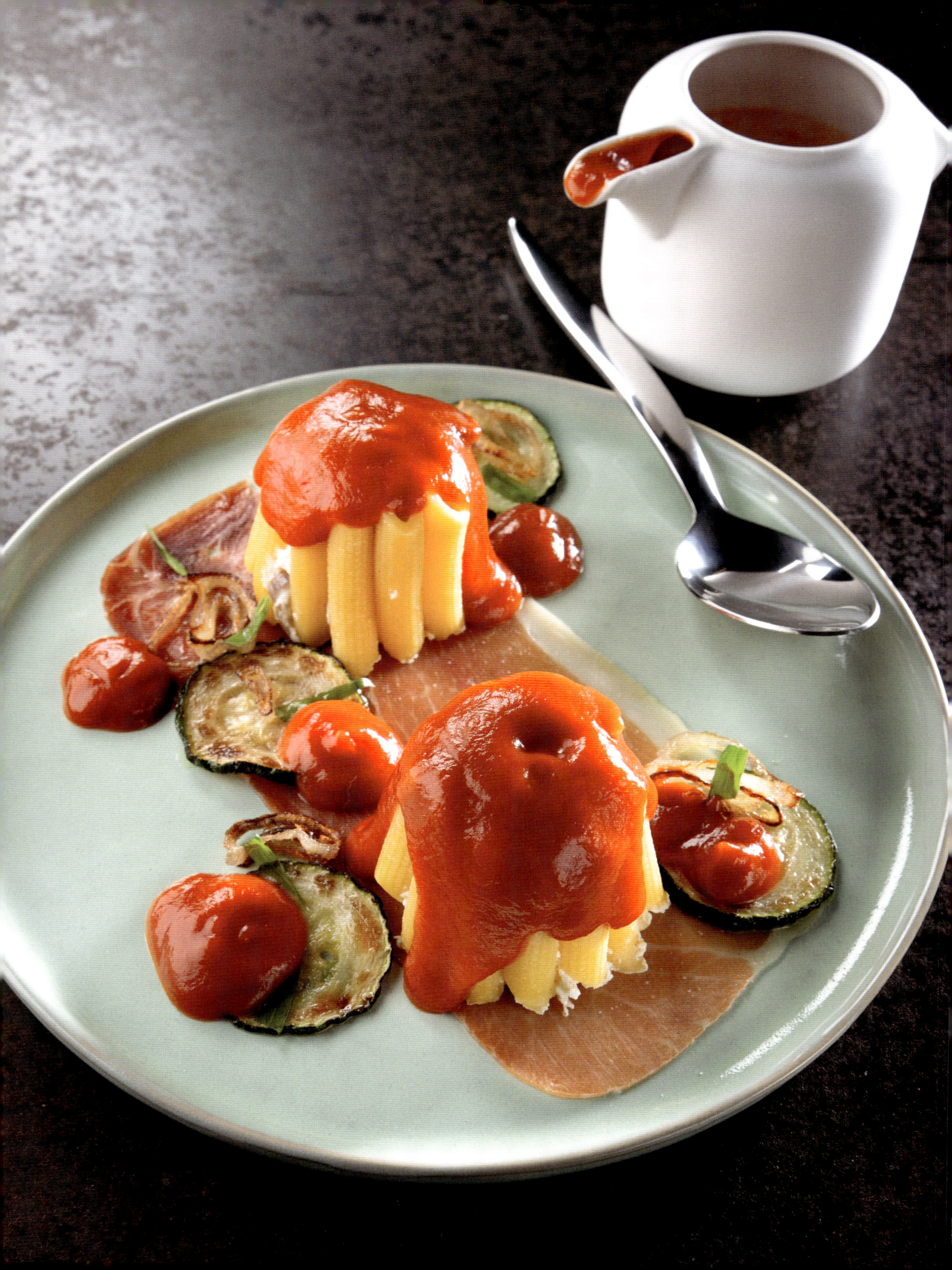

THE VOLCANO

MY ODE TO ALFONSO IACCARINO, ITALIAN TOP CHEF

INGREDIENTS
SHARING DISH FOR TWO

- 1 slice of Culatello di Zibello
- 24 al dente cooked penne (2 minutes)
- 2 dl [1 US cup] tomato sauce

FOR THE FILLING
- 2 shallots
- 50 g [2 oz] courgette, in cubes and 4 thin slices
- 5 cl [3 US tbsp] olive oil
- 160 g [5 ½ oz] fresh ricotta (preferably buffalo ricotta)
- 4 slices of Serrano ham
- 2 g [1 tsp] tarragon leaves, chopped

FOR THE TOMATO SAUCE
- 2 shallots, shredded
- 5 tomatoes, type Toma'Gusto, cut into cubes
- 1 red pepper, deseeded, cut into cubes
- 5 cl [3 US tbsp] olive oil
- 4 dl [1 ⅔ US cups] chicken stock
- 100 g [3 ½ oz] tomato paste
- pepper and fine sea salt

PREPARATION

- Clean the shallots and cut into fine rings. Stew them together with the courgette in the olive oil, fry the courgette slices and keep them together with some shallot separately as a garnish.
- Mix the shallots and courgette with ricotta, the Serrano ham sliced into fine strings and the tarragon.
- Place the penne into bowls smeared with olive oil and fill the penne with the ricotta mixture. Bake in a preheated oven at 160° C [320° F] for 6 minutes.
- Warm the tomato sauce, but do not let it boil.

PREPARATION

- Let the shallot turn glassy in the olive oil. Stew in the chopped tomatoes and peppers. Pour the stock and the tomato paste over it and leave to simmer for twenty minutes.
- Mix in a blender until smooth and pass through a fine sieve. Season.

SERVING INSTRUCTIONS

- Place a slice of Culatello di Zibello on a hot plate with two demoulded pasta timbales on it.
- Finish with slices of courgette, fried shallot and tarragon leaves.
- Pour the tomato sauce over it like a volcano that is erupting.

TIP Alfonso Iaccarino is chef-owner of hotel-restaurant Don Alfonso 1890** on the Gulf of Naples. Iaccarino is one of the greatest ambassadors of South Italian cuisine. One of his signature dishes is the image of the Vesuvius as it erupts, called the Vesuvio di Rigatoni. This original dish that was served to Italian soldiers has become world famous. Hence my version ...

BRUSCHETTA PARTY

INGREDIENTS

- slices of ciabatta
- olive oil
- thyme leaves
- slices of Parma ham
- slices of Parmesan cheese
- green olives with pimento
- sun-dried tomatoes

PREPARATION

- Preheat the oven to 200° C [390° F].
- Spread the ciabatta slices with the olive oil and sprinkle some thyme leaves on them. Place Parma ham and Parmesan cheese on them. Finish with the olive rings and a sun-dried tomato.
- Bake briefly in a preheated oven.
- Enjoy with a nice glass of Italian red wine from the Parma region.

POTATO, OLIVE OIL AND IBERICO DE BELLOTA

INGREDIENTS

- 4 large potatoes, such as Belle de Fontenay
- nutmeg, freshly grated
- 2 dl [1 US cup] olive oil
- 200 g [7 oz] Iberico de Bellota, in wafer-thin slices

PREPARATION

- Peel the potatoes and cut them into cubes. Cook until well done in boiling salted water. Drain and dry briefly on the burner.
- Mash the cooked potatoes with a fork and season with olive oil and freshly grated nutmeg.
- Serve the mashed potatoes in the middle of the plate with the fantastic Iberico de Bellota ham on it.

TIP Belle de Fontenay is a French potato from the region of Orleans. It is known for its tasty nut aroma that combines fantastically with the Iberico ham.

AUBERGINE PUFFED IN THE OVEN WITH GRANA PADANO CHEESE AND PARMA HAM

INGREDIENTS

- 2 large Italian aubergines (eggplants)
- 1 dl [½ US cup] olive oil
- fleur de sel
- 50 g [2 oz] Grana Padano cheese
- 100 g [3 ½ oz] Parma ham in slices

PREPARATION

- Preheat the oven to 250° C [480° F].
- Cut the aubergines in half and carefully cut grooves in the flesh diagonally without puncturing the skin.
- Pour the olive oil over them and sprinkle with fleur de sel.
- Bake in a preheated oven until the flesh is nice and soft.
- Cover with the Grana Padano cheese and slices of Parma ham.
- Serve with ciabatta as a tasty snack.

169

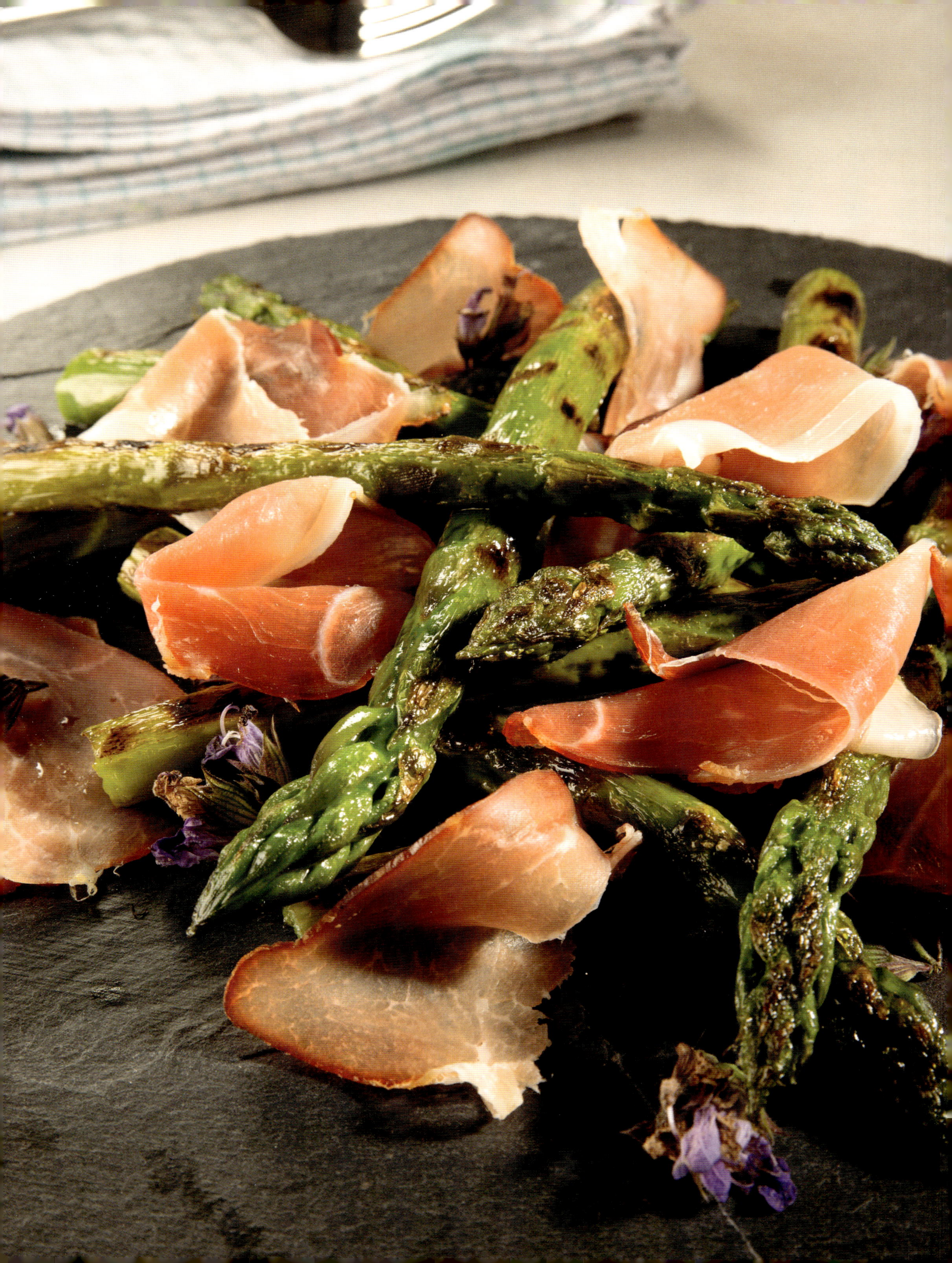

SNACK OF GRILLED GREEN ASPARAGUS AND BLACK FOREST HAM

INGREDIENTS

- 20 green asparagus, cooked al dente
- 1 dl [½ US cup] olive oil
- coarse sea salt
- 200 g [7 oz] Black Forest ham, in fine strings
- blossoms of sage or young sage leaves

PREPARATION

- Heat the grill pan.
- Dip the asparagus in oil and grill them on the hot pan.
- Finish with some coarse sea salt.
- Arrange them with the Black Forest ham on a sharing platter.
- Finish with the sage blossoms.

TIP Enjoy with a delicious glass of Riesling wine from the Pfalz region of Germany.

WATERMELON WITH GANDA HAM

INGREDIENTS

- 1 small watermelon
- 1 red onion
- 8 slices of Ganda Ham
- 4 cl [2 ⅔ US tbsp] balsamic glaze
- 2 g [½ tsp] black poppy seeds
- shoots of olive herb
- anise flowers

FOR THE SOUP
- pulp of watermelon
- 5 cl [3 US tbsp] gin, type Tanqueray
- juice of 2 pink grapefruit (ca. 2 dl [1 US cup])

PREPARATION

- Peel the watermelon and remove the seeds. Cut 20 nice little bars of watermelon of 2 × 4 cm.
- Peel and cut the red onion into fine rings.
- Make the soup: Place the rest of the watermelon with the gin and grapefruit juice in a blender and mix finely. Pour through a fine sieve and then through a kitchen towel to obtain clear soup. Let the onion marinate in it for 20 minutes. Put in the refrigerator.

SERVING INSTRUCTIONS

- Arrange the bars of watermelon in a chilled serving bowl with strips of Ganda Ham and some rings of red onion.
- Pour the soup over it and finish with the balsamic glaze, poppy seeds, olive spice and some anise flowers.
- Fantastic dish for a sultry summer evening, served with a delicious Tanqueray gin and finished with grapefruit juice.

TIP Fantastic dish for a summer evening, served with Tangueray gin and grapefruit juice.

TIP Ice plant (BlinQ Blossom is the commercialized name) is an original South African plant that also thrives in Mediterranean areas. It is fantastic with mussels and other salty products; red meat is also a pleasant flavour partner.

ZEELAND MUSSELS, GANDA HAM, TOMATO AND SAFFRON

This is a revision of my classic mussel dish from the Mosselboek [Mussel book].

INGREDIENTS

- 200 g [7 oz] samphire, cleaned
- 2 ripe tomatoes, type Toma'Gusto, skinned
- tufts of ice plant (BlinQ Blossom)
- 4 leaves of radicchio (red lettuce)

FOR THE MUSSELS

- 50 mussels from Zeeland Jumbo, debearded and washed
- 1 onion
- 1 dl [½ US cup] Chimay Tripel
- 14 slices of Ganda Ham

FOR THE SAUCE

- 4 dl [1 ⅔ US cups] mussel liquid
- 1 g [¼ tsp] saffron threads
- 50 g [2 oz] cold butter

PREPARATION

- Clean and cut the onion fine. Put together with the mussels in a mussel pot and pour the Chimay Tripel over them. Poach them done until the shells open (about 7 minutes). Remove the mussels from the shell and collect the liquid.
- Poach the samphire in the mussel liquid. Scoop it out and rinse with ice-cold water.
- Make the sauce: Bring the mussel cooking water to a boil with the saffron. After about 5 minutes, thicken by letting the butter dissolve little by little in the sauce. Stir constantly and make sure you do not let the sauce boil.
- Roll the mussels up in strips of Ganda Ham.
- Cut the tomatoes into thin slices.

SERVING INSTRUCTIONS

- Arrange 5 slices of tomato on a hot plate. Place 10 Ganda Ham mussel rolls on it.
- Finish with the samphire, ice plant and pieces of radicchio.

SOUTHERN RATATOUILLE ... FROM THE CARTOON

Ode to Thomas Keller, The French Laundry and Per Se

INGREDIENTS

- 2 ripe tomatoes, type Toma'Rito
- 1 yellow courgette
- 1 aubergine (eggplant)
- 2 dl [1 US cup] olive oil
- 8 slices of San Daniele ham
- fresh basil leaves

FOR THE TOMATO SAUCE

- 2 shallots, shredded
- 5 cl [3 US tbsp] olive oil
- 5 tomatoes, type Toma'Gusto, cut into cubes
- 1 red pepper, deseeded, cut into cubes
- 4 dl [1 ⅔ US cups] chicken broth
- 100 g [3 ½ oz] tomato paste
- pepper and fine sea salt

PREPARATION OF THE TOMATO SAUCE

- Let the shallot turn glassy in the olive oil. With it stew the chopped tomatoes and peppers. Add the broth and tomato paste and let it cook for about 20 minutes.
- Mix until smooth in a blender and pass through a fine sieve. Season.

PREPARATION

- Preheat the oven to 180° C [355° F].
- Cut the tomatoes, courgette and aubergine into thin slices. Arrange overlapping in turn (8 times 3 slices) in an oven dish and drizzle with olive oil. Place in the preheated oven for about 10 minutes.
- Cut the ham and basil into thin strips and mix.

SERVING INSTRUCTIONS

- Start with a spoonful of tomato sauce and arrange the ham / basil around it.
- Serve the ratatouille in the middle.

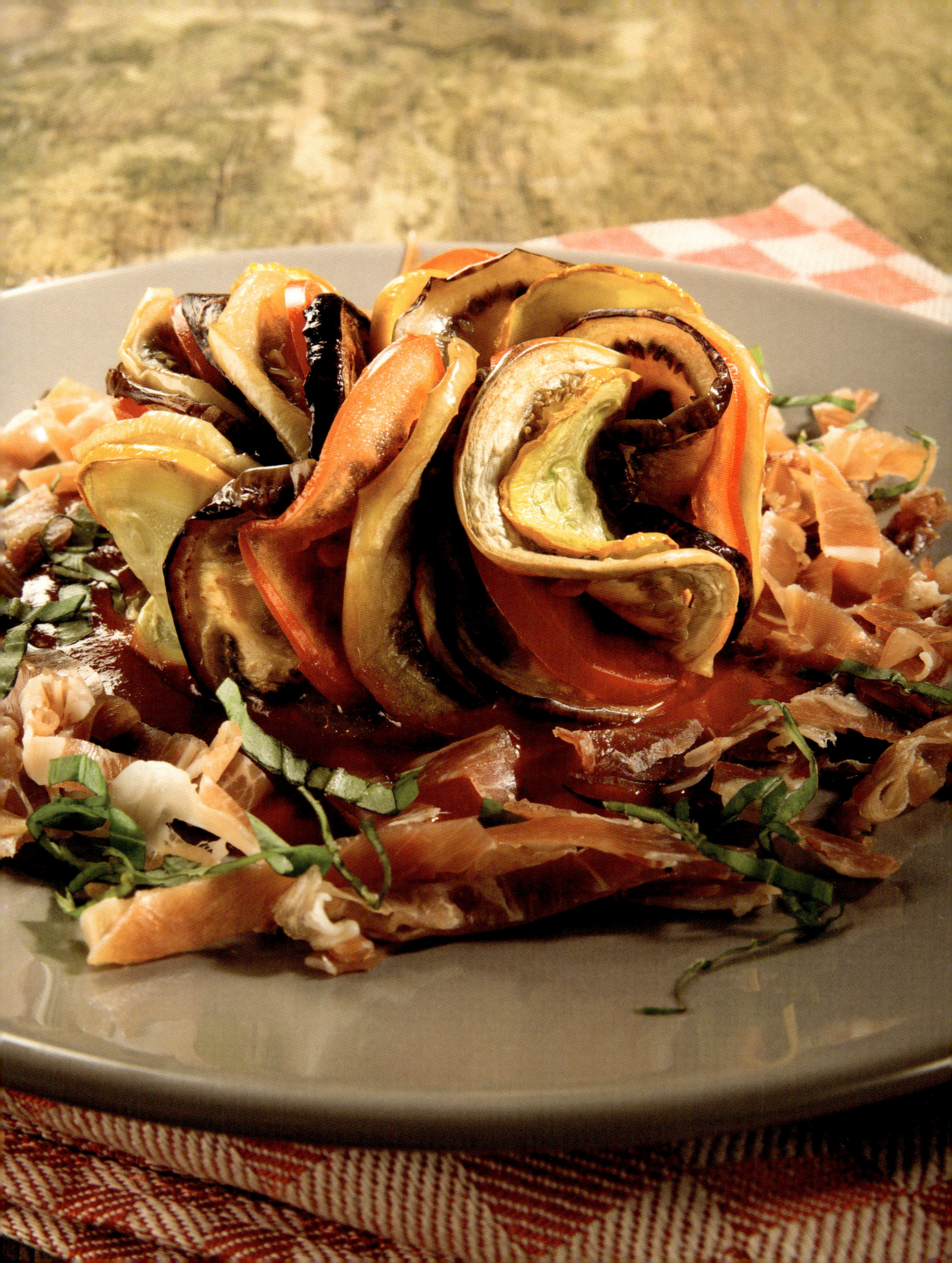

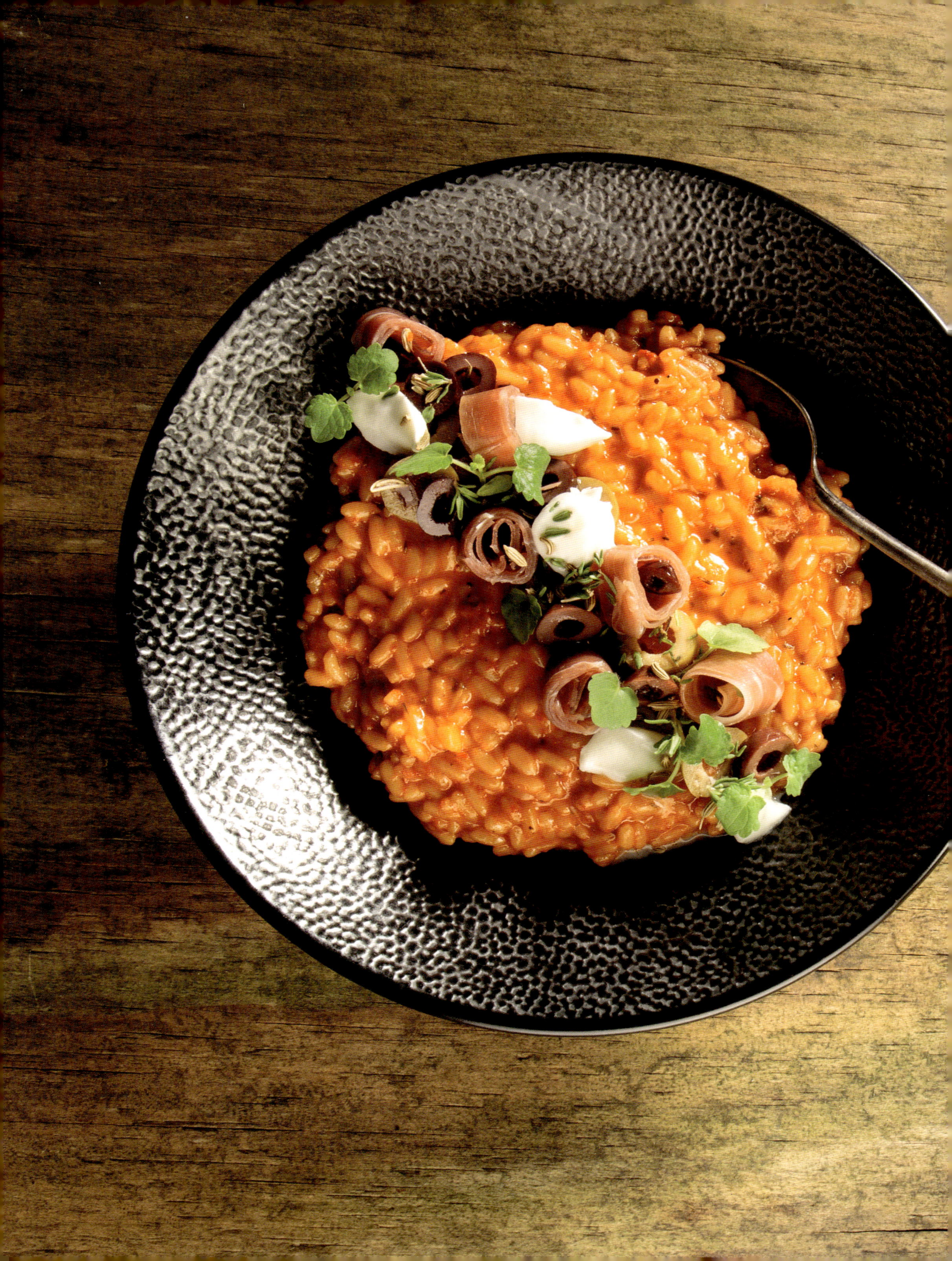

RISOTTO WITH PARMA HAM, TOMATO AND MOZZARELLA DI BUFALA INGREDIENTS

INGREDIENTS

- 8 dl [3 ⅓ US cups] vegetable and tomato broth (vegetable broth finished with passata of tomato – 6 dl [2 ½ US cups] broth and 2 dl [1 US cup] passata)
- 1 dl [½ US cup] dry white wine
- 1 banana shallot
- 20 g [½ oz] butter
- 250 g [8 ½ oz] risotto rice (round grain such as arborio)
- 100 g [3 ½ oz] grated mozzarella
- 50 g [2 oz] butter
- black pepper from the mill

FOR THE GARNISHES

- 8 slices of Parma ham
- 1 scoop of buffalo mozzarella
- black and green olives, type Calamata
- fresh thyme leaves
- ground fennel seeds
- 1 box of Atsina® cress

PREPARATION

- Make the risotto: Heat the broth with the white wine. Cleanse and finely chop the shallot. Stew in a pan adding butter and sprinkling in the risotto rice. Let the rice become glassy. Moisten each time with a spoonful of broth and let it boil gently. Stir occasionally, keeping the heat low so the rice does not burn.
Repeat until the stock has been absorbed and the rice is smooth. Test a grain: if the grain has a soft, crispy dot inside, the rice is cooked. Remove from the heat and finish with the cheese and butter. Season to taste with some black pepper from the mill.
- Cut and roll the Parma ham, pull the mozzarella into small pieces. Cut the olives into slices.

SERVING INSTRUCTIONS

- Serve the risotto and finish with the different garnishes.

CARAMELISED CHICORY, JAMBON D'ARDENNE, THREE KINDS OF CHEESE FROM CHIMAY

INGREDIENTS

- 12 stalks of mini-chicory
- 100 g [3 ½ oz] butter
- juice of ½ lemon
- 1 red onion
- 4 thick slices of Jambon d'Ardenne
- small basil and rosemary leaves
- little blocks of Chimay La Dorée cheese

FOR THE CHEESE SAUCE
- 5 dl [2 ¼ US cups] vegetable stock
- 1 dl [½ US cup] whole milk
- 50 g [2 oz] butter
- 50 g [2 oz] plain flour
- 150 g [5 oz] Grand Chimay cheese, diced
- 150 g [5 oz] Le Poteaupré cheese from Chimay, diced
- grated nutmeg, pepper from the mill, squirt of lemon juice

PREPARATION

- Put the butter in a frying pan and let it brown slightly. Remove the bitter cores from the chicory stalks and brown them in the butter. Reduce the heat, turn the stalks and moisten them with lemon juice. Cover and let them cook until done on a gentle heat.
- Cut the red onion into thin strips.
- Heat the stock and milk, and poach the onion in it briefly.
- Make the cheese sauce: Let the butter melt and stir in the flour. Moisten with the warm stock and let it thicken. Remove from the heat and finish with the cheeses. Season with pepper, nutmeg and a squirt of lemon juice.

SERVING INSTRUCTIONS

- Serve a slice of Jambon d'Ardenne on a warm plate and place three chicory stalks on it.
- Finish with the sauce, fresh herbs, onion and cubes of Chimay La Dorée.

TIP Drink a tasty Chimay Dorée here. Since 2001 I have been a Creative Chef at *Les Bières et les Fromages Trappistes de Chimay*.

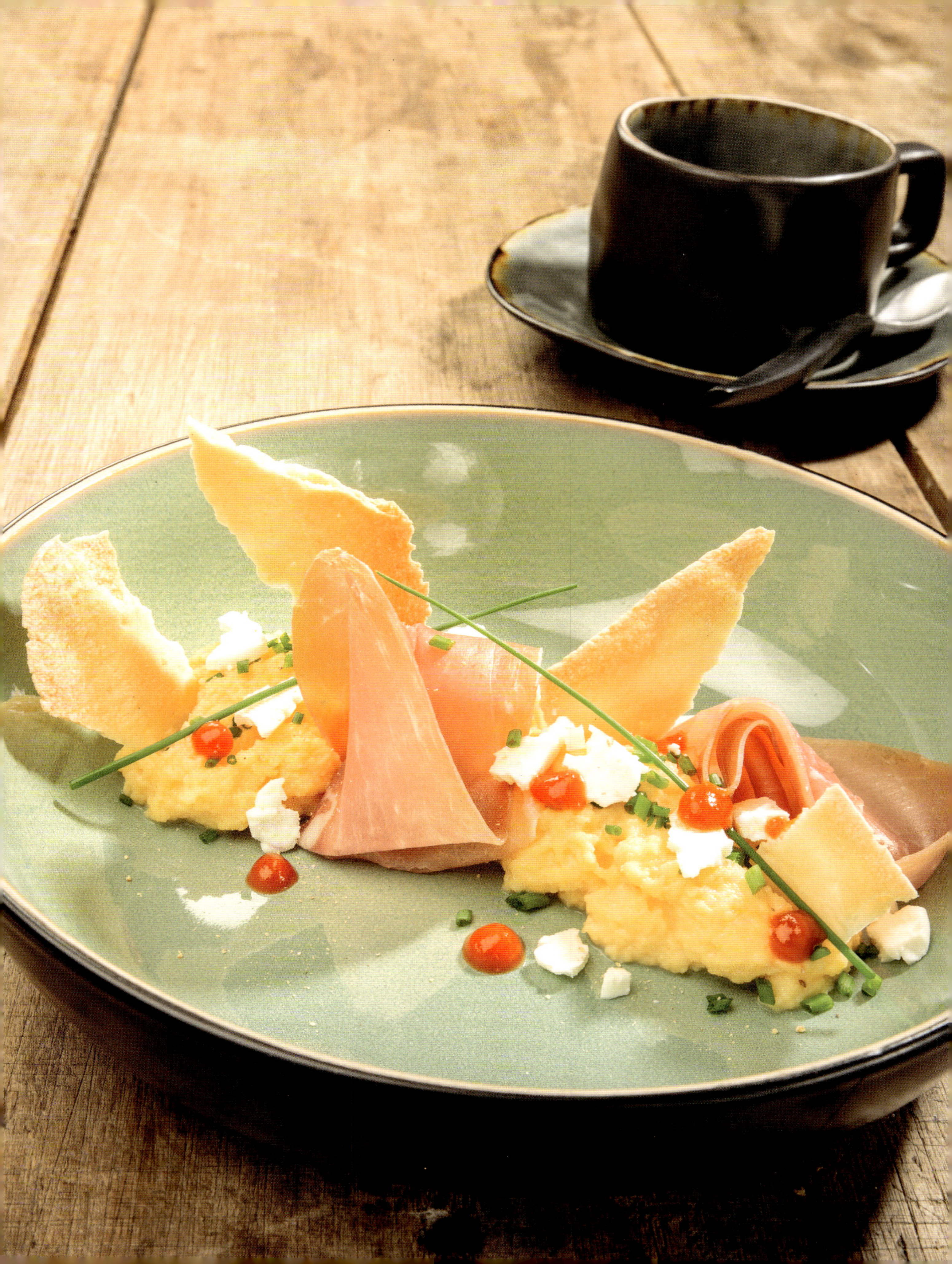

SCRAMBLED EGGS, GANDA HAM, AND KETCHUP

INGREDIENTS

- 7 free-range eggs and 2 yolks
- 20 g [½ oz] butter
- pepper from the mill, coarse sea salt
- 4 Italian bread crackers (Lingue di Suocera or Mother-in-Law's Tongues)
- fresh chives
- 100 g [3 ½ oz] Greek cheese, in cubes
- 8 slices of Ganda Ham
- 2 dl [1 US cup] Heinz tomato ketchup
- 3 g [¾ tsp] celery seeds

PREPARATION

- Make the scrambled eggs: Melt the butter and stir the eggs on a low heat. Let them bind and stir in the 2 yolks at the end. Season with pepper and sea salt.

SERVING INSTRUCTIONS

- Serve the scrambled eggs and arrange the broken crackers, chives, cubes of Greek cheese, 2 slices of Ganda Ham and tufts of ketchup.
- Finish with ground celery seeds.

LITTLE ROLLS OF BAYONNE HAM AND BASQUE PIPERADE

INGREDIENTS

- 4 unsweetened pancakes
- 8 slices of Bayonne ham
- 200 g [7 oz] cheese curls, type Ardi Gasna or Idiazabal (semi-hard Basque sheep cheese, Spanish manchego is a possible substitute)

FOR THE PIPERADE

- 1 red onion
- 1 red pepper
- 2 cloves of garlic
- 1 dl [½ US cup] olive oil
- 50 g [2 oz] sun-dried tomatoes
- 10 black and 10 green olives
- 40 g [1 ½ oz] pine nuts
- fresh oregano

PREPARATION

- Make the piperade: Clean the red onion and the peppers and cut into small cubes. Stew together with the shredded garlic in the olive oil. Add finely chopped tomatoes, olive rings and pine nuts and leave to continue cooking briefly. Finish with young oregano leaves.
- Heat the pancakes and top each pancake with 2 slices of Bayonne ham and some curls of Basque sheep cheese. Roll up and keep warm.

SERVING INSTRUCTIONS

- Serve the piperade with the lukewarm pancakes cut into equal rolls.

PUFF PASTRY WITH BAYONNE HAM AND SPINACH

PREPARATION

- Preheat the oven to 190° C [375° F].
- Arrange the puff pastry on baking paper on an oven plate. Brush with water and sprinkle with the sesame seeds. Season with salt and pepper and prick with a fork. Cover again with parchment paper and cover with an oven plate. Bake in the oven for 15 to 18 minutes, until crispy.
- Warm the mascarpone and add the spinach. Season with a few drops of lemon juice and nutmeg.

INGREDIENTS

- 1 slice of puff pastry, circle of 30 cm in diameter
- 5 g [⅕ oz] sesame seeds
- black pepper and coarse sea salt
- 8 slices of Bayonne ham

FOR THE SPINACH

- 250 g [8 ½ oz] mascarpone cream cheese
- 500 g [18 oz] of young leaf spinach
- a few drops lemon juice
- nutmeg

SERVING INSTRUCTIONS

- Spread the spinach on the crisp puff pastry and then place the Bayonne ham on it. At the last minute grate some nutmeg on top.
- Divide and enjoy.

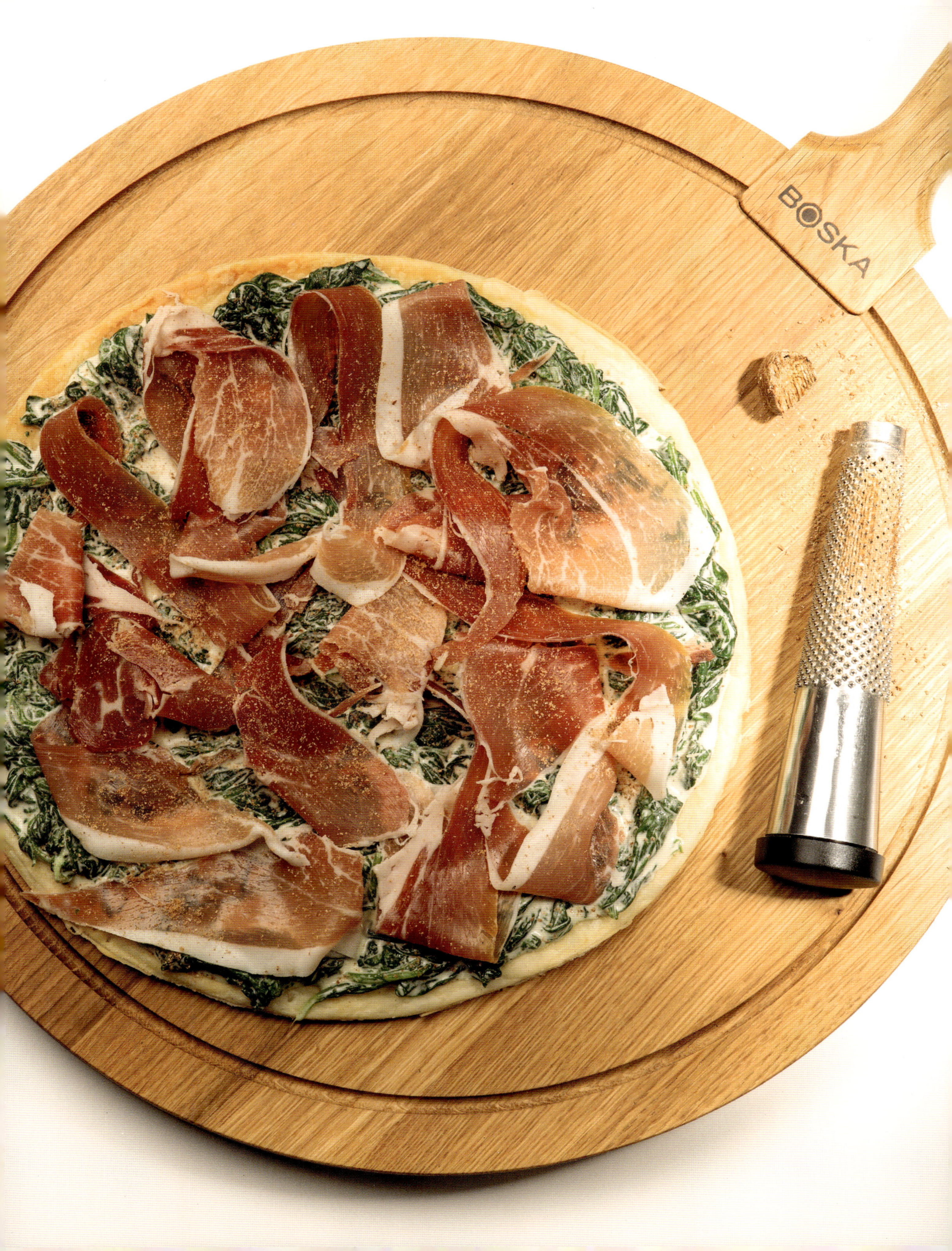
BOSKA

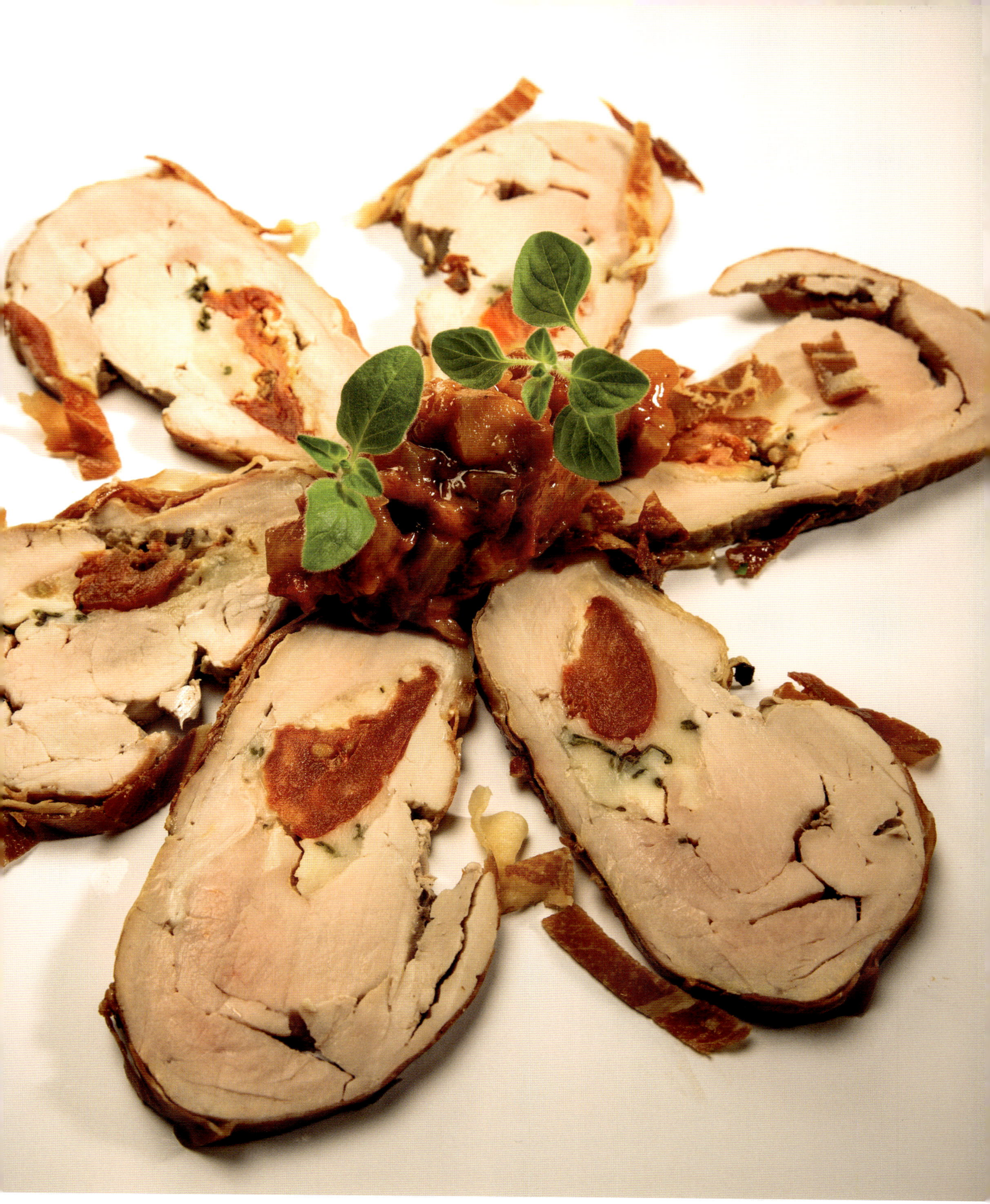

ROLLED PORK TENDERLOIN ROAST, CHIMAY CHEESE AND JAMBON D'ARDENNE

INGREDIENTS

- 1 rolled pork tenderloin roast, with the tendon and skin removed
- 10 slices of Jambon d'Ardenne
- 200 g [7 oz] sun-dried tomatoes
- 200 g [7 oz] Chimay à la Rouge cheese, cut into bars
- 10 g [⅓ oz] sage leaves

FOR THE SALSA
- 1 onion, shredded
- 100 g [3 ½ oz] courgette cubes
- 100 g [3 ½ oz] eggplant cubes
- 100 g [3 ½ oz] yellow and green pepper cubes
- 100 g [3 ½ oz] tomatoes, in cubes
- 1 dl [½ US cup] olive oil
- fresh oregano

PREPARATION

- Preheat the oven to 200° C [390° F].
- Cut open the tenderloin open into a flat piece. Place on it 5 slices of Jambon d'Ardenne with the sundried tomatoes, the bars of Chimay cheese and the sage leaves on top. Place it close together on the rest of the ham and roll into the fillet. Brush with some olive oil and cook in the preheated oven for 25 minutes.
- Make the salsa: Stew all vegetables in the olive oil, cover and let cook for 20 minutes. Finish with picked oregano leaves.

SERVING INSTRUCTIONS

- Serve fine cuts of tenderloin with the salsa.
- Serve with baked potato or tasty pasta.

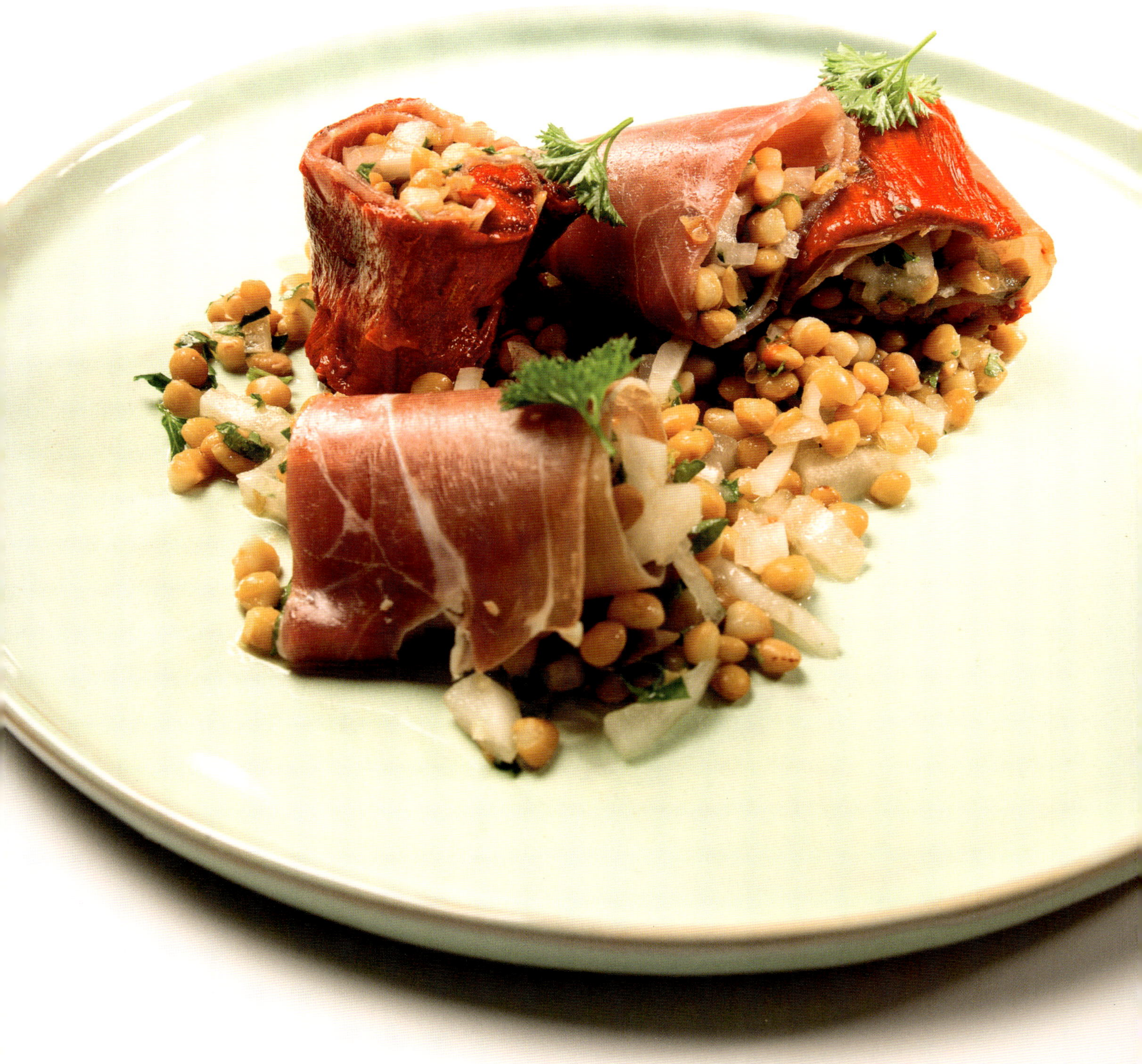

LENTILS WITH HAM ROLLS

INGREDIENTS

- 200 g [7 oz] lentils
- 1 litre [1 US quart + 5%] vegetable stock
- 1 onion, finely shredded
- 10 g [⅓ oz] mild mustard
- 5 cl [3 US tbsp] Chardonnay wine vinegar
- 1 dl [½ US cup] olive oil
- 20 g [½ oz] freshly chopped parsley
- 4 paprika, peeled and seeds removed (or 4 piquillo peppers, drained)
- 10 slices of Ganda Ham
- 100 g [3 ½ oz] curls of hard cheese (e.g. Bellie cheese from the Belgian cheese cooperative "Het Hinkelspel")

PREPARATION

- Rinse the lentils under cold water and let them soak for an hour. Drain them. Cook the lentils in the stock for about 40 minutes until done. Drain and mix in the shredded onion. Let it cool down.
- Mix the mustard with the vinegar, oil and parsley. Pour over the lentils and mix well together.
- Place a piece of paprika on a slice of ham and scoop a spoonful of lentil salad on top, distribute some hard cheese curls over it. Roll up and cut in half. Repeat with the rest of the raw ham.

SERVING INSTRUCTIONS

- Serve some lentil salad with the different ham rolls on it. Finish with some parsley plumes.

MY FAVOURITE HERRING

PREPARATION

- Preheat the deep fryer to 170° C [340° F].
- Clean the herring and roll the fillets into the Ganda Ham. Cut these into three equal pieces each time.
- Make the croutons: Cut the garlic in half and rub it on the bread. Cut the slices into equal cubes. Warm the olive oil and fry the bread in it. Pour on a kitchen towel and season with salt and pepper.
- Mix all ingredients for the vinaigrette.
- Cut the onion into fine rings and fry until crisp in the deep fryer. Let drain.
- Slice the lemon into equal thin quarters.

SERVING INSTRUCTIONS

- Serve the green beans with the herring ham rolls.
- Add the onion, croutons and lemon.
- Finish with the milk vinaigrette and dill plumes.

INGREDIENTS

- 4 Dutch young herring
- 8 slices of Ganda Ham
- 1 large onion
- 1 lemon
- 200 g [7 oz] green beans, cooked al dente
- fresh dill tufts

FOR THE CROUTONS

- 2 slices of white bread, without crust
- 1 clove of garlic
- 5 cl [3 US tbsp] olive oil
- coarse salt and pepper

FOR THE YOGHURT MILK VINAIGRETTE

- 100 g [3 ½ oz] natural yogurt
- 5 cl [3 US tbsp] whole milk
- 3 cl [2 US tbsp] Chardonnay wine vinegar
- black pepper from the mill

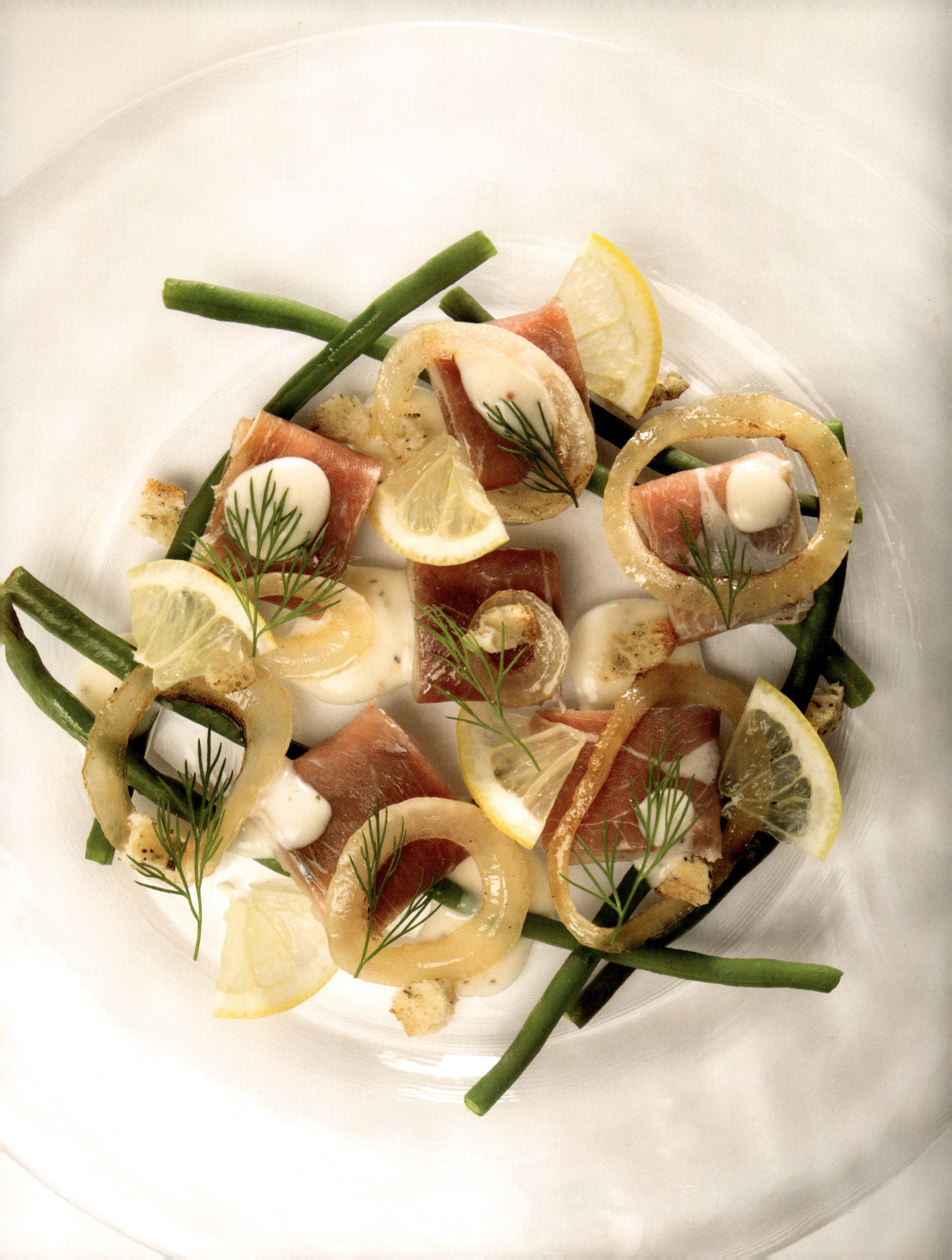

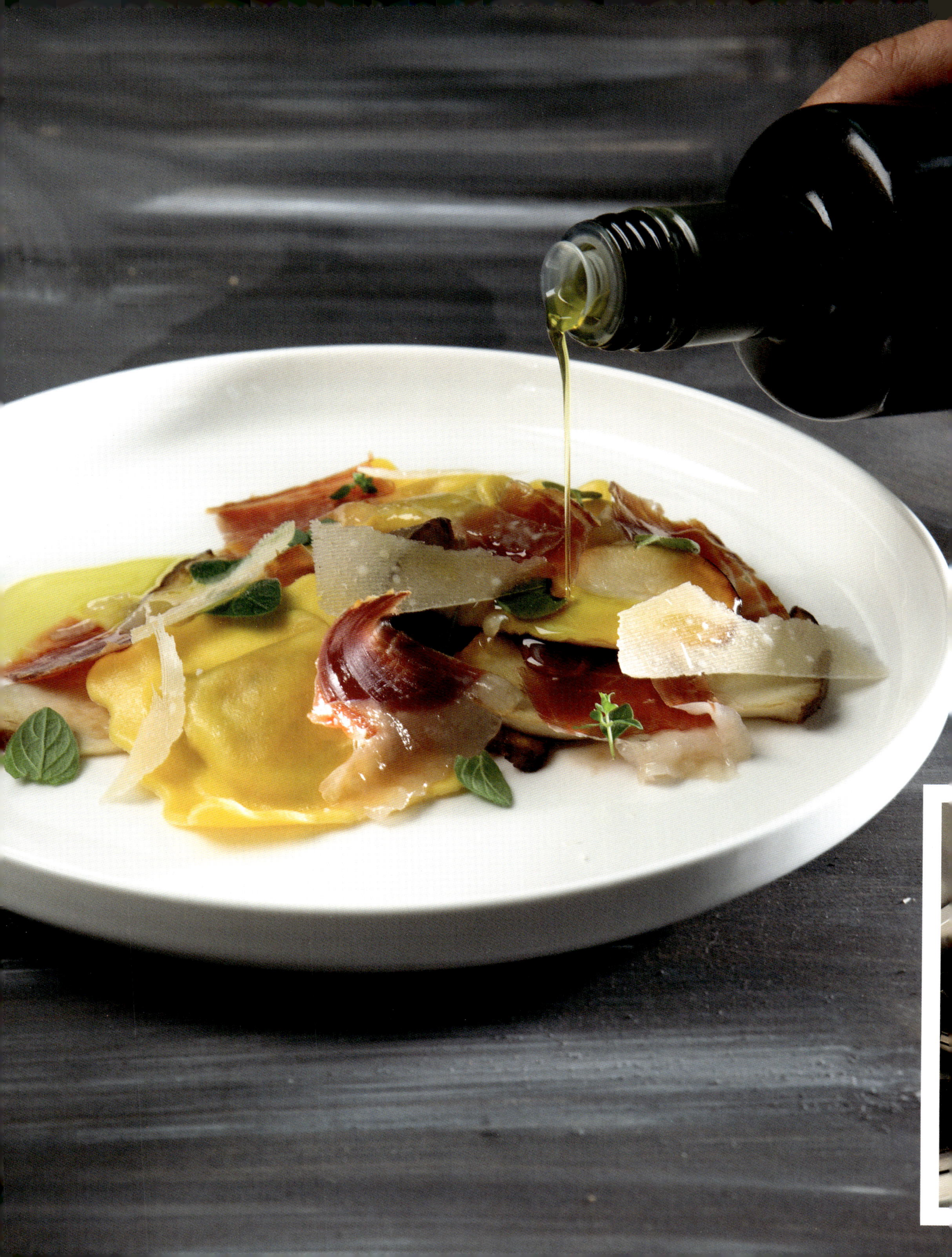

RAVIOLI WITH MUSHROOMS AND PARMA HAM

INGREDIENTS

- 2 porcini mushrooms
- 4 slices of Parma ham
- 40 g [1 ½ oz] curls of Parmesan cheese
- young sage leaves
- 1 dl [½ US cup] olive oil from the first cold pressing

FOR THE PASTA

- 400 g [14 oz] Italian pasta flour 00
- 4 eggs
- squirt of olive oil

FOR THE FILLING

- 1 shallot, shredded
- 1 clove of garlic, shredded
- 5 cl [3 US tbsp] of olive oil
- 250 g [8 ½ oz] mix of porcini and chestnut mushrooms in small cubes (brunoise)
- 2 sage leaves, finely chopped
- 50 g [2 oz] ricotta

PREPARATION

- Make the filling: Fry the shallot and garlic briefly in the olive oil and add the mushrooms. Remove from the heat and finish with the sage. Mix the mass through the ricotta.
- Make the pasta: Arrange the flour with an indent in the middle and break the eggs into it. First knead carefully and add the olive oil. Now knead firmly for about 6 minutes into a nice elastic dough. Make a ball and wrap in plastic foil. Let rest for 20 minutes in the refrigerator. Now roll out thinly with the pasta machine at position 5 or a few millimetres thick [⅛ of an inch]. Lay out a piece of pasta dough and cut into strips of 4 cm with a serrated knife.
- Spoon some filling on every 3 cm [1 ⅕ inch] and put a new layer of pasta dough on it. Press around the ravioli and with the serrated knife cut into 4×4 cm [1 ½ × 1 ½ inch] squares. Dust with some flour and allow to dry for a while.
- Cut the porcini mushrooms into slices and fry briefly in the olive oil.
- Bring well-salted water to a boil and cook the ravioli until al dente, maximum 4 minutes.

SERVING INSTRUCTIONS

- Arrange the ravioli with the porcini.
- Finish with the Parma ham, a few curls of Parmesan cheese and young sage leaves.
- Serve and finish at the table with tasty olive oil.

FINGERFOOD

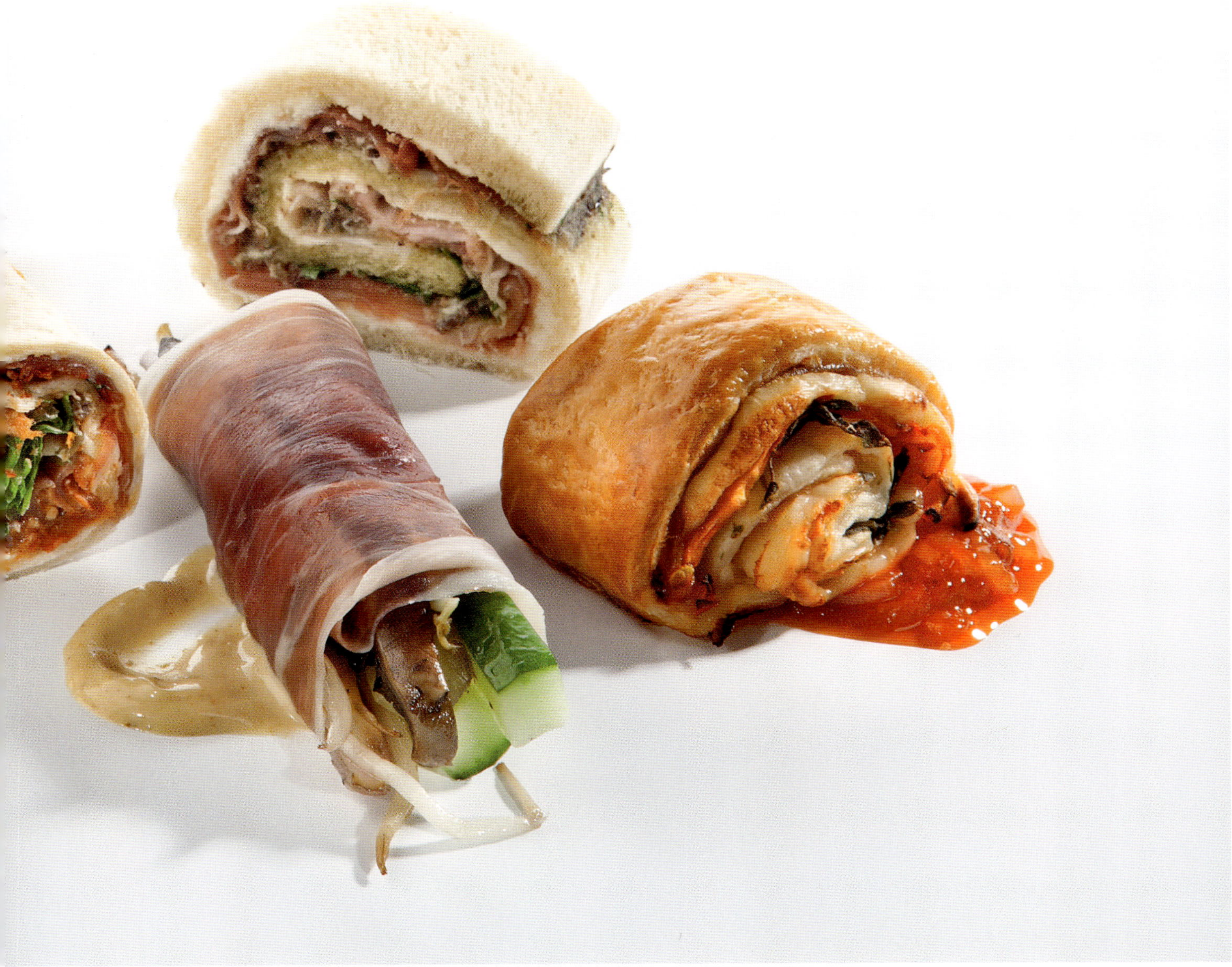

GANDA HAM ROLL-UPS

INGREDIENTS FOR 5 ROLL-UPS

- 1 slice of tramezzino bread (long Italian bread without crust)
- 100 g [3 ½ oz] Le Larry goat cheese
- 4 slices of Ganda Ham

FOR THE PESTO
- 3 cl [2 US tbsp] olive oil
- 1 large shallot
- 5 anchovies, marinated and drained
- 5 black olives, pitted and finely chopped
- 20 g [½ oz] rocket

PREPARATION AND SERVING INSTRUCTIONS

- Put all ingredients for the pesto in a blender and mix.
- Smear the pieces of tramezzino bread with goat cheese and place slices of Ganda Ham on them. Smear on the pesto and roll up.
- Roll in plastic foil and leave in the refrigerator for an hour.
- Cut the rolls into slices, pierce with sticks and serve.

WRAP ROLLS WITH GANDA HAM AND LE LARRY GOAT CHEESE

INGREDIENTS

- 1 tortilla
- 50 g [2 oz] tomato tapenade
- 50 g [2 oz] Le Larry goat cheese
- 3 slices of Ganda Ham
- 6 corn chips
- 20 g [½ oz] rocket

PREPARATION AND SERVING INSTRUCTIONS

- Coat the tortilla with the tapenade and goat cheese. Arrange the slices of Ganda Ham on it.
- Garnish with crushed corn chips and rocket.
- Roll up and cut into wrap rolls (with or without sticks).

ROLLS OF HAM

INGREDIENTS

- 1 slice of Ganda Ham
- 3 leaves of rocket
- 10 g [⅓ oz] aubergine (eggplant) paste or grilled aubergine
- 10 g [⅓ oz] Le Larry goat cheese
- 1 grissino breadstick
- a few drops of olive oil

PREPARATION AND SERVING INSTRUCTIONS

- Take a slice of Ganda Ham, place the rocket, aubergine and some goat cheese in the middle of it, place a grissino and roll up.
- Cut in two and serve with a few drops of olive oil.

ORIENTAL GANDA CANNELLONI

INGREDIENTS

- 3 cucumber strips
- 10 g [⅓ oz] soy sprouts
- 10 g [⅓ oz] shiitake mushrooms, in slices
- 10 g [⅓ oz] red onion, in rings
- 3 cl [2 US tbsp] peanut oil
- 1 slice of Ganda Ham
- fresh chives

FOR THE SAUCE

- 20 g [½ oz] mayonnaise
- 3 g [¾ tsp] of curry powder
- 2 cl [4 tsp] soy sauce

PREPARATION AND SERVING INSTRUCTIONS

- Stew the vegetables briefly and crispy in the oil and place them on the slice of Ganda Ham. Roll it up.
- Mix the ingredients for the sauce.
- Place the rolls on a stripe of sauce and finish with some chive stalks.

CRISPY GANDA HAM ROLL-UPS

INGREDIENTS

- 4 sheets of brik dough (malsouka)
- 8 slices of Ganda Ham
- 200 g [7 oz] Le Larry goat cheese
- 24 mini green asparagus, cooked al dente
- butter

FOR THE SALSA

- 1 large tomato, skinned and diced
- 2 dl [1 US cup] Heinz tomato ketchup
- 1 finely chopped red onion
- 10 green asparagus, cooked al dente
- 10 g [⅓ oz] dried oregano
- 3 cl [2 US tbsp] balsamic vinegar
- 1 g [¼ tsp] cumin powder
- 1 g [¼ tsp] curry powder

PREPARATION AND SERVING INSTRUCTIONS

- Lay the sheet of brik dough open and distribute the Ganda Ham, the goat cheese and the green asparagus over it. Brush with the butter and roll it up. Bake in a preheated oven or frying pan.
- Mix all ingredients for the salsa.
- Serve the roll-ups cut in two with some salsa.

SAVOURY STRUDEL

INGREDIENTS

- 1 sheet of puff pastry, 20 by 30 cm [8 by 12 inches]
- 8 slices of Ganda Ham
- 8 slices of Grand Chimay cheese
- 4 tomatoes, in thin slices
- 10 g [⅓ oz] oregano leaves
- 1 egg yolk and some water
- pepper and salt
- 4 shallots
- 1 dl [½ US cup] olive oil
- 5 dl [2 ¼ US cups] Heinz tomato ketchup
- 10 g [⅓ oz] oregano leaves, finely chopped

PREPARATION AND SERVING INSTRUCTIONS

- Lay the puff pastry sheet open and cover half of it with Ganda Ham. Place the cheese on it with the slices of tomato and sprinkle with oregano, pepper and salt.
- Spread the remaining part of the puff pastry sheet with egg yolk and water, and roll up. Coat with egg yolk.
- Place in a 190° C [375° F] oven for about 20 minutes.
- Make the salsa: Cut the shallots into thin slices and put them in the olive oil. Finish with the ketchup and some oregano.
- Serve the strudel slices with some salsa.

TIP: Replace the Chimay with Le Larry goat cheese and serve as an appetizer.

BRUSCHETTA GANDA HAM WITH GREEN OLIVES

INGREDIENTS

- 3 slices of ciabatta
- 60 g [2 ⅕ oz] Le Larry goat cheese
- 90 g [3 ⅕ oz] green olive tapenade
- 3 slices of Ganda Ham
- grilled and preserved yellow paprika
- oregano leaves

PREPARATION

- Spread half of the ciabatta with the goat cheese and the rest with the tapenade.
- Place a slice of Ganda Ham on it and finish with the yellow pepper and a sprig of oregano.

GANDA HAM WITH TASTY TAPENADE

INGREDIENTS

- 3 slices of white baguette or ciabatta
- 60 g [2 ⅕ oz] Le Larry goat cheese
- 90 g [3 ⅕ oz] tomato tapenade
- 3 slices of Ganda Ham
- basil leaves

PREPARATION

- Spread half of the ciabatta with the goat cheese and the rest with the tapenade.
- Place a slice of Ganda Ham on it and finish with a leaf of basil.

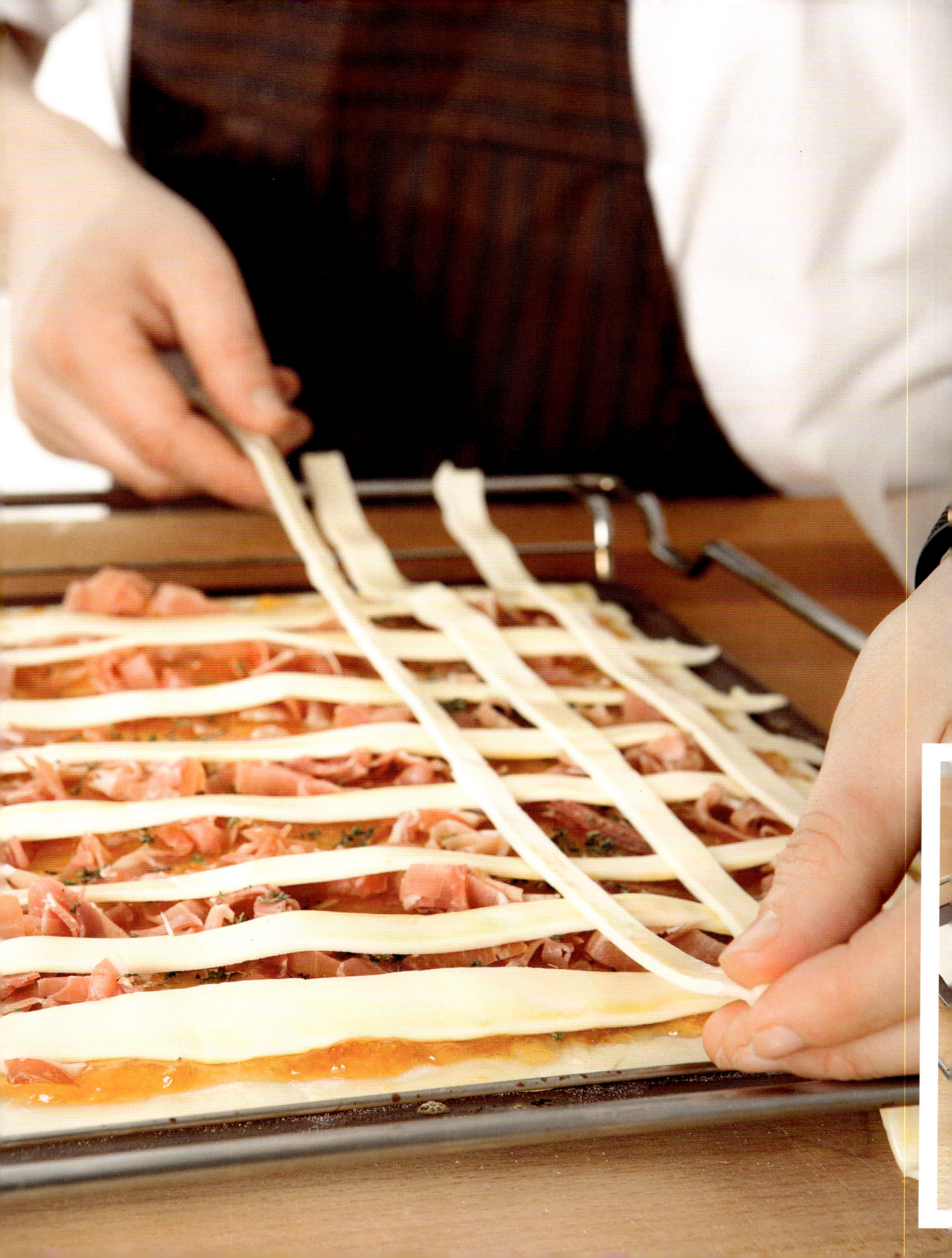

SWEET-SALTY-SOUR, MY JAM PASTRY

INGREDIENTS

- 2 sheets of puff pastry, 20 by 30 cm [8 by 12 inches]
- 250 g [8 ½ oz] apricot jam (e.g. Belberry)
- 8 slices of Parma ham (12 months)
- fresh young thyme shoots
- 2 egg yolks and some water

FOR THE CREAM

- 1 can of apricots
- 250 g [8 ½ oz] sour cream

PREPARATION

- Preheat the oven to 190° C [375° F].
- Arrange a sheet of puff pastry on a silicone mat or parchment paper and pierce it with a fork.
- Brush the sheet with the apricot jam.
- Cut the ham into equal strips and finely chop the thyme. Distribute the ham and the thyme over the jam on the pastry.
- Cut the second sheet of puff pastry into strips and coat with a wash made of egg yolks and the water. Also rub the edges of the pastry with the egg wash.
- Arrange the strips of puff pastry on the tart and press.
- Place the tart in the oven and bake 15 to 18 minutes until it is golden brown.
- Cut the apricots into small cubes and mix them with the sour cream.

SERVING INSTRUCTIONS

- Cut the jam pastry into the desired shapes, serve lukewarm or at room temperature and finish with a spoonful of apricot cream.

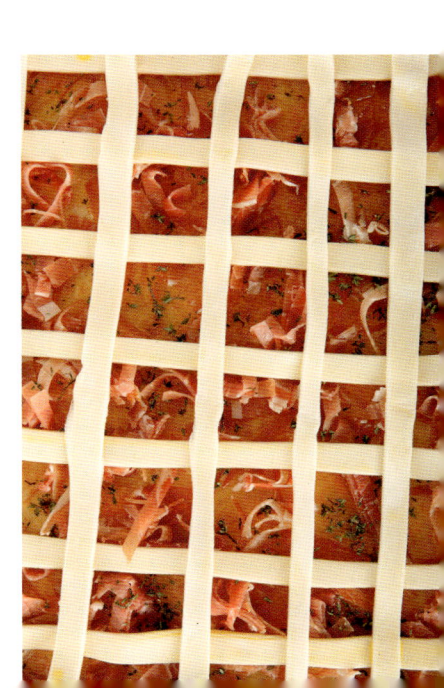

SALAD AND TOAST WITH MUSHROOMS AND IBÉRICO HAM

INGREDIENTS

- 600 g [21 oz] chestnut mushrooms
- 2 large banana shallots
- 100 g [3 ½ oz] salted butter
- 1 dl [½ US cup] cream 40%
- 5 cl [2 ⅔ US tbsp] Madeira wine
- slices of Ibérico de Bellota (24 months), hand sliced
- 80 g [3 oz] yellow raisins (sultana or eleme raisins) soaked in the Madeira wine
- 4 slices of nut-raisin bread
- young leaves of blood sorrel

PREPARATION

- Cut the brushed mushrooms into quarters. Clean the shallots and cut into fine slices.
- Melt the butter 'noisette' and fry the mushrooms and shallots in it. Cook for a moment and extinguish with the cream and a dash of Madeira wine.
- Boil down. Finish with the soaked raisins.
- Toast the bread golden brown and cut into the desired shape.

SERVING INSTRUCTIONS

- Serve the mushrooms. Finish with the Ibérico ham, blood sorrel and slices of bread.

SALAD NIÇOISE

INGREDIENTS

- 4 slices of Bayonne ham (12 months)
- 4 pieces of 100 g [3 ½ oz] of tuna fillet
- 20 g [¾ oz] baharat spices, mixed with 1 dl [½ US cup] olive oil
- 8 quail eggs

FOR THE GARNISHES

- 4 piquillo peppers, rolled up in slices
- 8 cherry tomatoes, in quarters
- 2 banana shallots, in ultra-fine slices
- 200 g [7 oz] of green beans, cooked al dente
- 4 ratte potatoes, cooked well-done, peeled and sliced
- 8 conserved and stretched anchovy fillets
- rucola shoots

PREPARATION

- Heat a cast-iron frying pan. Dip the tuna in the herb oil and fry briefly in the hot pan (for a few seconds on each side). Allow to cool and cut the fillets into four equal pieces.
- Fry the quail eggs in the hot pan with a stainless steel egg mould.

SERVING INSTRUCTIONS

- Serve a slice of Bayonne ham with the four pieces of tuna on it.
- Finish with the different garnishes and a squirt of olive oil.

TIP Baharat is a widely used blend of herbs from Arabic cuisine and is popular around the Persian Gulf, in the Middle East, northern Africa and southern France. Baharat has a complex, savoury taste and a warm and sweet aroma, just like the Arabic cuisine. It literally means 'spice' in Arabic and is one of the oldest Arabian herbal mixtures.

My thanks go to:

Dirk Cornelis and the Ganda Ham-team – www.ganda.be

Mathias Verbeke and the Joka-team – www.jokajoka.com

Johan and Heidi of Lannoo Publishers for their confidence and patience

Joran of Butchery Delbaere with the best blood sausage in Belgium – www.slagerijdelbaere.be

Geert Van Hecke, Massimo Bottura and Piet Huysentruyt, top chefs whom I admire

Stefano Montali of S.Ilario

Mr Federico of Galloni in Langhirano – www.galloniprociutto.it

Mr David Rodriguez Suarez of Jabugo De Ley – www.jabugodeley.es

Ruben Brabant of Menapian pigs and Piet De Kersgieter,

for the pictures – www.menapii.be

Signor José Luis and Yolanda Escuredo – www.lajabuguena.com

Tom, Bart and Sven, who have an incredible ability to capture images

and to present my dishes in an exceptional way

Steven & Thijs, for the fantastic layout of the book

Stefaan Van Laere, for organising my chaotic texts

Jeroen Staes, for the information about Over the Edges and a few pictures – www.smak.be

Johan Walravens of Elishout, for his encouragement

And of course Ella and all my tasters at home, Ferran, Jordi,

Arnau and Miro, and Petra, who enjoy good food.

www.lannoo.com

Register on our web site and we will regularly send you a newsletter with
information about new books and interesting, exclusive offers.

Text: Stefaan Daeninck

Photography: Tom Swijns, Bart Van Leuven, Sven Everaert

Graphic design: Steven Theunis & Thijs Kestens, Armée de Verre Bookdesign

If you have observations or questions,
please contact our editorial office:
redactielifestyle@lannoo.com

© Lannoo Publishers, Tielt, 2018

D/2018/45/556 – NUR 440 – ISBN 978 94 014 4921 2

All rights reserved. Nothing from this publication may be copied, stored
in an automated database and/or be made public in any form or in any way,
either electronic, mechanical or in any other manner without the prior
written consent of the publisher.

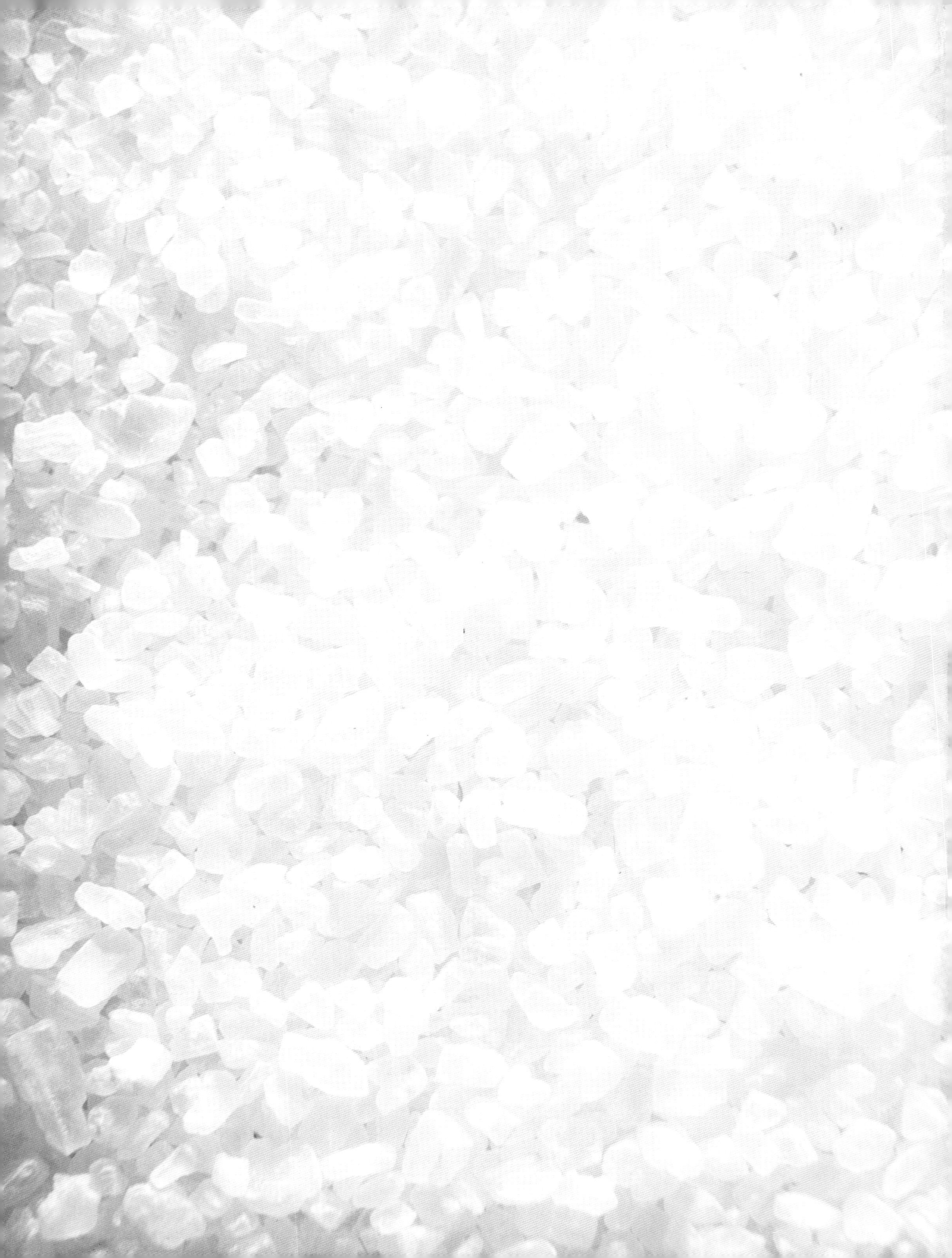